Linda Perlstein

NOT MUCH JUST CHILLIN'
The Hidden Lives of Middle Schoolers

INSIDE THE MOST CRUCIAL—AND LEAST UNDERSTOOD—YEARS OF CHILDREN'S LIVES

Suddenly they go from striving for A's to barely passing, or obsessing for hours over "boyfriends" they've barely spoken to. Former chatterboxes answer in monosyllables; freethinkers mimic their peers' clothes, not to mention their opinions. Bodies and psyches morph under the most radical changes since infancy. On the surface, they're "just chillin'." Underneath, they're a stew of anxiety and ardor, conformity and rebellion. They are kids in the middle-school years, the age every adult remembers well enough to dread. No one understands them, not parents, not teachers, least of all themselves—no one, that is, until Linda Perlstein spent a year immersed in the lives of suburban Maryland middle schoolers and emerged with this pathbreaking account.

The book traverses the school year, following five representative kids—and including the stories of many more—as they study, party, IM one another, and simply explain what they think and feel. As Perlstein writes about what she saw and heard, she explains what's really going on under the don't-touch-me façade of these critically formative years, in which kids grapple with schoolwork, puberty, romance, identity, and new kinds of relationships with their parents and peers. *Not Much Just Chillin'* offers a trail map to the baffling no-man's-land between child and teen, the time when children don't want to grow up, and so badly do.

LINDA PERLSTEIN is an award-winning education reporter for *The Washington Post* and a 1984 graduate of Mapledale Middle School in Milwaukee.

6 x 9 / 304 pages
0-374-20882-4
$24.00/$39.95 CANADIAN

not much just chillin'

not much just chillin'

the hidden lives of middle schoolers

LINDA PERLSTEIN

Farrar, Straus and Giroux

New York

JAN 1 0 2007

Farrar, Straus and Giroux
19 Union Square West, New York 10003

Library of Congress Cataloging-in-Publication Data TK

Designed by TK

www.fsgbooks.com

1   3   5   7   9   10   8   6   4   2

The names of the children and their families have been changed out of respect for
their privacy. Everything else remains unaltered. The few conversations and situations presented that I did not witness firsthand were related to me soon after, by
one or usually more participants.

For Rachel and Noah

Contents

s p r i n g

not much just chillin'

at least they can't shove me in

You can eat french fries for lunch every single day, if you want. There's something really cool, too, about having a locker, your very own parcel of the earth to which nobody else knows the code. In middle school, you don't have to walk through the halls in hushed, prissy lines. You get to cook food and saw wood and still make it home in time for the end of *CatDog*.

What else the kids filing into the half-lit cafeteria have heard about middle school: If you stand in the long line for fries, you might not have enough time to eat them before recess. The teachers can be mean, and the homework so hefty it really cuts into your valuable time. You have to change for gym, in front of everyone. Barely any fun stuff, like the gingerbread house your fifth-grade class made last Christmas. Worst of all: The eighth graders like to jam sixth graders inside lockers.

As the two hundred almost-sixth graders—girls with wet ponytails or freshly knit braids, boys with gelled spikes and droopy shorts—find their friends and settle into rows of blue plastic chairs for Wilde Lake Middle School orientation the Thursday before school starts, they greet each other loudly and think silently:

After finally persuading Mom to replace my dorky snakeskin binder with the black kind you can write on with milky pens, will those all of a sudden be out of style, leaving me one step behind the school-supply trends yet again?

Should I risk getting my butt kicked in lacrosse this year, since all the other boys look like they gained four inches on me this summer?

Can I wear my American-flag shirt from Old Navy on Monday, even though Dale insists it really only works on the Fourth of July? "We have to go in looking cool," she said. "We have to go in with style."

Could I rig some sort of basket inside my locker door with suction cups, so my friends can drop notes in there? Will my friends be in my classes? Will my friends be my friends?

Am I really going to start thinking, "Eww, Mom, you're weird, go away"? Is middle school really my last chance to be a kid?

The parents share those last two concerns, and others. Their minds are filled with equal parts worry and nostalgia about their children's entrance into this baffling no-man's-land between child and teen. Most adults say the most humiliating experience of their lives took place in middle school (or junior high, as it was called then), and many parents in the cafeteria remember their own preadolescence as the worst time of their lives: The awkward changes of puberty and the obsessions that entailed. The fumbling steps toward independence. The cliques. Being too embarrassed to sneeze in public. Constantly checking the armpit. Thinking everyone else was smarter, happier, better.

The men remember the time they asked out a girl they didn't want to be seen with, and the women remember the time they showed up at school to find all their friends wearing matching jeans and matching sandals and matching blazers with matching patches on the elbows. "Guys," today's mothers pleaded, "why didn't you call me?" They remember blindly joining the boycott of the benevolent redheaded girl who went, in one school year, from eating lunch with the most popular clique to eating lunch with the special-ed students, for no reason she (or anyone, for that matter) could discern. They remember when they stopped doing homework for a month, because they discovered that in the all-important world that revolved around their friends, there was nothing cool about getting A's. They remember telling their classmates that they'd been sick for a week instead of the truth—that they'd been in Greece with their parents—because if you're eleven, there are seventy-three ways you can make fun of someone just because he went to Greece.

How strange they were then. When they were twelve, they couldn't believe Styx would ever be oldies music; they were appalled at the gauchos they wore even one year before but couldn't imagine that what they had on at the moment would ever go out of style; they actually wanted braces and glasses, until they had to have them.

Maybe they don't remember. Maybe they've blocked it out. But at the parent meeting in the spring, they heard Wilde Lake's principal, Brenda Thomas, warn, "There are some poor decisions made at this age. If anyone gets through unscathed—I don't know them." When puberty's all over, she said, you'll get back a person much like the one you used to know, in personality much the same as before. "Eventually that child is going to be exactly who you raise it to be," she told them. But in the meantime . . . The meantime. While her own daughter was in middle school, Thomas called her Regan, after the possessed child in *The Exorcist*. Horror-movie mood swings, sudden demands for privacy, defiance, pushing away. Each public hug the parents have gotten this week is, they fear, the last. Will kids be mean to their child? Or worse: Will their child be the mean one?

Most of these parents have read the newspaper. They've read that middle school is an "academic wasteland," the new ground zero for state and national school-reform efforts, the point at which a child has to start thinking about *college*. In some ways, America's twelve and a half million middle schoolers are growing up faster than ever, their workload piling on as quickly as their distractions.

A few of the parents have even read what little "literature" is out on middle schoolers. They've learned that their children are about to go through the greatest period of physical and emotional growth, after infancy, that humans experience—years during which no significant part of themselves will go unchanged. They've read that the irresponsibility, the selfishness, the boredom their kids are about to exhibit are signs of progression, not regression—no, *really*. They've read to expect contradictions: Children start to fix their values and figure out who they are independent of their families, at the same time they are too timid to set themselves apart as individuals. Twelve-year-olds are eager to turn everything into arguments but don't have the cognitive skills to win them. They are at once submissive and defiant, idealistic and materialistic. The titans of commerce have started rearranging their world around the shopping habits of "tweens"—who are thrilled to be targeted, except they don't make their own money. They want to be cuddled. Except when they don't.

More than anything, middle school pulls in children and pitches back teenagers. It is a time of change, which means, at this age, many things.

For Eric Ellis, an eighth grader, change means going from striving to please his teachers and mother to realizing that there's not much room in his life—what with skating and video games and dealing with his family—to aim for A's, and that if work is boring, which it often is, it is in his power to simply not do it.

For Jackie Taylor, a seventh grader, change means going from someone who not long ago invented a playground-wide inoculation against boy germs to spending a major chunk of time obsessing over and writing notes about her and her friends' serial crushes, recounting soap-operatic plot lines that are agonizing to them and utterly mystifying to everyone in their lives (usually over the age of thirteen) who thinks you actually have to *talk* to a boy to be his girlfriend.

For Elizabeth Ginsburg, also a seventh grader, change means going from chattering on about life's rich details in the car to swim practice and asking her parents for help with just about everything to all of a sudden shrugging off their suggestions, demanding to be left alone, invariably answering "Nothing" to the daily and now useless question, "What did you do at school today?"

For Jimmy Schissel, who is starting sixth grade, change means living through strange, uncomfortable alterations to the way his body works—inside and out, from sleeping to eating to thinking to sitting to running—and forever wondering both what is normal and what comes next.

For Lily Mason, also in sixth grade, change means experiencing a new intimacy with her friends and a new absorption in where she stands among them, such that to peek underneath her easygoing persona is to witness a constant effort to wear the right clothes and say the right things and not make one single move to stand out, lest she drop a notch in the eyes of the girl she considers her best friend.

The teachers in their matching white polos take the stage one by one to lay the first of a yearful of transparencies on the overhead projector and lay down the laws of sixth grade: You may go to your lockers only before school, before lunch, and after school. No sticky book covers—they ruin the textbooks. Travel at all times with your agenda, a spiral-bound date book that serves as both assignment log and hall pass. Classes rotate every other day, four on A-days, four on B-days, eighty minutes each— don't worry, you'll get used to it. The kids are given orientation folders, and page through them.

"What's on the next page?" a mother says to her daughter, who clamps it shut. "What, is it a secret?"

One little brother, a third grader with a sitcom child's knack for one-liners, is not too young to sense the tension. "What if I skip middle school," he suggests, "and go straight to high school?" His mother is one of the many who linger at the sides and back of the cafeteria, clucking their tongues, shaking their heads, smiling frowny smiles: "It seems like *yesterday* he was graduating from *kindergarten*." They make mental notes to take a photo this weekend, in case their children grow that fast. They look around and are not quite able to picture gangs in this cafeteria, arson in the trash cans, like the rumors had it. Wilde Lake lies at the heart of Columbia, Maryland, a suburb between Washington and Baltimore created in the late 1960s as developer James Rouse's original planned community, a tree-thick, sidewalk-lined town made up of individual "villages" where people of all races and social classes would live in harmony and chat and swap tools at communal mailboxes. Even though it's relatively progressive, things haven't quite worked like Rouse envisioned; Columbia has been suffering from a nationally pervasive suburban white flight, whereby more prosperous residents flee places like this for the outer, more pastoral, less eclectic villages. The parents who remain have heard that this place is a little "rough" for a suburban school in such an affluent county, and parents with children still uneasy about cooties wonder if this is where it all starts: Drinking. Smoking. Drugs. Sex.

Not to mention indifference to schoolwork.

"She's worked so hard," one mom tells her friend. "I don't want her to lose any gains."

"Is she going to get so defiant," the other says, "and not be my quiet, studious little girl anymore?"

Homerooms are announced by surname, and after packs of friends bless or curse the accidents of the alphabet that keep them together or separate them, they are sent to walk through their class schedules and—

finally!—try their lockers. The lockers aren't even six inches wide, so everyone can't fit at once. Some parents crowd in, some force themselves to stay back. Kids bounce on their heels trying their combinations, ten times in a row. The parents stand mute, until they can't any longer.

"We'll stay here until you can do it five times by yourself." (Sucked teeth.)

"Abby, can I come in and help?" (No answer.)

"Why don't we walk your schedule and come back and try when there are fewer people here?" ("One more time.")

From inside a classroom, an eighth grader who came to spy on the new kids perches on a desk, swinging her long legs, and watches. As the kids in the hall talk about skateboards and locker combinations and summer camp and the 'N Sync concert—they look so *small*—she tilts her head side to side. "I've been waiting for this day for years," she says. "I'm going to own this school."

Lily Mason tries her locker combination several times as her best friend, Mia Reilly, sits next to her on a high ledge, paging through the papers they've been given. A newsletter called *Middle Years* gives instructions on Backpack Safety. *Please*, Mia thinks. Lily's face practically touches the dial as she spins slowly—right, left, right, stop—and each time she tugs on the little metal handle, nothing.

"My camera makes little sticky pictures," she tells Mia. If she ever gets her locker open, she can paste them inside. Her father, standing a few steps behind, asks, "Do you want me to help?" Since it's a matter of the locker being stuck, and not a matter of getting the combination right, Lily figures it's not immature to let him unjam it.

The girls make plans to meet right here the moment middle school starts for real, and Mia goes to open her locker. Eight times she tries, quiet and serious. The crisscross of her swimsuit straps show above her tank top. Her mother, Leigh, would like to help but can tell Mia wants to do it herself—which she finally does. *Such an accomplishment*, Leigh thinks. A bigger accomplishment is when Mia tries to sidle into the locker. All that fits of her four feet nine inches is one tanned leg.

"Well," she announces, "at least they can't shove me in."

autumn

why is it that when we are mad at someone

we tend to wait right by the phone for them

to call and tell us that they are off but they

never call and you mad at them and you

chapter one

i can't believe the day's almost over

On Monday morning some mothers drive their children to the bus stop, where they achingly resist the urge to hug their babies. Instead they settle on forehead kisses so quick as to be nearly invisible. One boy stands slumped, breathing in the muggy air slowly, tired from being kept awake most of the night by lingering images from *The X-Files*. A mom rolls up in a Suburban and leans out the window: "Brittany, did you remember your keys?" Brittany scrunches her face, mortified, and rolls her eyes to Mia. Mia's got on a camouflage tank top, khaki shorts, two old string anklets, and white, silver-striped Adidas with the laces tied under the tongue. (White Adidas are the best shoes you can wear; Vans or Skechers are okay, too. If your Adidas are colored because your mom says white gets ruined too soon, you may as well be wearing Stride Rites.) Having decided that a sixth grader has to care more about her looks, Mia took a while getting ready today. She had her mom blow-dry her shoulder-length chestnut hair pouffy, but not too pouffy.

As Mia pushes her hair behind her ears, the seventh graders, weighed down by enormous backpacks, grill her:

"Do you like school?"

"Yes."

"Well, you won't by the end of sixth grade."

One of the most popular kids in her elementary school, Mia has the confidence that comes with having popular jocks as older brothers, plays soccer (the coolest sport), isn't afraid to try a never-before-seen hairstyle, and sasses just enough to crack the class up but still get away with it. She was the only girl not to cry at the end-of-fifth-grade pool party. So none of her classmates would guess that Mia Reilly has worries, too.

The only reason she didn't cry at the pool party was that she got it all out in private, the day before. She's anxious about middle school. If only she could wear her tall hidden-roller-skate shoes—then she might not be the shortest in the school. After being with the same group since kindergarten, she's looking forward to meeting new kids from the two other elementary schools, but that's also what scares her: "How will I know I can trust them?" She's concerned about times tables and about teachers "from the Black Lagoon."

Another huge issue: Mia has to broker peace between Lily and their friend Alexandra, who aren't speaking after a fight this summer. They ended fifth grade best friends—quite an accomplishment for Lily, who arrived, quiet and Southern and with no Adidas, in the middle of December. Lily and Alexandra spent practically all of August together, until one day Alexandra wanted to go outside to dance and Lily didn't. They argued and stopped talking to each other, completely. "Alexandra has to be the boss of everything," Lily says. Seems to Mia like a stupid thing to fight over, but there it is. Getting them to make up "might take a little bit of time," she says, but "it's crucial, because I can't spend time with just one."

Dropped off by the buses but not allowed inside until the eight-forty-five bell, the students swarm outside the school building, a flat, cream brick hexagon that lies in view of the big high school and the strip mall. A few eager boys peer through the front doors. They half shake hands or don't touch at all. The girls touch each other's hair. "Fine, don't say hi," one girl says to another. "I *did* say hi." The bell goes off and the students push their way inside, where Ms. Thomas snatches hats off heads. Teachers stand in the hall with homeroom lists, filtering kids down one hall or the other.

In homeroom Mia finds her assigned seat, up front. Lily sits in the back corner, wearing turquoise-plaid shorts, a white T-shirt, and a navy cardigan from The Children's Place. For an eleven-year-old she rarely slouches, conditioned from the discipline of ballet and gymnastics and a desire to one day be Miss America. Her dirty-blond hair spurts from a little ponytail; she hates the way it styles and wishes it were thinner. Her blue-gray eyes are always either cast down bashfully or (when she is sure they are not looking) studying the people around her, for clues on how to act. When her face is at rest, like now, it is inscrutable, but she will tell you she's pretty happy today. Last night she and Mia went to the Aaron Carter concert and screamed. Middle school all sounds interesting to her—the lockers, the teachers, getting to sew in home ec—and anyway, she doesn't fashion herself a worrier. Her answer to an annoyingly large number of questions is "I don't care," whether it's her mom asking what she wants for dinner or a friend asking what game she wants to play.

Split personalities are common among middle schoolers, Lily included. At home she is chatty and confident, not a hint of self-consciousness about her. She is an able caregiver to her siblings, nine-year-old Gabrielle, five-year-old Sean and the foster newborns who arrive one, two, three at a time without names. Among the neighbor kids she is something of a mother hen, leading the skit-writing and fort-building and chalk-drawing. When she is alone with Mia, hyperactivity takes over. Heady with the companionship of a true friend, Lily gets wacky. She cannot stop moving, talking, touching, goofing. At school—in any large group, in fact—Lily rarely speaks, so her teachers would laugh if you told them this. Not Lily! Since she got to Maryland it's only every two months or so Lily figures she has something amusing to add to a lunch-table conversation. In the rare instances when, having appraised the sentence thoroughly in her head, she judges it worthy of emitting, everyone is like, "Uh, yeah."

Whereas Mia looks forward to meeting new kids, Lily doesn't much care about making new friends. She learned the sign-language alphabet so they can communicate during class. Mainly, when Lily talks about friends, she is talking about Mia. "We're best friends," she's explained, "and we're the same height and same age. Our noses come up to the same place and so do our eyes. Her birthday is the day after my birthday. We were born twelve hours apart. So when my mom was having me her mom was in labor. I call Mia 'M' or 'MM' or 'Mi' or 'Mia.' She calls me 'Lil' or 'Lily.' I have four names for her and she has two for me."

Lily has only one name for Alexandra—"Alexandra"—and though the two saw plenty of each other during orientation last week, she didn't use it once. When Alexandra came into the cafeteria that day, instead of seeking out Mia and Lily, she bounced over to Tamika, one of the few other black girls from their elementary school, which was somewhat of a relief to Lily, because she sees Alexandra as competition for Mia's attention. At the same time she was a little insulted. Today Alexandra is late; she is supposed to occupy the empty seat in front of Lily, who eyes it nervously.

The school computer has run Lily's first and middle names together: Lilyelise. During roll, when the rest of the kids are offering up corrections and nicknames to Mrs. Stokes, Lilyelise is too shy to say anything about it. The students are silent, and efficient Mrs. Stokes is already going over schedules—no warm "Hi!" or "Welcome to middle school!"—when Alexandra walks in, wearing a white button-down, a plaid miniskirt that wouldn't pass the fingertip test, and chunky black-heeled loafers. She finds her seat in front of Lily, who watches and then tilts her head down and keeps it there, through morning announcements, through Mrs. Stokes reviewing all the papers that need to be signed, through the questions about gym shoes and recess and what if my backpack doesn't fit in my locker, through the explanations of Homework Hotline and hall passes, until the bell finally rings and the kids set out on their favorite task of the day: unloading backpacks into lockers. The girls walk through the hall with Mia in the middle, Alexandra and Lily talking to her from either side, but not to each other.

When they walk into the cafeteria for lunch, the swim-team girls at one round table, already making progress on their bagels and sandwiches and Trix yogurt, call out for Mia. They've saved her a seat, but she leads the way to an empty table. Everyone there except Alexandra brings lunch from home; when she returns with fries, they are dispersed, and enthusiastically approved of. Lily listens as the girls discuss Mia's blue Kool-Aid, the classmate whose new house has closets the size of bedrooms, and Brittany's mother's bus-stop appearance. In the telling, "Did you remember your keys" has become "*DID YOU REMEMBER YOUR KEEEEEEYS*," but the girls still agree that this was preferable to a hug.

Ms. Thomas comes by the table and asks, "How was your first day?"

"Good."

"Did they stuff you in the locker?"

"Too small."

She laughs. New sixth graders are just the cutest. Later in the year they'll turn a corner, and the teachers will wonder, "Who are you?" But for now most of them are overwhelmed, sweet, taking it all in soundlessly. In the cafeteria they raise their hands for permission to use the bathroom. The noise is one-fifth what it will be during seventh-grade and eighth-grade lunch. When Ms. Thomas counts down from five into the microphone, the room falls utterly silent, for which she congratulates them. "Welcome," she says. "It's nice to see people from all the feeder schools, and all over the world."

At recess, some boys chase a shopping cart. Mr. West, the assistant principal, quarterbacks a football game. Mia marches to the soccer field with the swimmers, where they play against the boys and her shoe keeps flying off. Alexandra and Lily are left alone on the blacktop to speak their first words to each other in a month.

"What do you want to do?" Lily asks.

"Nothing," says Alexandra.

"I can't believe the day's almost over."

"Like my new watch?"

"Don't tell me—you got it at Kohl's. I put the pink one on hold, but I can't decide." Maybe this isn't so hard.

When the whistle calls everyone inside, the boy who played Robin Hood in the fifth-grade play passes by. "Hey, Joel," Alexandra calls, "nice tights!"

Lily rolls her eyes—at the boy having worn tights once, at Alexandra taunting him, at all of it.

At eighth-grade lunch, Eric Ellis and his friends are discussing whether the plane crash that killed the R&B singer Aaliyah will affect the Video Music Awards and whether it's okay to cry if you're injured (only if there's blood involved), when Mr. West sits down and asks what grades they're going for this year. Liam, who always gets A's, says "A's." Chris, who wants to stop being the class clown so he can play football in high school, says "A's." Shawn, who thinks he's too dumb to get A's but is not too dumb to know what the right answer is here, says "A's."

Eric figures he could make A's if he really wanted to. But with skating and paintball and missing his mom and getting along with his dad's girlfriend and improving at saxophone, he says, "It's too hard to get A's. My brain is too full. I'm gonna get B's."

Sixth and seventh grade, Eric pretty much lay back, did what he was told. This year, there's a little excitement at being at the top of the school, an "I'm not a little kid anymore" feeling—for once, wanting to succeed not just for Mommy but for himself. This is a typical shift in attitude among eighth graders, as they prepare for the big league of high school. But in Eric and most of his classmates, it does battle with an equally strong attitude: ambivalence. The collective eighth grade of the United States could be labeled "Doesn't work to potential." Decline in motivation from elementary school to middle school is universal and documented. Thirteen-year-olds can't get interested in anything that bores them, no matter how many times they're told, *This is important, you'll see why in ten years.* In the preteen years, the brain's gray matter has almost fully thickened, but it is not yet pruned to its most efficient level of activity. All of a sudden there's a vast overproduction of brain cells and connections—by the time puberty is done, only some will have survived—and quantity trumps quality. It's not a particularly spectacular time to soak up information, because, even though emotional centers closer to the core of the brain have developed well by now, capacity for skills like logic, organization, and judgment, centered in the still-immature frontal lobes, is poor.

Eric's level of effort is typical for his age: Sometimes he does his work, sometimes he doesn't. Sometimes he pays attention in class, sometimes he doesn't. He likes school, and he doesn't like school. He likes his teachers, he thinks they're shrews. He thinks he's very bright compared with Chris and Shawn, and tells them, "You'll be sorry when you're out there asking for pennies on Route 40." Because teachers tell him so, Eric assumes he could get A's whenever he wanted, but when he's bored he can't pay attention, and when he's frustrated he can't either. "I want it to challenge me," he says, "but not to be too hard." He doesn't want to be too smart, "just a little intelligent." If you're too smart, people talk behind your back—"He thinks he's all that," and so on, like they do about Liam—and he's heard it's even worse if you're an adult. What would be best, he figures, is if everyone were born just smart enough so that school didn't have to exist.

Adults love Eric, who knows when to "sir" and especially when to "ma'am" and never curses above "Dag!" or "Snap!" In conversation Eric shows genuine interest, looking straight at them with his dark-ringed eyes and nodding and laughing along. He escapes the torture normally directed at a boy of his substantial weight, partly because his chubbiness doesn't prevent him from attempting the normal physical adventures of boyhood (as proved by the topography of scars on his legs) and partly because Eric is kind to everyone who doesn't cross him. He is black, but the racial divides of friendship don't apply to him. White boys in younger grades argue about who was friends with him first.

All in all, Eric does okay in school, particularly when his mother gets on his back about it, and when he has a teacher he adores, like Mr. Shifflett in seventh grade, who was really into sharks and always made science fun. Eric briefly had a 104 average in that class and once had all B's on a progress report. He was invited to the Most Improved pizza party, which felt good, though he didn't appreciate his friends calling him "Teacher's Pet" and "Egghead." There are always dozens of sixth graders at functions like that, but often by the time kids get to eighth grade they've banished A's to the same black hole where they keep their Backstreet Boys CDs. Despite the teasing, Eric really would like all B's again, although he has no idea how hard it's going to be this year to make that happen.

Last year he lived in a townhouse with his mother, Tenacious, and his half-brother on his mom's side, Tim, who's eighteen. They were evicted from their townhouse over the summer and Tim left for college, so Tenacious has moved in with friends in Baltimore, where she works as a health counselor in the jail. Eric has moved in with his dad, William, an over-the-road trucker; his fiancée, Beulah; and Eric's half-brother on his dad's side, nineteen-year-old Thomas. Their townhouse is only a half-mile from Wilde Lake Middle and barely a mile from Eric's old place, but it may as well be in another state. Without a ride, he doesn't see his old neighbors. Nobody around here walks that far. His new neighbors—not that he wants to be friends with them anyway—go to a different middle school. (Eric is breaking the districting rules, but nobody will complain.)

More significant, Eric is separated from his mother for the first time ever. She still plans to stay in control of his schoolwork. She figures she'll be more lenient about his time now that he's in eighth grade. "I'd prefer he do his homework right away," Tenacious says, "because that frees his afternoon up, but if he calls and says he's getting a snack or needs to unwind, that's okay." Since Eric will be reading *Romeo and Juliet* this year in English, she has bought a copy.

"It's a great love story," she says.

"Yuck," he says.

On the days he c omes home, Eric's father may ask if he's done his homework, but he never questions the "yes," is usually too tired to check, doesn't make Eric talk about school. "I don't talk about work if I don't have to," William says. So Tenacious plans on driving a half-hour from Baltimore to Columbia each morning by six-forty-five, to check Eric's work and take him the half-mile to school. And she has made her expectations clear: "The absolutely lowest grade you can get is a C. B's are great, just as good as A's to me. C's are beneath you, but I'll accept them. D's are out of the question." William, too, says anything less than a C is unacceptable.

It's also unacceptable to the powers that be. Concerned that middleschoolers were allowed to coast in mediocrity for too long, last year the school-board members of Howard County, which encompasses Wilde Lake, implemented strict rules: A student can't move from eighth to ninth grade without passing state reading, writing, and math tests designed for high schoolers. If he has below a C average or even one F, the principal can hold him back, or bar him from sports and extracurricular activities in ninth grade. Ms. Thomas, the principal, is serious about helping kids over the bar, and it breaks her heart—and theirs—when they don't make it. Last year thirty eighth-graders were put on the no-sports list, and eleven were held back. So far, Ms. Thomas thinks the new policy is working, that kids have seen enough classmates retained to focus far more on their grades. When she tells parents about the new policy, she says of the students, "They do understand that academics are number one—that's why we're here."

In Eric's mind, academics aren't number one. That spot is reserved for God. They're not number two. That's his mother. Music and the rest of his family—tied for third. Skating is fourth, paintball and video games are fifth. But Eric does know that, in order to satisfy the Lord, Tenacious, and the Wilde Lake High School marching band, he has to do his homework.

Eric's science class is two hallways and a universe removed from the hush of the sixth grade. The eighth graders have dropped their forbidden backpacks on the floor—they are supposed to be kept in lockers—and laugh and taunt and fiddle and compare who grew over the summer and who didn't. They keep finding reasons to go in and out of the room, and they ask things like, "Do I need to do all this?" Ian Garvey zips off a section of his cargo pants, tosses it in the air, and says, "Look, my leg came off."

Most kids arrive at Wilde Lake behaving just fine, but there are enough who are so inattentive to direction—enough Ians—that the whole first week is spent going over school rules and philosophies. Students take quizzes on the importance of their agendas, perform skits about the school motto, and answer questions like, "Which is the most important rule and why?" They highlight key sentences from an Ann Landers passage called "How to Fail" and parse the school's Mission Statement:

> WLMS staff, students, family, and community members will work together to create a supportive and stimulating school environment for all. This will enable students to achieve academic excellence, demonstrate cultural sensitivity, provide service for the community, and develop the skills for lifelong learning.

For the many children who have never acted up in class—who still respond to "Boys and girls, raise your hands if you're waiting quietly," or "Put your hand on your head when you have your name on your paper"—all this emphasis on rules is overwhelming, and boring, and they wonder how they'll ever finish the curriculum at this rate. To be told you have to raise your hand before answering is like being told you have to put the toilet lid up before you sit down. When they are debriefing over dinner after school the first night, the main thing Lily and her friends tell their parents, aside from which friends are in which classes and the unfairness of the no-spaghetti-strap rule, is that some of these kids are just plain *rude*. At Clemens Crossing Elementary, disobedient kids might talk in between what the teacher was saying, but not *over* it. And sometimes the teacher doesn't do anything about it!

Though Eric, too, finds these sessions numbingly tedious, this year he has decided to be Mr. Participation. So he alone volunteers to read aloud from the worksheet and to answer every question of today's lesson, positive and negative consequences.

"What would a negative consequence be?" Ms. Drakes asks.

With the pants leg balancing on his head—sending it there will get Ian no negative consequences—Eric raises his hand.

"Eric?"

"A negative consequence would be getting punished. I can't do nothing. I can't even play with Power Ranger toys," he jokes, and plucks the pants leg from his head.

"What's a positive consequence?" she asks.

Eric's hand is up again. "Get a piece of candy?"

"What's one positive consequence you want to earn? Eric?"

"Positive phone call home."

"What would you have to do to earn that?"

"Pay attention in class and keep up with homework and stuff."

Ian announces, "I was good once. I went to the Capitol. I still have the ticket in my wallet. It was free. See?" Next to him, Eric drums a sophisticated beat with his knuckles and fingers.

"Okay, Eric, stop." Ms. Drakes stands up front and folds her fingers down, one at a time. "Five, four, three, two, and one. One, two— You went two past my countdown. You shouldn't. Ian, turn around."

After the class has listed more positive consequences of doing schoolwork ("ice cream," "pizza party," "extra recess"), the students complete a worksheet. Eric fills in the blanks: "My goal for this year in order to *earn good grades* as a positive consequence is *to study and work hard*." When Ms. Drakes asks if anyone wants to share, Eric reads what he's written.

Good grades alone as positive consequence? He may as well have written "know a lot." Ms. Drakes suggests, "Maybe the consequence you would want is the honor-roll breakfast or something."

It doesn't take long to know what a class is going to be like for the rest of the year. By the second week at Wilde Lake, Eric's hand is already cramped from writing class goals and expectations, and he has made some assessments:

Science, she's no Mr. Shifflett. Too many worksheets, not enough labs.

Band should be good. The new teacher was visibly impressed when Eric, the best sax player in the school, said he had taught himself to play in only two years. Sometimes he gets bored with band, but Mr. Vega seems enthusiastic, and, anyway, his mom would be crushed if he quit. Music, she tells him, is his special gift, even at age two, when he would pull the pots and pans out of the cupboard and entertain himself for hours.

English might be cool, *Romeo and Juliet* notwithstanding. Mrs. Brown has set the bar high—"Eighty and above, that's success"—but she also lets them set expectations for *her*: Be prepared, don't pick favorites, don't go too slow, don't go too fast, don't punish the whole class for the misdeeds of a few, and, from Eric, make sure you understand a kid's question before you answer. Also, Mrs. Brown and Eric share a passion. One of the first days, she asks, "Does anyone like auto racing?" Eric, who has sweated with excitement each of the nine times he's watched *The Fast and the Furious*, shouts "Yes!" and stops tapping his pencil. Mrs. Brown tells about one of her favorite authors, who spent eight years studying auto racing for a novel, and she answers Eric's questions about NASCAR superstar Dale Earnhardt, even though they're irrelevant.

Eric's not sure about academic enrichment, a class where students who aren't taking a foreign language learn study skills and review subjects there's not time for in other classes. He likes that Mrs. Cook seems stern and caring at the same time, that it's instantly clear she's determined her students turn out good citizens. She already has the class totally under control. "When it's time to work in her class," Eric says, "you work." But he goes blank at the topics she announces they'll learn: Microstudio and PowerPoint and Hypertext and Concept Mapping, whatever all that is.

He has Mrs. Cook for reading, too. Reading and English classes are a lot alike, and for Eric that two just combine to mean too many books. Even though his mother tried to pass on her passion for books to Eric, and he fondly remember their Peter Rabbit moments, officially Eric says that no book is good unless it's about cooking, cars, funny stuff, or skateboarding. Unofficially he really liked two books he read in sixth grade: *Freak the Mighty*, a novel about a midget kid and his grotesquely huge friend Max, whose dad killed his mom, and a biography of Langston

Hughes. When they read how Hughes was treated poorly in his new all-white neighborhood, Eric says, "That related to me. When I lived in the city everybody was black, and then when I moved out here—aside from Shawn and James; they were like, 'What's up?'—everybody else was like, they already had their little cliques, and I had to find somebody else to be friends with." Eric's thinking he might not hate reading so much this year, because they're going to write a research paper on whatever they want, which for Eric is cars, and for class he has written a poem he's pleased with, called "I Am":

> Soft, friendly sometimes, mamas boy, easy!
> Who discovered, that its hard to be popular in a variety of cultures in a
>   school
> Who feels alive, brainy, curious
> Who fears breaking another bone, failing, parent-teacher conferences
> Who loves my rollerblades, sportscars, and my parents
> Who wants 99.9 million dollars, a fully equipped car

Eric thinks America is one of the best countries in the world, even though for its celebrations Africa has cool decorations like beads made from animal skin and "we just have that flag." But he's not pleased with American-history class. First of all, Eric hates the way Shawn copies from his homework. His classmates cheat a lot; there's a homework worksheet being copied at half the cafeteria tables every day. Eric doesn't have a problem with people copying off him, but only when he gives permission. He hates the way Mrs. Conroy capitulates to the girl who complains, "Obstruction of justice! I know my rights, and I have a right to go to the bathroom!" and the way she seems to just stand up there at the front of the room smiling, calling on them, and referring to the book. Still, Eric raises his hand to answer all the time, as if a pulley attached to the ceiling were jerking his wrist.

Ms. Adams, the new, youngish math teacher, who wears a different pair of funky glasses practically every day, intrigues Eric; he touches her long blond ringlets and says, "Your hair is mad curly!" Sometimes her lessons are cryptic, though, or incomplete. The first day, in an attempt to interest the many black students in the class, such as Eric, she asks what "40 Acres and a Mule" means. After some guessing (Eric: "Oooh, did the slaves use mules to fight back?"), she explains. She adds, "Everything we do in here is not necessarily what you'd think is math," though why they're discussing forty acres and a mule, beyond the fact that forty is a number, never becomes clear.

Within days Eric realizes that when he's not in a math mood he can talk about Red Lobster or *Gridlock* with the kid sitting next to him, or watch the girls across the room stick tape all over a boy's ears and face. "Do you not know better?" Ms. Adams says. "Do you not know better? You owe me a roll of tape." Still, when Eric feels like working, he wants to get it right. One day in the second week of school, the drill for the day is written on the overhead:

1. What day followed the day before yesterday if two days from now will be Sunday?

Eric says to himself, "Wednesday. Yep, that's easy."

2. A math teacher drove by a playground that was full of boys and dogs. The teacher happened to notice that there was a total of 40 heads and 100 feet. How many boys and how many dogs were there?

Eric doesn't know where to begin on this one. He guesses fifteen dogs, in which case there's twenty-five boys. Too many. He shakes his notebook. There are kids working; there are kids talking. Eric picks some numbers randomly and figures them in his head, but they don't work. "I don't get number two, Ms. Adams, so I'm quitting because I'm getting frustrated and then I'll get mad." He pounds the desk: "How many legs on the goddamn dog?"

3. Replace A, B and C with numbers so that $A{\times}A = B$, $B{-}A = C$, $A{+}A = C$.

Last year Eric's half-brother Tim, a college freshman, taught him tricks to figuring these kinds of expressions, but variables don't make sense to him. Can you own "A" CDs? Invite "B" people to your birthday party? Are there "C" days till Christmas? Ms. Adams tries A as one, then two, then three. Bingo. "I still don't get what you're doing," Eric says.

Ms. Adams, a twenty-five-year-old who spent the two years before teaching school as an exercise physiologist, doesn't totally get it either. In the last two weeks she's been learning the rules, too. Don't stand on a desk to put up your bulletin board. Check the duty map to see when you have hall patrol. Write comments to parents every week on the agendas, and phone if a grade goes down. Make sure kids don't fill out their hall passes in pencil. Keep your eye out for bandanas, hats, purses, Palm Pilots, spaghetti straps, pagers. Follow the official levels of discipline intervention laid out in this fat binder—don't make up your own system.

Last year Ms. Adams student-taught sixth graders in a prosperous middle school near Pittsburgh; here, the amount of time spent going over the discipline policy has made her fearful for what the teachers call "our population." She can't pronounce the foreign kids' names ("Give me a vowel, just one vowel"); she worries black kids will call her racist; she doesn't know much about geography, which she has to teach in addition to math; she doesn't know how to plan for an eighty-minute class, because she's used to fifty; she rear-ended a Cadillac on the Beltway and can't afford the five-hundred-dollar deductible (in addition to the five-hundred-dollar deductible from when she was rear-ended herself); she's already missed a day of school to fight a speeding ticket; her neck hurts; she can't find an affordable apartment that will take her dog and cat, so she's staying on her boyfriend's brother's girlfriend's couch; and she's realizing that eighth graders are way different from sixth graders, even when they're at the same place mathematically. They look ready to tear her apart. She wonders if she can help them.

"Eric," she says, "explain to me what's confusing."

"Everything."

everyone else thinks it's a stupid plane crash

On picture day, a Tuesday morning in September, students are called to the cafeteria, class by class. The sixth graders take the occasion very seriously, and several, on their mothers' request, wear collared shirts, which they change out of right after photos. Most of the eighth graders aren't buying their pictures. They can list every nonawful photo ever taken of them, and school photos are never among them. Just as well, since several eighth-grade boys made themselves pass out at recess yesterday (lean against the wall, take ten quick deep breaths, have someone press a fist into your chest), and their foreheads are bruised from hitting the asphalt.

Seventh graders still care about their pictures, but even more they care about having a half-hour out of class with their friends.

"Last year I looked retarded."

"Are there bags under my eyes?"

"Man, it stinks!"

"Eww!"

They all wave their order forms under their noses and eye a girl in a messy orange T-shirt, who says, "I did not fart, I swear."

One boy does a karate chop to another's neck, because his brother in the Army said you can stun someone that way. Onstage, in front of screens painted in some disco-cheesy way to look like they're emanating light, the photographers from their fingers into "L"s and angle them, but

the kids remember how stupid their heads looked tilted in last year's photos, as if they were all going to topple off the yearbook page, so they resist.

As one boy settles into the stool, his friend grabs his crotch and says,
"Go like this!"

"That's not funny," a teacher says.

"It *was*."

"But was it appropriate?"

"Last year I looked like an insane clown," Michelle says. "My hair
was all lumpy from the ponytail the night before."

"Are you going to go out with Adam?" Ann thinks this one kid,
Adam, is cute and funny but is taking into account that the last time they
went out, he dumped her.

Across the street Ms. Thomas is sitting in a room full of principals listening to a talk about emergency procedures when, shortly after nine, the assistant superintendent comes in and announces that an airplane has hit
the World Trade Center. It's part of the meeting, they think, a sneaky
practice drill. No, he insists, this is real, and the meeting is disbanded.
Ms. Thomas's older daughter comes up from the train into the World
Trade Center every morning on the way to work. Ms. Thomas goes
home to check CNN: It's real, all right. Futilely she dials Ashley's cell
phone, Ashley's friends, Ashley's work. She heads to school.

Just yesterday there was a staff meeting about the emergency-
procedures manual: how to do a lockdown, how to evacuate, where the
orange vests are kept. Clearly this is an emergency, but what kind? There
may or may not be problems in Baltimore, a half-hour away. There may
or may not be problems in Washington, forty-five minutes away. This
isn't in the manual.

By late morning, the teachers have started to hear the news, and
many parents show up for their children. Ms. Thomas wants to keep the
kids out of this. She agrees to let them be released but makes parents wait
outside; she tells the staff not to congregate in the halls; she pulls one
who is crying into her office. She struggles to keep her composure, worried desperately about her daughter, and her six hundred other children
too. Televisions next door at the high school play CNN, and the students

watch and cry, but mass terrorism, Ms. Thomas decides, is something twelve-year-olds should hear about from their parents. The day will be as normal as possible.

So the sixth graders go to lunch oblivious. They talk about Round-wiches, those new packaged peanut-butter sandwiches without the crust; they talk about the truck accident they saw from the bus this morning; they talk about everything, nothing.

"Mia, I have another plum if you want it."

"You want to hear something traumatizing? I left my book in the eighth-grade pod and I can't get it back."

"This school is so cold compared to Clemens."

Ms. Thomas's daughter has finally called, so while Ashley is telling her, with sirens in the background, how she was in the towers just hours ago, how from where she stands blocks away "it looks like a nuclear disaster," Mr. West goes to the cafeteria to fetch the kids whose names come over the PA.

"If you hear me," he says from the center of the room, "raise your fingers. I need you to use elementary-school voices today, because there are important announcements I need to hear. Please whisper." When the names penetrate the buzz of lunchtime one by one, Mr. West finds each child and says, "Your parents are here to pick you up."

"Oh, cool," says one girl at the table as she fumbles with her Sprite and applesauce. "I get early dismissal." Onstage, the photographers roll up their screens, and the wondering grows loud.

"Maybe there's a bus broken down so they can't get home."

"What's going on?"

"Anyone named Jeff is a geek."

"My mom never packs me enough food. Does anyone have any money?"

"Something must be going on."

"Remember the snow days last year? Remember we did the snow dance?"

"Why are so many people leaving?"

"Maybe something happened at the high school."

"All voices off," Mr. West says. "I have a serious announcement. As you noticed, a lot of your classmates have had early dismissal. There is something taking place across the nation. It is a crisis including Washing-

ton, D.C., and New York City. We are confident that you are safe. You
will be dismissed a half-hour early."

"YES!"

"Please. Today is the day to have your attention. Something has transpired across the nation. We don't have any information now. Trust us
that we would tell you. Please act like the mature sixth graders that you
are. You're not in elementary school anymore. I need voices to be *this
quiet*. We're not going to have snack or recess today."

Groans.

Mia isn't concerned about snack, or recess. She's concerned about
her father, a college professor who, like many Wilde Lake parents, works
in Washington. *Oh my God,* she thinks. Lily can't think of anyone she has
to worry about, but most of the kids come up with someone—a baby
cousin in Brooklyn, their moms at Fort Meade. They figure that if Mr.
West knows "something has transpired across the nation," he knows exactly what it is, and he should tell them. Especially since Brittany is crying!

Softly, she says, "My grandma lives in Queens."

"Anyone want a chewy granola bar? Hey—maybe the president was
assassinated!"

"Yay!"

"Maybe it's World War Three!"

"I hope it's not the end of the world," says Lily.

"My dad's in Washington, D.C.," Mia says. Next to her, a girl shiv-
ers.

"I heard in health that a terrorist plane crashed into a building,"
Jonathan says. He is one of only two sixth-grade boys brave enough to sit
with girls at lunch, but right now his eyes are red with fear.

By eighth-grade lunch many parents have picked up their kids, so the
cafeteria is half empty. A guidance counselor told some of the boys what
had happened, the little he knew. In the back corner Eric worries about
his father, who drives between Baltimore and Washington all the time,
and his brother, who plays college football. "They travel to the different
states," he says, "and he might catch a plane."

"Death is my biggest fear," Malik says, and his friends nod. "Planes all around us crashed. Are you afraid they're going to hit us? They were saying the last one was eighteen miles away."

"Our humanity: lost!"

"Why are you sitting there? You didn't sign the paper."

"I wasn't here that day and Ms. Thomas said sit anywhere."

"Tara, I hope your boyfriend didn't die."

Mr. West tries to silence the room. "One, two." he says.

"Are we going to die?"

"Three."

"There's a rapist in the school."

"Four. Five. A lot of you have been hearing information. We're not going to share too much with you." But he's shared enough that even the tough boys have wide eyes. Mr. West continues, "This is not a drill. This is not fake. This is real. When you get home, ask your parents. There have been bits of information given to some of your—I don't know if that's factual. When you get home, you'll have all the information you need."

Eric's head is in his hands. Shawn comes up and asks, "Pal, you okay?"

"Everyone else thinks it's a stupid plane crash," says Liam.

Eric lifts his head, shakes it. "I wonder if it has to do with Aaliyah. Who are the idiots doing this? These people have no reason to live." He wants more from Mr. West, who says, "I'm sorry, Eric, this is all I can read to you."

When the bell rings for the day, Ms. Thomas herds the children right outside. She won't let them go to their lockers for books. Some of the kids have heard there's no homework, but Lily isn't sure. She asks the music teacher, who tells her to ask Ms. Thomas, who is standing in front of the office with a group of teachers. Lily can't get up the nerve, and leaves. She feels stupid.

It's quiet on the buses. Once home, kids dial their mothers' cell phones, with little success. Nobody's home at Eric's, where he flips through BET, *Rugrats*, MTV. It's practically impossible to find a channel without the World Trade Center footage, which is getting more explicit each time more video is found, so he rides his bike to McDonald's.

Mia watches with her dad, as one simple thought loops through her head: Oh my God. Oh my God. When the CD she is listening to before bedtime ends, the radio comes on, and a man with two five-year-olds pleads for someone to find their mother in the wreckage. At this she cries, and clings to her mom. Cartoons can't take her mind off the possibilities: What if it happened at BWI? What about Grandma and Grandpa, who are driving back to Ohio? Why didn't anyone ever tell me what a terrorist was before?

Howard County schools are the only ones in the Washington area open Wednesday, which Ms. Thomas is glad of—it sends the right message to terrorists. Although she hates dressing up, she wears the black suit she bought as a joke last year for a colleague's fiftieth birthday. "We don't know which of our kids will be affected," she tells the staff before school, "but there will be some for sure. No reaction is a wrong reaction. Allow them to go to guidance. I'm not going to say you can't discuss it, I'm not going to say you should discuss it. I just ask that you not tune in to TV, these tragic visions again and again. If kids are laughing, don't come down hard on them. Many of our students are Muslim; make sure they are not blamed. We are all here to support each other."

The kids arrive looking a little shell-shocked, tired, the hair not quite as neat as normal. A group of eighth graders waits under the half-staff flag for the doors to open.

"Doofuses. They were dumb. Do you think they'll rebuild the World Trade Center? It'll take a year or so."

"I bet they're going to Chicago—to the big tall one."

"The Sears Tower."

"I think the president is a stupidhead, putting a Christian spin on his speech. He should have said, 'Don't blame Muslims.' " Max and Malik, both Muslims, start to tussle. Max calls Malik "Bin Laden wannabe." Malik calls Max "Turbanhead." A teacher intervenes: "Not today, guys."

"Or tomorrow," one girl adds. "And the day after that? Not so good either. Oooh, there's a plane!"

The eighth graders, more mad than sad, want to get to the bottom of this. Today the students in Mrs. Conroy's gifted-and-talented class raise their hands at every question. A typical middle school has very little time—often none—to teach current events, and this is the most rapt they will be all year, meandering through not just the horror of the carnage but its geopolitics.

"We know this will be in the history books," Mrs. Conroy says quietly.

"Are they going to hit anyone else?"

"My guess is not at this time, because we are all on alert."

One after another, the students say where they heard the fourth plane was headed: Camp David, Baltimore's World Trade Center. "I heard on the news," one boy says, "that they got threats three weeks ago but nobody took it seriously."

"There are always threats we don't know about," Mrs. Conroy says.

"Lateshia's mom's co-worker's daughter was on the plane, and she called on her cell phone."

"I hear they might have killed people right away because none of the panic buttons were pressed."

"There is that theory," Mrs. Conroy says.

"Who bombed the World Trade Center a couple of years ago?"

"Bin Laden," she says. "He has openly said we are evil."

"They found a van in Boston with instructions on how to fly the plane."

"A news agency did an undercover test about whether you could get through security in the airport, and you could, twenty percent of the time."

As always, a girl named Daisy pops her head in the door and says, "Hi, everybody!" For once she is ignored.

"My mom says someone in her office was in some religion that said Tuesday was War Day."

"The date was nine-one-one."

"It was exactly three months after McVeigh was executed."

"It could be Americans. After the Oklahoma City bombing they captured all Muslims, and it turned out not to be them."

"U.S. terrorists usually don't kill themselves," Mrs. Conroy says. "There's no glory or reward for Americans who kill themselves. How many people watched the president's speech?" Everyone. "Who else is he holding responsible?"

"Those who supported them."

"The news said the airport would be running at noon. Wouldn't that be a bad idea if they were working from within?"

"I suspect," Mrs. Conroy says, "they won't open them till they think they're safe."

"Why were they telling everyone where the president was?"

"Maybe," she says, "they wanted people to know the president was safe, that we are not going to hide. Girls," she tells a group in the back, "share with everyone."

"We both saw a plane flying over our neighborhood last night. Why was it flying there?"

Mrs. Conroy can't answer every question, she will never be able to, but she has always thought that eighth graders are ready to become engaged citizens and that her job is to get them there. "This has changed our culture now," she says before flipping on the overhead to reveal the daily drill question: "What document guaranteed all Christians the right to worship as they choose?"

"This has changed America. You have just lived through a historical event."

"Cool," the students say.

It is not, the way the eighth graders see it, about them—it is about the world beyond their own five square miles. This is a perspective most sixth graders aren't quite mature enough to grasp. They're not used to discussing current events, and in this case their loved ones are okay, so for many the news, and the sorrow, sit in their heads only briefly. If any time is spent dwelling on the tragedy, the thoughts are mostly about the personal losses, the broken families.

Mia, one of the hundred students absent today, believed her mother when she said it wouldn't happen again, because the FBI is on the case, but still she was too upset for school this morning. It didn't feel right yesterday, trying to kick a medicine ball over other people's heads in PE when what she really wanted to do was visit the guidance counselors for comfort. Had she known them, she would have. At home she cries, as hard as she tries not to, the plane crashing into the tower over and over in her head. She decides she'll find work around the house and in her mom's dental office so that she can sponsor a cute poor girl she saw on a TV commercial for eighty cents a day.

At school, her classmates are evenly divided between those who want to remember and those who want to forget. Last night three of the swimmers assembled in a bedroom lit with candles and sat around the best-smelling one, thinking, What are we supposed to do about this? They pulled out the big children's Bible and found the pages with the prettiest pictures and read aloud. They discussed forgiveness, and agreed to disagree. But today one of them says, "I just want to move on. This happened before, at Pearl Harbor, and they didn't get all worked up about it."

Her English class has voted to forget—to debate, as scheduled, whether the government should rate music. There is a boy in the class whose father, a Baptist pastor, came home warning of an apocalypse. Today the child wonders, to himself only, if a nuclear bomb is the size of his car, or his apartment building, or bigger. With low, brassy squawks coming from the band room next door, a sixth-grade music class discusses what the word "opera" makes them think of ("Opera Winfrey," "people breaking glasses," "fat ladies screaming at the top of their lungs"), and why in the old days sopranos were fat ("because the noise echoes in their stomachs," "they show up better," "they hold more air").

Those who have voted to remember—and avoid a math worksheet—discuss whether braces will set off an airport metal detector and who "that big terrorist guy" is. "The leader of Afghanistan," the teacher says, which is in either the Middle East or Asia, she's not sure. In another class they write to firefighters. "Can we draw fire in the background?" one boy asks, and his teacher says, "That's not appropriate. We want to get their mind off what they're doing and show how much we appreciate them." So they write things like "Dear Fireman, That was really sad what those guys did. Thanks for being brave," and "I know that because of the tragic things that happened Tuesday, you have been working hard. USA!"

Talk at lunch is about whether people are still buried in the rubble at the Pentagon, whether anyone has tried a turkey-and-ketchup sandwich, whose uncles worked in the World Trade Center, and whether you would rather die from a gigantic fireball or jump out a window on the hundredth floor. Lily found out last night that her cousin had flown one of the F-15's that accompanied President Bush, but she doesn't mention this. Jonathan pokes fries into his ears, then eats them, then says to Lily, "You're invited to my birthday party." Lily has worn a new knee-length maroon sweater from Candie's with a fake-fur collar, and she does a model's twirl for her friend Maddy. The rest of the girls are still immersed in talk about defenestration when Lily asks, "Is anyone going outside? Is anyone going outside? Is anyone going outside?"

Lily has an idea about identifying the terrorists, that you could pause the video of the plane crashing into the building and zoom in real close. After the sermon in church about what happened Tuesday, Lily's sister, Gabrielle, who is in fifth grade, is inspired to write a musical about patriotism and freedom. So the girls open the cover of Lily's binder, which is coated with photos of Britney Spears and Christina Aguilera even though she thinks they've gotten ugly, and go to work. In the play, George Washington declares war on the British, becomes president, and throws a party. "Food all over," the stage direction says. A soldier collapses. In death, he says, "I see a bright light."

Other than that, Lily doesn't have much time to think about global terrorism. She is too busy serving as the poster child for middle-school self-absorption.

When she thinks about anything—not like she stresses; nothing, she claims, gives her stress—she's thinking about Halloween. She doesn't want to trick-or-treat, since her sister already claimed the pale-blue pageant dress Lily wanted to wear, and anyway Mia has other plans. So Lily decides to set up a haunted house and Creepy Maze in the yard and starts by drawing diagrams and making to-buy lists: dry ice, red candle wax to drip for blood.

She's thinking about Wesley, one of the foster babies, whom the Masons are thinking of adopting.

She's thinking about Abigail Werner, who has a locker next to hers and, because it's too cramped for them to get their books at the same time, always stands there with her arms crossed over her chest, threatening to get inside Lily's locker and change the combination. "She knows how," Lily says.

She's thinking about the way that everyone in home ec, kids she barely knows, looks at her when Mrs. Brodian announces that Lily can help with sewing if anyone needs it. "Stop staring at me," she wants to tell her classmates, "and don't call me Miss Lily anymore."

She's thinking about how already Wilde Lake is harder than her school in Louisiana, and even though she pays attention, whenever teachers call on her she doesn't know the answer. She likes being quiet, because you never get in trouble and you never get made fun of and nobody much cares what you say or what you think, but it also means teachers call on you more, because they know you'd never raise your hand.

She's thinking about Eric Ellis's friend Chris, who pulls scrunchies out of girls' ponytails on the bus. He may not be trying to hurt anyone, but a kid who's six feet—"his Afro is, like, two feet tall"—can cause pain even when he's not trying. He gets Lily across her eye and bops her on the head, and she almost cries. Her mother, Avy, and two other moms call the school, and Chris is suspended from the bus. Lily just hopes he never finds out who tattled.

She's thinking about the way her mom will only let her wear lip gloss and a teensy bit of eye shadow, not that she cares about wearing it to school, because none of her friends do, but still. And her parents made her pay three dollars every time she butted into their conversation from the back of the van on the way to Niagara Falls—"Whatchou talking about, Mama? What'd you say?"—and when Avy calls "Lily!" up the stairs she has to respond with "Ma'am?" instead of "What?" or "Yeah?" like every other kid in the state of Maryland. Her parents can feel the changes coming on, the way a tickly swallow portends a sore throat. Cheekiness has started to seep through Lily ever since they moved from Louisiana six months ago. Avy—who tells her kids even the word "butt" is "ugly talk"—has a feeling that during middle school it's going to be some kind of struggle to preserve what's left of Lily's Southern gentility.

More than anything, Lily's thinking about her friends, a tiny bit about the ones she left in Louisiana and a lot about the ones here. Social scientists explain that being eleven means that you put friends number one on your list of priorities, that for the first time you perceive intimacy as a desirable state, not just within your immediate family but in your very own world outside it, that what you're doing is less important than whom you're doing it with. You pick your friends not just because they live near you or happen to be in your ballet class but because, well, *you pick them*. You want to share. You learn that making them happy makes you happy. Parents lately have read a lot about the vicious nature of schoolyard exclusion, and mean girls, and much of it is true. But even if a middle-school girl is as well situated as Lily—she hates nobody, and is hated by nobody—the ebb and flow of her friendships consume her to a mind-boggling degree.

So she's thinking about recess. Most of the girls follow Mia to play soccer, but Lily is terrified of "anything with the last name Ball." Alexandra double-dutches, switching easily between the black girls' jump rope and the white girls' jump rope, but Lily doesn't like jumping rope, and besides, she doesn't know those girls. She doesn't try to. On Friendship Day, during the scavenger hunt, when you find people in the class who share your birth month or favorite food or what have you, Lily is too shy to approach many people, and her sheet never fills up. The Masons go to her sister's friend's house for dinner, and a boy there asks, "Do I know you?"

"I'm in your homeroom," Lily says. Thanks a lot.

Lily is not, she insists, thinking about Alexandra. Or maybe she thinks about her, but she doesn't care, which are two different things. "I'm never mad at people," she says, "so it doesn't really matter." Still, she notices that Alexandra doesn't eat at their lunch table anymore; usually she eats with the tall girls, or the black girls.

More than anything, Lily's thinking about Mia and how to keep her close, how this new math class she's just moved up to seems hard but at least they're together, and how she really wants a double birthday party in February, in Mia's new basement, because you can wipe up spills easier on a concrete floor.

Jackie Taylor is thinking about her birthday party, too, but that doesn't mean she ever stopped thinking about death. A couple days after the attacks, Miss Colton writes on the overhead, "September 11, 2001 will prove to be an important day in American history. It will also be remembered by the writings of those who lived through it." "You can write a letter, poem, story, whatever," she tells the seventh graders. "But you have to write something, because your reflections are important. Each of you should have something to say about it, because it *did* affect your lives."

My life was affected because I got out of school a half hour early.

I was saying no more World Trade Center that is bad, but as long as I am okay, and my family.

Jackie's mom had just done some work at the Pentagon offices before they were destroyed. One of her acquaintances there had heard about the World Trade Center during her commute and phoned her colleagues with a premonition. "Please," she urged, "come out into the parking lot." They did, then the plane crashed, and Jackie fills up a whole page with this story, which Miss Colton asks to keep.

In the hall after class, her friend Judy keeps directing her hand downward like a crashing plane and saying "Zoom! Zoom! Zoom!" "That's not funny," Kelly tells her. The girls complain that they're the only county to have school today. Jackie tells how her mom worked at the Pentagon, and Judy demonstrates dominoes with her hand, the rooms collapsing.

The zooming, the dominoes: Though Jackie doesn't say anything in the hall, it's not funny to her either. Over and over she thinks, We're not safe anymore. Even before yesterday, Jackie had been thinking about mortality a lot, and though it doesn't take up quite as much space in her brain as wondering what other kids think about her, particularly the boys, particularly Jay Starr, it still feels like a lot. Too much. Sometimes she tells herself, "You're twelve, you don't have to worry about this now," but she can't help it.

Thoughts of death—their own and their loved ones'—weigh heavily on many children as they approach puberty, though they rarely let on. For some kids, like Jackie, these thoughts are part of a broader onset of spirituality and seeking. For all of them, it's about fear. They fear more than anything the death of a parent. When their parents are ill, they lie awake anxious. Those with older fathers grimly calculate how old they will be when their dads die. Sad, they know, but they are certain. One boy came to school the day after his mom died of a heart attack, and his classmates couldn't even imagine it. When Jackie is annoyed with her mother for not letting her walk to the Giant, she thinks about her sick, with breast cancer maybe, like their next-door neighbor, and then she stops being mad, at least for a little bit.

Her father went through thoughts like that when he was Jackie's age, but her mother never did, and would be stunned to know that in her journal Jackie writes pages upon pages of questions about death. What if her soul can't escape her body? What if it does, and then winds up in some third grader's science project? What if heaven is a myth? Really, who can say "ribbis" and priests know any better than anyone else? What if she dies? If a genie floated down to grant Jackie a wish, she'd choose to live forever. If there were a giant question box in the sky, to which you could submit any query without fear of embarrassment, Jackie would ask two things: *How do you make out?* and *What happens after you die?* Jackie remembers what it felt like to be unborn. She wonders: Will it be like that? Will it be like heaven, or will it be black? She believes you are reincarnated until you fulfill your goals—not including your goals about Jay Starr.

chapter three

any girl will obsess over at least 1 guy in their life

After death, Jackie's biggest worry is whether Jay likes her, pretty much par for the course for a twelve-year-old. Jackie plays drums in the school band and has a good mind for canasta and imagines having a house with every room a different color, red and silver in the dance room and blue in the aquarium room. One day on the swings, she thinks, she'll flip clear over the top. Her parents love this sense of adventure—"spice and zing," her mom calls it—thought they worry a little when she lies back on a skateboard and luges, fast, down the steep sidewalk.

"It's so great to be popular!" Jackie declares once at the lunch table, hands thrown in the air, apropos of nothing. She is at the less socially advanced end of the group, which means she is always the one dispatched to say "So-and-so is mad at you." She doesn't get into fights and is proud that she can, and will, carry on a conversation with someone she's doesn't even know, unlike her friends. They're always "in a band," though they never play music—just make up songs and band names over the phone, like "Obsession," the "i" dotted with a rose. Jackie's typical report card is one or two B's, the rest A's. Her shiny brown hair would fall straight down her back if she didn't tie it up all the time; in her wildest dreams it is streaked green, or the very least it's thick and curly like the girl's in *The Princess Diaries*, or at the very, very least it's redder. Her orthodontist and her grandma and her friend Kristina's mom say she should be a model, but her mother won't let her sign up on the Barbizon Web site, "so I'm obviously not a model right now." Jackie is tiny, thin, flat; even though her hips are lower than the hurdles, during gym class she floats right over them, to her surprise.

In Jackie's house, her dad, Mike, stays home with the baby, and her mom, Sara, an interior designer, drops Jackie at the bus stop, goes to the office, and makes it home in time to be the boss. Mike and Sara have raised Jackie to stand up for herself, and she was into the surface notions of girl power even before the Powerpuff Girls told her to be. In third grade she announced to the class that she wanted to be quarterback for the Miami Dolphins, and when one boy protested that girls can't do that, she hit him. It bugs her that there's never been a female president, that women barely show up in her history textbooks, and that so many people assume men are stronger, not just physically but mentally. She wears a T-shirt that says "Girls are the best. Boys are OK" and really wants this calendar with a picture of a gingerbread man that says, "The perfect man: He's quiet, he's sweet, and if he gives you any grief you can bite his head off." On her mom's computer in the basement, Jackie has created a PowerPoint presentation about boys that she calls her Web site. It urges, "Always remember to put your self ahead of your guy no matter what!" and lists reasons girls are better than boys:

- They scream higher than we do.
- We get better test scores.
- We're better. Face it.

Sara said no to *CosmoGIRL!* magazine and its French-kissing tips, and fortunately even Jackie disdains the concept of *BoyCrazy!* trading cards and magazine—which doesn't even pretend to have articles about anything else—but Sara yielded to pleas for a subscription to *YM*, which promises better living and better boyfriends through low-rider jeans and always knowing just the right thing to say. Sprawled on her waterbed, surrounded by a kittens-in-a-basket poster and a slew of spent glow sticks and Dolphins pennants and ink-on-loose-leaf pronouncements of her musical tastes taped to the door (Sum 41, Linkin Park, Incubus) and forty Beanie Babies piled on a shelf, Jackie loves to read the embarrassing moments column. A twelve-year-old lives in perpetual fear of being embarrassed. She always feels like an audience full of people is watching and judging her, worries they'll think her outfit looks gay, and, in Jackie's case, even feels like someone's peeping through her window. Still, some sense of schadenfreude draws her to the magazine accounts of spilling punch in front of a crush, losing a bikini top after a dive, peeing in the pool and trailing an inky tail from the gotcha chemicals. The one that cracked Jackie up the most was the girl who was at her boyfriend's for dinner and the toilet clogged so she threw her poop out the window and went back to the table, where everyone was laughing because they saw it hanging off the telephone pole. Jackie always scores in the just-right realm on the quizzes—"Sincerely Yours" on the lying quiz, for example, instead of "Pants on Fire" or "The Truth Hurts"—and she gives her own advice to girls who write in:

"My guy friend puts his arm around me a lot—does this mean he likes me?"

"No! 'Cause Brad does that to me. Brad does that to me all the time and he's going out with Mimi."

What little most teen-girl magazines have to say about sidelines like school, they do through the prism of guys—"What do boys' lockers tell you about their personalities?" Jackie may say she likes *YM* for the horoscopes, which, she insists, "really work," and boasts about owning only one dress, and expresses relief that her baby brother, Kyle, is not a girl, because then she might have to play tea party instead of army men, but for all her tomboyhood and feminism and independence Jackie exhibits a good share of the signs of preteen boy-craziness—and, like most girls her age, is not sure why. She says guys are the second-most-important thing in her life, after friends and before family, school, and shopping. Her girlfriends generally rank life the same way.

For most children, middle school is a time when the hormones bubble, when boys and girls notice each other *that* way. Some Wilde Lake girls, like Lily and Mia, are focused fully on schoolwork and girlfriends and hobbies and are not interested in boys at all. Some Wilde Lake girls have been put on the Pill by their worried mothers and are either having sex or very close to it. The majority of the girls are somewhere in between: simultaneously boy-crazy and boy-phobic, yearning for love but clueless about how to attain it. Their dramas are serious and absurd: Who can help laughing at the way a preteen girl obsesses over a "boyfriend" with whom she has never had a conversation? The way she writes "I ♡ Danny" on her hand in black marker and then hides it in her sleeve so nobody can see? And who can help feeling sorry for her pain when he ignores her, and worrying that her insecurities won't go away when the crush does?

A girl on the cusp of adolescence has this need to branch out from familiar, familial relationships and create an independent universe of allies and adversaries. She needs to test fidelity and see, in the starkest way, what others think of her. Although boys and girls may never be more fickle than at this age, they may also never have more capacity for devotion. Above all, according to what little research exists on the subject, having romantic relationships—even if the concept is used loosely—exalts boys' and girls' status among their peers, as long as they choose correctly. Crushes give girlfriends something to conspire about.

"It is a proven fact that any girl will obsess over at least 1 guy in their life," Jackie writes on her "Web site," and she's already got that covered. Last year she had a crush on the lead singer of Blink 182 and in real life went out with Dan Arnstein, who called her every day (she had to do the talking), then Dan Pryor, then Kevin Heneman. Kevin was three times, for a total of three months, which she'll never understand; she suspects all the milk she'd been drinking might have warped her brain. She started this year with a thing for the lead singer of Linkin Park, and all September, though Sara doesn't like Jackie to write on herself—it's one of those I-just-said-sos she tries not to mandate too often—the acronym of Jackie's longing is inked onto the fingers of each hand: J-A-B

Jay Starr.
Anton James.
Brad Aronson.

Jackie's friends, at age twelve, span the spectrum from prim on one end to boy-crazy on the other, from well rounded to hobbyless, closely supervised to unbound, polite to mouthy, engaged to indifferent. Kristina and Celia say they got caught passing themselves off on the Internet as eighteen-year-olds from Las Vegas and another friend tells her dad, in a fit of peevishness, "Why don't you go sixty-nine Mom?" Jackie whines a lot, but it's doubtful she will ever instruct her parents to perform sex acts.

Even though they're not *doing* much, these girls talk all the time about boys and romance; lesbians come up a lot. They speculate that one female rabbi is gay and might hit on a girl while she reads the Torah at her Bat Mitzvah.

When Jackie meets Kristina and Celia at the mall, she hitches a Betty Boop beeper (no batteries, no phone number) to the back pocket of her sparkly jeans. She laughs with them at the key chains at Spencer's, especially the one that says "I'll be your 6 you be my 9." Jackie spots a pimp Halloween costume. "This is Anton! This is Anton!" She buys two stickers for her binder that say "Warning: HEARTBREAKER" and "I Recycle Boys." Over cookies in the food court, Kristina complains about how the terrorist attacks are on television all the time. "I don't really care about it, because it doesn't affect Maryland," she says, to which Jackie replies, "We're going to *war*, Kristina." Then they discuss Kristina's new boyfriend, for whom she has written on her hand, "I love Scott 4ever." "He has a nice personality and the nicest ass," she says. They compare numbers: Kristina has had twelve boyfriends, Jackie seven, and Celia five. Jackie has kissed one boy, though not French.

Jackie is in the norm for preteen sexual experience, or lack thereof, and has no plans to go further. Who has done what at this age can be discerned mainly from anecdotal evidence, since researchers are rarely permitted to ask children so young about sexual experience; it is, however, generally held that most girls and boys Jackie's age have been kissed, but nothing more. Barely a quarter have been on either end of breast-fondling, and far fewer have had intercourse, oral or otherwise—second base, third base, and a home run, respectively (it is either comforting or not that some lingo will never change). Nearly all middle schoolers have had some sort of crush, and one-quarter of twelve-year-olds report having had a "special romantic relationship," though at this age, given their psychological immaturity, that term doesn't have too much meaning. Generally they just realize the roles they are supposed to play and pretend to do so.

It's the sexually active minority that gets discussed, though, not just in the newspaper (for a while it seemed, from reading the papers, that you couldn't pass through seventh grade without participating in oral sex on the playground) but at the lunch table. Who's a slut, who's a player, who gave a hand job in the bathroom next to the band room: There are plenty of children who never get near this kind of talk, but in a popular crowd like Jackie's, sex and its accoutrements make up a large part of conversations. Girls that supposedly go all the way are looked down on; boys are not. Celia and Kristina enthusiastically list the kids at school they think have had sex, including an eighth grader with, supposedly, two abortions and a miscarriage.

Eww. The way Jackie sees sex—well, she doesn't want to do it. Maybe when she's thirty, when she doesn't have the drive anymore. Or maybe she'll never do it and just adopt, which is probably better for the world's children anyway.

"You guys," she says, "we're too young to even think about that."

On a dare once at a party, Celia showed Jay her breasts and he showed her his penis. This, Celia says, was the worst day of her life; she took a knife, barely, to the soft white skin on her arms afterward; but still, her fingers read "J A Y." Jay knows there's a club called JSC but doesn't know it stands for "Jay Starr Crushers." If he did, he'd add it to his mental list of the weird ways girls obsess about boys. Jay hears about these crushes and doesn't quite understand what the fuss is about, why at a sleepover the biggest laugh of the night is when the girls kiss the wall, pretending it is him. Don't get him wrong—he thinks about girls and loves to flirt. But it's not like he is particularly nice to them or cares about his looks. "I don't even comb my hair in the morning," he says. He doesn't realize he exudes cuteness—his freckles are cute, his grin is cute, even his name is cute, the way it pops out all at once, like a spotlight. The girls call him the "pervertedest of the perverted," like how when they flirt on instant-message he will write things like, "The fat rabbit is getting fatter."

"He used to be my best friend," says Celia, "and he was really nice then, and I just can't get over him." The thing she says she wants most in the world is "That Jay would at least think of me the way he thinks about Kristina."

A few days later, at school, two girls slip Jay a note in careful cursive, the "i"s dotted with hearts, the mistakes blotted out with Liquid Paper.

When I am with you, the caterpillars in my stomach turn to butterflies. I want to give you oral sex. I really want to suck on your head.

Love,

Daphne

Jay's shown it around, and when Daphne finds out, she's pissed. On the playground she points at Kristina and circles her. "You tell me who wrote this! You tell me! I did NOT write this. I will kick their ass! I'll wipe the floor with their ass. There will be blood."

A crowd has gathered. The girls who wrote the note stand off to the side laughing, then are scared away by bees. Jackie stands next to Brad, the "B" on her fingers, a little guy who serves as a sort of mascot for the girls. She leans on his shoulder, which is just the right height, and watches.

The girls appear to be the stars of middle school's romantic dramas. But the boys deserve equal billing. Even though they don't draw hearts on their tennis shoes, they occasionally draw them at home, when nobody's looking. There was more than mischief behind the forays they made a couple of years back across the playground, in order to shove a girl. They strut, they act ambivalent, but really they're anxious. They feel like girls know so much more about romance than they do. Boys certainly don't spend as much time with each other analyzing it; God forbid they admit their vulnerability . . . or *feelings.*

Because they aren't so comfortable with intimacy as a social skill, the romance thing can be more difficult for them and even, in the end, without as much of a support network to help them bounce back after rejection, more damaging. It's painful even thinking about girls, despite the lack of interaction. Strutting masks true emotion, which once in a while they go out on a limb and show. A sixth grader named Brendan was going out with one of the swimmers, and when somebody told her he liked someone else, she broke up with him. "She thought I didn't care," he says, but he did, he totally did, and he ached over the fact that all the girls, especially her, were mad at him. He spent many hours on instant-message pleading for their respect. A seventh grader named Nathan beat up his best friend since kindergarten not because the kid tried to pants him in front of a girl but because he tried to pants him in front of a girl Nathan really, really likes. Some care about what girls think of them so much that in class they cannot keep their minds on anything else.

Many sixth-grade boys have learned that the crushes that would have lasted one day last year stick around for at least a week now, and the ones that once lasted a week now last a month, and, more often than one would imagine, their crushes last years. Jimmy Schissel has had a crush on Mia since third grade, even though the last time he asked her out she called him a freak. Last year he carved a wooden bird emerging from an egg to give her at the end-of-fifth-grade party. The whole night went by, the swimming, the food, the DJ, and when everyone was leaving, his mother finally said, "Aren't you going to give her the bird?" He did, then rushed off. His friend Will didn't fare any better with the stuffed otter he'd brought back from Alaska for Mia's friend Marnie. "Stop trying," she told him.

For the Wilde Lake magazine sale, Jimmy studies the prize catalogue with his dad, figuring out exactly what he wants—Spy Ears, the ten-foot snake, the Magic Ball—and how many subscriptions he has to flog to get it all. He sells $519.36 worth of magazines, the most in school, and in the end gravitates toward the bubble machine, because he heard Mia wanted it. "Here," he says by the buses, and hands it over.

By seventh grade, many boys have learned to protect themselves, fast withdrawing unreciprocated affections. Kristina liked a boy named Stephen for a while, but he didn't like her back "like that." Then he did, and she told him she only liked him a little bit, not enough to go out. So he instantly shut off his feelings for Kristina. A year ago, he says, he would have pined. If it sounds fickle, that's not how Stephen sees it. "It wasn't just, like, one day I like her like that and the next day I don't. It's just, two weeks I like her like that, then the other month I don't, then the other month I do."

Sometimes the stars converge and a boy and girl actually go out. "Out," these first times, would better be described as "in," either because of discomfort or lack of opportunities. A few awkward phone calls, a lot of empty instant-messaging, a mildly flirtatious note or two, a slow dance at the school social, no kisses, no dates. Still, the elation can be immense, and the heartbreak inevitable, rejection being the most miserable thing imaginable. Whether the romance includes actual involvement and ex-pressions of affection or it's just people passing each other in the hall, its importance is as massive as the planet. Especially for a girl less confident than Jackie, euphoria at being chosen can cloud her judgment. She officially likes the guy even when he's an out-and-out jerk and ignores her. She wonders, after they've broken up, why he's going around calling her a slut, when she wouldn't even do anything. He wonders, too. In a sense, the ways boys and girls try out romance and adulthood are fundamentally at odds, according to the enduring philosophy of the psychoanalyst Erik Erikson: Girls step toward womanhood by attaching themselves to others of the opposite sex; boys step toward manhood by breaking away from such ties.

It can be a brutal combination.

Jackie doesn't see it that way. Adolescent romantic relationships are the subject of much sociological study, in which some researchers contend that the selection process and image-obsession and stress involved, particularly in breakups, is not worth the anxiety and depression it produces, whereas others conclude that the stress is motivating and the experience good for a kid's self-worth. Jackie sides firmly with the latter camp. To her, the breaking-up stuff is hard, but the going-out part, the "mmm, someone likes me," really makes her feel "self-esteemish," as she puts it. Somehow Jackie always manages to run into the cutest guys—her friend Leslie tells her to travel with a Polaroid—though she often displays an ability uncommon among her more boy-crazy peers to just not get too worked up.

Part of it can be attributed to her parents, who work nonstop to make sure Jackie doesn't grow up too fast, "cramming as much crap into her head as possible and hoping to God it sticks," as Sara puts it. Unlike her friends, Jackie doesn't have cable, so she can't watch throngs of bikini-clad dancers writhe around the gold-crusted rappers who call them ho's; she doesn't have the Internet, so she can't spend hours bantering with boys who ask her bra size; she's not allowed CDs with a "Parental Advisory" sticker, so she doesn't hear singers brag they're "gonna tap that ass soon"; she can't watch any movie rated PG-13 for sexual content, so she has never seen a boy masturbate into a pie. Even on prime-time television, deviance has been defined down, way down, so Jackie's parents watch with her.

They are her authorities on values.

They don't allow her to walk to the Giant, where the other seventh graders meet at the fountain and flirt and ride bikes and get into trouble when a gym mat outside the high school is discovered aflame and buy condoms on a dare. ("Don't be embarrassed," the cashier says. "At least you're using protection.") Sara would never let Jackie wear a stretchy, deep V-neck like Celia's or a bra-strap-baring tank like Kristina's or fishnets like Leslie's.

Jackie's body has a purpose: jumping, flying, spinning. When Celia and Kristina and Leslie walk around the track during gym class, she runs. She trampolines competitively, moving like an old-time movie speeded up, bouncing halfway to the gym ceiling, doing double tucks and layouts with tight, zippy twists. The very most popular girls in seventh grade, Jackie has noticed, don't do sports. "Maybe they think since they're popular they don't need to do anything else," she says, "because they've already fulfilled their lifetime dream."

Her period, which she's been told she'll get when she's fifteen or sixteen, can wait: "I'm in no hurry to pee blood." Breasts, though—she'd like breasts. Her doctor says she's only in stage two, two stages away from actual breasts, but Jackie thinks she might be able to will them to grow, like this monk she heard of who changed her own eye color through meditation. Unlike Celia, who got her period at age eight, or Kristina, whose breasts surprised her in fourth grade and haven't stopped growing since, Jackie's body does not yet draw attention from boys, like when one guy calls to Kristina, "Omigod, you have a nice ass," and smacks it, or another guy tweaks Celia's breasts and says, "Squeeze squeeze!" Celía and Kristina respond with faux, flirtatious dismay.

Jackie doesn't get this. "I'd hit anybody who touched my boobs," she tells them.

The home-economics room is crowded, and Mrs. Brodian can never really get control of the class. She's calling kids up one by one to discuss progress reports as the others laugh and argue at squished-together round tables. At Jackie's table, a boy named Kendall says, "Anton doesn't like you. He likes Amy. Do you know Amy?"

"Amy Anders?"

"Yeah."

"Shut up—you don't know anything about relationships because you've never been in one." Jackie absently runs a rubber band up and down her family-tree poster for French, which is rolled in a tube.

Justin raises his eyebrows. "I like the looks of that."

"Pervert!"

While Mrs. Brodian is still on the D's, Justin tosses Lauren's pen under the table so she'll look at his and Kendall's naked penises, which they've pulled over their low-slung pants and boxers. Jackie knows something's going on under the table but not that it's naked penises; Justin tells her to stomp her feet if Mrs. Brodian comes, but she never does. Lauren, Kendall, and Justin arrange to meet in the boys' bathroom at nine-fifty. When she goes there is groping, and over twenty minutes, she leaves and goes back twice. Through the wall, a friend in the girls' bathroom hears Lauren laughing. When they see each other in the hall, the friend tells her to come back to class, but Lauren says she's having fun. Afterward she says the boys pulled her into the bathroom, and her friends are appalled. "Uh, Lauren, that's rape!" they yell.

Jackie doesn't know exactly what went on in the bathroom. One minute she's saying of Lauren, "She didn't ask for that." Next minute she says, "She brung it on herself."

chapter four

stop! don't touch! get out!

When Jackie's mom drops her at the bus stop the next morning, another mother tells her that there might or might not have been a rape in the bathroom at school.

Horrified, Sara asks Jackie, "Do you know anything about this?" Jackie heard the gossip, she knows the players, she was practically *there*.

"No," she says.

These newly private middle schoolers are the same children who two years ago clogged the air in a room with detailed narratives of their day. All of a sudden a parent must develop the sensitive ears of a Kremlinologist, praying for emissions from accidentally loose lips. You learn of the change in your little girl, who not long ago said "Yech!" at any mention of kissing, the first time you hear her say, "He's hot!" about a guy who pops up on television. You pick up on pieces from your son's conversations in the back seat during carpool. They give, then take away: In sixth grade, when they tell their mothers whom they like, they use first names. Seventh grade, first initials. Eighth grade, "some kid," or nothing. Jackie used to reveal her "crush of the moment," as Sara calls it, but not so much this year. With Sara so good at "sucking the details out of me," Jackie finds it easier to stay mum.

Elizabeth Ginsburg, also a seventh grader, feels that way, too. In sixth grade, when Eugene bought her a bracelet and wrote her notes like,

"Let me express how much I love you," she asked her mother for advice on how to rebuff him. This year, she's getting unwanted attention from Mitch—Why, Elizabeth wonders, are all the guys who like me stupid?—but she doesn't bother asking her mom for advice. That might encourage a line of inquiry about whom Elizabeth "*like*-likes," which she hates, because why does everybody insist she has to like-like someone at all?

One of the other girls in the home-ec room saw the penises, and Ms. Thomas tells her that her mother has to know. The girl is worried about worrying her mom, who has enough on her mind. "She can't handle that," she says. Ms. Thomas thinks: And you can? She sends a note home to all the parents about the incident, saying that the parties were consenting but, still, it was totally improper. Wilde Lake has worked hard to improve its reputation, and this doesn't help. Moreover, she writes, it's disturbing the way some girls are flattered by the inappropriate attention boys give them.

At school that day, conversation is all about the rumors: A boy got beat up in the bathroom, according to Jonathan. A girl got raped in the bathroom, according to Jimmy. Lauren has apparently told her friends that the boys forced her into the bathroom. This is the version Eric believes, and calls it "mean and desperate." Jackie's lunch table discusses the difference between rape and sexual assault and sexual harassment, though they really don't know. If something like this happened to her, Celia says, "my dad would stick a gun up their butt and pull the trigger." In art class an eight-grade girl says, "Well, she wasn't screaming," and the teacher, Mr. Mitchell, listens to the kids' discussion—the anger and the sexuality, the old arguments about sluttiness and she-asked-for-it-ness alive and well—and is appalled. He wonders if he should ever reproduce.

Elizabeth, too, has been discussing what happened, how creepy it is that something like that could go on at their school. Her friends are scared, but she says that if two boys pushed her into the bathroom—this is the operative rumor at lunch table 6D—she would kick and scream. When her parents read the note from Ms. Thomas that evening, she is lying amid the stuffed animals on her big cloud-sheeted bed. "The letter," her dad says to her from the study, then comes into her room and sits on the desk chair. "What do you know about the letter?"

"I don't know," Elizabeth says. "Nothing."

He bends down and picks up an inside-out T-shirt from the floor.

"Stop! Don't touch! Get out!"
And he does.

For their only child, Joseph and Ellen Ginsburg hoped for a girl. They got what they wanted, and since then a sheepdog, Rosie, and a guinea pig with several names have joined them in their 1970s split-level, nestled in a wooded cul-de-sac. All of a sudden Elizabeth is taller than her friends, and catching up to her parents. Last year her skin had pimples, but now it's ideal, rosy and smooth. Everything about her face evokes roundness: her cheeks, the tip of her nose, her brown eyes, her arched hairline. Her long curly hair is always knotted into a sturdy brown braid—a rope you could climb up if you had to. If you compliment Liz on any of this, she'll tilt her head, smile her huge metal-filled smile, and say, quick and high-pitched, "I know." Her child's voice seems out of line with her developing face and form.

On Elizabeth's bedroom doorknob hangs a fuzzy pink sign that says GO AWAY on the side you see all the time and ENTER on the side you don't. On another sign Elizabeth has written KNOCK in huge letters and "please" in tiny ones. Ellen is good about knocking and waiting, but Joseph will knock and come right in; once Elizabeth was half naked. "I'm like, '*Daaad*, the whole point of knocking is so I can say "Come in." ' "

Elizabeth hides cookies in her underwear drawer and a mess of candy in a deep drawer of her night table, behind the organized piles of magazines, which range from *Disney Adventures* to *Seventeen*. Her dolls sit atop the bookshelves, including Emily, whose brown eyes have turned an eerie red over the years. Ellen hates the clutter covering up Elizabeth's newly painted lavender walls but indulges it: *Buffy the Vampire Slayer* posters, a Polaroid of Joseph with Santa, synchronized-swimming posters, ribbons from her meets.

On the wall of the study, Joseph and Ellen have hung writings from when Liz was little:

My mother is the most wonderful mom in the world. She's as pretty as me. She weighs 90 pounds and she's six feet tall. Her favorite food is lobster. I wish Mom would take me to school every day. I wouldn't trade my mother for my special stuff.

Happy Mother's Day, Love, Elizabeth.

I like winter because I like when my daddy lets me play in the snow and make big snowballs. Weight 22 pounds height as tall as the swings. He makes pancakes for breakfast. Thank you for loveing and caring for me.

Ellen and Joseph are nostalgic for the days when Elizabeth would proclaim her affection in ways that could be hung on the wall, when she was fun and funny in wide swaths instead of unpredictable slivers, when she hobbled sympathetically the time Joseph broke his foot or offered a hug just at the right moment before he delivered his father's eulogy, when Ellen could win affection through a Fluffernutter sandwich cut in tidy triangles. They're nostalgic for the way they knew what Liz was thinking, the way they knew what they were doing, even when they didn't.

These days, not only does Elizabeth not thank Joseph for loving her, she doesn't talk to him when he drives her the fifteen miles to synchro practice three times a week.

"How was school?" he asks in the car one October evening.

"Fine."

"Anything you want to talk with me about?"

"No."

"Do you have chorus three days a week?"

"Two or three."

"And home ec? What do you learn in home ec?"

"I don't know."

"What do you learn—how to clean? Using the washing machine?"

"No. You're annoying." The pop station he let Elizabeth choose plays into the silence.

It stings. Joseph tries not to cross-examine Elizabeth like his parents used to do to him, but she thinks any question he asks is a cross-examination. It's better during car pool, because the girls gossip in the back seat as if he's not there. Ellen gets yelled at when she calls Elizabeth by the nicknames Liz Whiz or Lizilia, which Elizabeth liked just a year ago. She used to enjoy the preschool songs her mom sang, and now she thinks they're "weird-annoying," and in front of other people they're "weird-embarrassing." Elizabeth learned they were weird-embarrassing when she sang them to her own friends, who told her so.

As for any parents of a twelve-year-old, life for Ellen and Joseph is a constant quest to figure out what their child is thinking—what they would pay to know this—and to decipher their status in her ever-changing mind. After the chorus concert one autumn evening, Elizabeth finds her parents in the audience, squeezes her tall, swimmer-firm body onto Ellen's lap in front of the whole grade, and lets her mother quiz her on Latin American capitals for tomorrow's Spanish test. Then, after three capitals, she says, "You're annoying! Stop!" and wriggles away.

All of a sudden, it seems, arguments with Liz have gotten circular; any criticism, however minor, is met by, "I don't do *any*thing right." She shuts off conversation in a snap, like the other day in the car, when Elizabeth was going on and on about how badly she'd do at the swim meet and Ellen said, "I only want to hear positive thoughts."

"We're going to be first," Elizabeth said. "Does that make you *haap*py?"

Feels to Ellen and Joseph like they've been here before, ten years ago. Middle schoolers share the most endearing traits of two-year-olds but also the most frazzling ones—whining and forty-three others. The desire to be a big girl and a baby at the very same time. Mood shifts, growth spurts, minuscule attention spans, temper tantrums. Inflexibility, egocentrism, defiance.

It's as if children operate on a loop, child development experts point out, but this time around the immaturity is less expected. The Terrible Twos are written about, but nobody tells you about the Terrible Twelves, so they seem less justifiable, even though they're not. And the Twelves aren't nearly as cute—those horrible clothes choices are easier to chuckle over when they're made by a toddler rather than by a gangly preteen.

Middle school is when the "Get out!" starts in earnest, and the natural reaction among parents who feel helpless is to do so, in many ways. The last thing they want to do is alienate their child more—she seems so fragile. They indulge her new mood swings more than they'd like; they waffle; they bail her out. The Ginsburgs care about their daughter—lovingly, excruciatingly so. But they are beginning to learn that raising a middle schooler—a species that hungers for freedom as it lives on reliance, whose location on the continuum from "baby" to "grown-up" seems to change constantly, and not just in the direction you'd think—is not only about what they *should* do, but what they *can* do. They are beginning to learn that parenting a preteen is a daily series of tests of their ability to trust their choices, and their child.

The couple were hippies once, and moved to Columbia for its planned-city promise. They've read all the books. They've read *Reviving Ophelia* and are conscious of the concept of the self you have for others, that a baby learns to laugh not just because she's happy but because she knows that's what you want her to do. So, although they want to think Elizabeth does well in school because she cares about her education, they can't help also thinking it's because she wants to please them, which weirds them out a little. They want her to live with free will. Last year, every month or so Ellen would get on a kick where she checked Elizabeth's agenda a few nights in a row. They don't bother anymore; she always seems to be doing her work, of her own volition, and she'll say she hasn't done it yet if that's the truth. Ellen knows Elizabeth shares her dangerous ability to do nothing for hours, so occasionally she shoos her off the computer for homework, but in general they leave her alone about the work. Elizabeth is pleased they trust her "to do it good and correct."

Ellen, a preschool teacher, went to middle school at a small private academy in Manhattan where she was the class Fatty and the class Four Eyes, and her parents let her do as she pleased. She did well in the subjects she liked and got D's in those she didn't. Joseph, who works in computers for a government health agency, remembers getting hours of homework each night at his Coney Island middle school. "I studied a lot," he says, "but look where it got me"—still bitter about growing up a miserable nerd with demanding and chilly parents.

"I'm doing everything I can," he says, "to not be like my parents, to have a better relationship with Liz than they did with me, but it's hard. My parents just leak out of me. You have a kid and you're like your parents. There's something you can't do about it. Maybe I should just be happy that she's happy."

Right now she's not. Elizabeth's plan to get all A's is being thwarted by the "stupidhead" strings teacher, who, she announces one day, is giving her a B.

"Why are you getting a B?" Joseph asks.

"I don't want to talk about it right now."

"I'd like to talk with Miss Colyer," Joseph says, then asks Elizabeth, "Do you want to talk with her first?"

"I think she should talk to her first," Ellen says.

"I wasn't asking you," Joseph says, "I was asking Liz." And that starts a parental argument about interrupting, after which Ellen lies down with Elizabeth and asks, "Can I fall asleep in your bed?" Elizabeth, who can't even imagine why two people would fight over something so minor, shrugs, and sleeps next to her mom.

Joseph worries that he's too worried about the B-ness of the B. The time Elizabeth got three points off her social-studies project for using lined paper instead of unlined, he made himself drop it, decided that instead of getting caught up in Elizabeth's grades he should be more concerned about whether she's learning how to learn and feeling good about herself. That's why it bothers him that Liz hates strings. He wants to ask the teacher, "How are you making this fun for the kids?" because here Elizabeth is choosing to play the viola instead of going to an ungraded study hall, and if she gets a B she'll be disappointed she can't go to the straight-A breakfast. "Let's make it fun," he says. "Let's keep the kids interested in music. I want to talk about bonding with the kids, if I can do it gently."

At the elementary school, the parents could have gone en masse to the principal to complain about a teacher. Neither Ellen nor Joseph finds it easy to be involved the way they were there, where they knew the other parents, where it was more of a community, where they knew Elizabeth's friends. They worry that the work in middle school is dumbed down to the lowest kids, that they don't get enough homework, that teachers teach to some pointless standardized tests, but they're not sure what to do about it. Joseph sits on the parent-teacher committee that plans the school's academic goals, though he doesn't always show up for meetings, because he thinks the principal "shoves her agenda down people's throats."

He and 250 other parents went to Back to School Night, where he found out that Elizabeth will study renaissance art and algebra and eating disorders and needs a seventeen-dollar gym suit; learned that the fundraiser wrapping-paper rolls are twice as long as the ones from CVS; was offered a pamphlet entitled *Think College? Me? Now?*; heard a talk about how 20 percent of Howard County eighth graders used alcohol in the last month, and that being a "hands-on" parent cuts underage drinking by one-fourth; and listened to one teacher review the dress code and another tell them to check their kids' homework even though they will resist and Ms. Thomas say, "This is not an easy age. They're going through tremendous changes. You ask why they made a decision they did and they say, 'I don't know,' and they're telling you the truth. You send us your best," she told the parents, "and we love them."

"I sent 'em my only," Joseph murmured.

All evening, various teachers said, "Your child should have shown you such-and-such," and the dads looked at the moms and the moms looked at the dads.

"Have you seen that?"

"No."

Children this age have a lot of things on their minds, and notes to their parents are not one of them. They don't make it home anymore, or they make it home crumpled in a crevice of the backpack, to be excavated in months. The preteen mind is weak on logic, very selective on memory. It drives Joseph and Ellen crazy the way they spent twenty minutes deciding with Elizabeth that she'll only do one swim meet this weekend, and then, the next day, after practice, she says, "Coach wants me to swim Saturday." Joseph says, "We agreed you'd only do one event, remember?" and Elizabeth says, "When?" Constantly losing things, too. "How can Jackie remember every word to every song Linkin Park ever made," says Mike Taylor, "but she can't remember her gymnastics jacket?"

The section of the brain where thoughts about notes and gymnastics jackets once resided is now occupied by thoughts about themselves. Which means that their parents' concerns are changing, too: Will I have to buy her another jacket? Will the kid eventually realize the world doesn't revolve around him? Once this year Avy Mason was so fed up with Lily's begging and me-me-me that she said, "For twenty-four hours, I don't want to hear about you." Five minutes later, as she headed out to the hairdresser, Lily asked, "Can you get me some mascara at Skinmarket?"

But the kids aren't always as clueless at it looks.

The day the back of the fish tank pops out in the Ginsburgs' family room, and everything is out of place when Elizabeth gets home from school, all she says upon seeing Joseph on the floor where the tank used to be is, "You're home?" Could she not have noticed the garage door up, the car and a weird vacuum machine in there, the sofa misplaced, the aquarium gone, *her father on the floor where the fish were?* Joseph is thinking, That's all she has to say? Hello, daughter?

He's right—Elizabeth didn't really notice the fish. What she was thinking is this: The last time her dad was in the living room when she got home from school, Ellen was at the hospital, sick.

chapter five

i'm scary enough as it is

Halloween night, Elizabeth comes downstairs in the hippie costume Ellen bought at Target, a snug halter and low-rider bell bottoms made of blue velvet and pink gauze. Ellen looks up from her salmon and says, as Liz covers it all with her bulky Adidas jacket, "Good thing I spent all that money on the costume." Elizabeth turns over her plastic witch's cauldron and last year's gummed-up loot tumbles onto the sofa.

"Anyone want some candy?"

"Let me take a photo."

"No."

Every year Elizabeth goes trick-or-treating with her neighbor Laura, her best friend. With the neighborhood growing older, there are no other kids in the dark cul-de-sac. As they wait for Laura and her father, Joseph looks up and announces, "This is the first full moon on Halloween in forty-six years, and the only one in your generation."

"Who cares?"

Like every year, the girls talk about which kids from school used to live where, pass quickly by the house where someone died, ring doorbells, and eagerly plop candy into their cauldrons. Elizabeth holds up the orange box she got at Sunday school and asks, "Would you like to support UNICEF? You don't have to. It's, like, for kids all over the world." The dads fall back, talking about the return of the neighborhood skunk and school-system redistricting and whether this retired meteorologist Bob knows would make a good caterer for the girls' joint Bat Mitzvah in the spring.

Something, though, is different this Halloween. Usually the girls run from house to house through the yards as if there were a deadline, tripping over their costumes, and the dads can't keep up. This time everything's slower; the girls defer to driveways and sidewalks. "They must be getting older," Joseph tells Bob, glowing a bit from his lantern.

Eric spends Halloween in his living room, watching television.

Lily's plans to build a Creepy Maze disappeared into whatever Bermuda Triangle eleven-year-olds' elaborate plans disappear into. Instead she decorates her porch with cottony spiderwebs and eyeball candles and jack-o'-lanterns and a cauldron of dry ice. While her mother hands out special Baggies of treats for the kids she knows and regular candy for the others. Lily dresses as a witch and goes trick-or-treating with a neighbor. She returns looking a little disappointed, especially when her sister comes and goes with her big, laughing group.

At a Halloween party in Dustin Fried's basement, Jackie and Celia are dressed in costumes they call "PJ Ho's," though Jackie has explained to her mom that she's a baby. They wear pajama bottoms and white long-sleeved T-shirts and suck on lollipops. It took forever at the mall to find a white shirt, because first of all every one Jackie liked wasn't on sale and second of all, even though Jackie knows that with Dad taking care of Kyle instead of working they can't just buy on a whim even if she says, "I love you, Mommy," real sweet, she saw a zillion things she had to beg for—a Sagittarius necklace, fancy jeans, a plaid purse with a planner inside, an oversize yellow hooded sweatshirt. "I had to wear Anton's sweatshirt today," she told her mom. Anton, Sara wondered, and said, "Put it on your Christmas list." At the party, during truth-or-dare, Kristina kisses Scott, and Celia kisses Brad and Jay, and one girl even has to lick a boy on the cheek. Jackie doesn't play. "I'm not kissing anyone," she says.

Jimmy Schissel goes trick-or-treating with a friend, for the first time without a costume. "I'm scary enough as it is," he says, only half kidding.

Even though Jimmy has just-right pumpernickel hair that lightens in the summer, and skin that's creamy where it should be creamy and pink where it should be pink, and lovely brown eyes with lashes as thick and even as the fringe on a flapper's dress, he can't think of one thing he likes about the way he looks right now. After he went to bed the night he and his parents made a personal-culture poster for social studies, his parents glued a fifth-grade school picture smack in the middle of the neatly typed passages about his interests. At school, he ripped it off.

At eleven, Jimmy can feel hints of it ending: the little-boy years when he was slender and nearly bionic, able to leap and dive and dart easily, comfortable with the way he looked, even happier with the way he moved. He was Superman when he wanted to be. Now he doesn't know where his body's going. "Those videos in health class, the *Your Changing Body* ones where they say, 'Puberty is the best thing to ever happen to you!'—they're so stupid," he says, the way they try too hard, propagandizing something that just isn't that cool. He has no sense that this upheaval is temporary. How can he? Underneath his ultra-baggy jeans, ragged at the hem, are feet that have stretched four sizes in three years—they are size-ten paws and he is the puppy who hasn't grown into them yet. A typical eleven-year-old has reached four-fifths the height he'll attain by adulthood but only half the weight—so here it comes, to his surprise. Whose flesh is this? Underneath his T-shirts—often a Superman shirt—that hang past his butt is a small belly that wasn't there before, small enough that you can't see it when he's clothed but big enough that he thinks maybe he should diet, or jog. He weighs 110 pounds, perfectly healthy for his five feet two and a half inches, but if he lost five pounds he'd weigh the same as his older sister, Brianna.

It happens at different times for everyone, which is why there are kids in sixth grade who look eight and kids who look eighteen. These physical changes are the greatest they've experienced since they were babies. This mysterious force that visits preteen boys' bodies, which causes blond hair to darken and easy grace to disappear in a tangle of limbs and skin to pock with pimples, is objectively something wonderful—growth! change! maturity!—but it infuses them with a profound, unidentifiable sense of loss, as they start to see their childhoods fall. They're not so cute anymore, and they know it. Their smells outpace their awareness of them, feet and armpits and breath, such that sixth-grade teachers wonder if they can tell their first-period classes to brush their teeth, or should they have the nurse do it? Eventually muscles will form, visible through forearms when fingers are flexed, but for now the bones come alone, and arms and legs grow faster than the brain's ability to track them. A boy hits himself on corners of doorways, bangs his funny bone. So many times, as he races to get his gym clothes off to catch the bus home, Jimmy gets his head stuck in his shirt, the pants in the shoes, so he's started to wear his gym clothes home. Entering puberty, a child grows so fast (three inches a year, on average, for boys) and so unevenly that inactivity is actually painful. He squirms after sitting still for fourteen minutes, which makes eighty-minute classes excruciating. Why do the teachers make you sit up straight? They think you can learn only if your body is propped a certain way?

And how quickly a swimming-pool party has lost its allure. Nowadays boys are bombarded with body-image obsessions almost as much as girls. Muscles. It's all about muscles. Some of Jimmy's classmates have started to lift weights. Some have grown a little hair on their chests, and though they've sort of been waiting for this, it's simultaneously maddening, because (as they see in the Abercrombie catalogue) body hair is just not cool. They shave surreptitiously in the bathroom. I am twenty, they think, in a moment of pride. I am a man.

Jimmy's not quite there yet. But puberty is an aggregate of physiological changes—many less visible than mustache fuzz—and Jimmy is embarking on many of them. He is tired when he is supposed to be awake, and awake when he is supposed to be tired. His attentions have begun to scatter, his temper has begun to grow. Hobbies and intellectual pursuits that once captivated him to no end have begun to strike him as childish. Some of his friends are about to strike him as childish, too. How he appears to others is suddenly a subject of great concern and mortification. His thoughts on girls are still chaste, though strong. Peter Parker, also known as Spider-Man, has had his crush since fourth grade, too. "Maybe I should get bit by a spider," Jimmy says during the movie. That would help, wouldn't it? His belly would morph into a six-pack, he could jettison the glasses, his brown eyes would turn blue—not to mention the impressive superpowers. Imagine.

Jimmy has notions of romance. In English class, he has to write a new ending to the Ray Bradbury story where a group of kids lock a girl in the closet while they enjoy the hour of sun their planet gets every seven years. Jimmy's classmates' endings involve a lot of tears and apologies after Margot gets out of the closet. One boy plots a prank involving toothpaste and hot sauce. Jimmy writes that Margot beats up the boy who trapped her, runs away to the other side of the planet and steals food that arrives on the landing pad. 'I need to leave this planet. If only I could hi-jack a rocket ship,' Margot always says." Then she meets an astronaut who takes her to earth, where she falls in love with the astronaut's son and marries him when they're old enough.

Jimmy figures he'll have a wife one day, but it's hard for him to imagine ever being as foolish as seventh graders on the subject of crushes. "Girls are all mean," Jimmy sometimes says, not just because of the way they treat him but because of the bratty way they treat each other, particularly since sixth grade started. First they'll set up a scenario to make someone look stupid; then, beyond the hurt of that, they'll call the person stupid for falling into the trap. Aside from his parents, he gets clues about what relationships are like from women on television, such as Anna Nicole Smith. "They use all their money to look good," he says. "Then they get a boyfriend and take all his money."

There's something comforting about a crush, like his on Mia, that is 100 percent unattainable. "What happens if they like you back and someone else likes you, too? Then you have a problem." There are a few girls in school he considers friends, kind of, girls he helps with homework or talks with during class. But he can't really have them over or anything, because then it's like, "She's your *giiiirlfriend*," which is what the boys say to Jonathan during lunch just because he eats with the girls.

The school bathrooms are locked for a while after the seventh-grade incident, and whereas he wouldn't have cared about it two years ago, Jimmy is too embarrassed to use the permissible toilet in the front office, so his bladder hurts, and his parents wonder why he has to pee the second he comes home. Jimmy now showers once a week, instead of taking a bath. Every day he washes his hair in the sink so it doesn't stand up, and if it's still sticking up when he's running out the door, he'll lick his hand and rub it down. (The comb is only for weddings and church.) He sometimes worries about clothes.

His parents worry about keeping him in clothes. With the growth comes an unbelievable appetite; like a dog, Jimmy would eat all the food in front of him until it was taken away. His favorite beverages are grape soda, orange soda, cream soda, Pepsi, Coke, root beer, Sprite, 7-Up, Sierra Mist, water, and the milk left over from a bowl of Apple Jacks. The food diary Jimmy keeps one day for home ec looks like this:

Breakfast—two Rice Krispie treats, milk
Lunch—peanut butter sandwich, pineapple, juice
Dinner—kielbasa, five carrots, sparkling water

Here's what he didn't mention: the venti-size caramel apple cider from Starbucks, two Cokes, three Hershey's kisses, two York Peppermint Patties, and seven handfuls of Doritos he ate after school. The cheese-filled Pillsbury rolls he tore through at dinner until his father said, "Enough croissants, Jimmy." And who knows when Jimmy ate the two puddings whose empty containers his mother found hidden behind the toilet in the downstairs bathroom, as if he weren't allowed the food.

The pineapples, too, are a white lie: Jimmy gives his fruit cups away every day. It's not uncommon, particularly among the girls, for middle-school lunches to go uneaten save four bites of apple. Even though the cafeteria teems with hungry, growing children, at least fifty parent-hours of slicing and spreading are dumped each day into the Wilde Lake Middle School garbage cans. Ms. Thomas figures that if the kids just handed over their sandwiches when they walked into school in the morning, she could give them to a soup kitchen and solve whatever hunger problem there is in Columbia.

When Jimmy ordered a large gym suit at the beginning of the year, the PE teacher said, "You're living dangerously. Bring it back if it's too big." Mr. Jackson scared the boys a bit that day when he warned that kids sometimes reach into the locker-room baskets and pick pockets or knot shoelaces together. Each day when the boys come out of the locker room, they tear around the gym in their baggy Wilde Lake shorts, chasing, sliding, jumping over one another onto the mat. Girls clump and talk. As the door shuts to separate basketball from field hockey, they run up and scream, "Bye!"

Some boys look surprised if their shot makes it into the basket; others get nothing but net. Jimmy is not a star, but he plays fine. He blocks Alexandra, who is good, forcing a turnover. Occasionally he bloops the ball errantly into the air, but just as often he makes it. When he does, his friend Will, who stands in the middle of the court picking his fingernails, calls out, "Nice shot, Schiss!"

Everybody ran around in elementary school, but in middle school kids clearly separate into jocks and not-jocks. Many of the not-jocks have mistaken their temporary clumsiness and weakness for permanent lack of ability, or they simply can't bear the taunts when they can't keep up. Children arrive at a point where they decide they are athletic, or they are not, and this dichotomy holds until adulthood, when they realize they can enjoy sports again even if they suck at them. For the moment Jimmy still sees himself as athletic; he doesn't notice what his parents are just starting to: that his growth is making him a little clumsier, weighed down. He enjoys PE even though the girls beat him, and most of the boys in his class, in running, sit-ups and push-ups. He thinks he'll play lacrosse again.

In gym, Jimmy likes Ping-Pong best. "I sweat more in this than in basketball," he says as he hits the ball back and forth, hard, with Will. When Mr. Jackson says, "No smashes," they bounce the ball off the walls. "Oops," Jimmy says, "I caught it in my ding." The ball rolls away to two boys who play keep-away. Jimmy begins to push one of them into a tall stack of chairs but stops himself and instead says, "We're going to tell Mr. Jackson."

Last year Jimmy and his friends played four-square and freeze tag at recess, but now they mostly stand against the wall, because there's not enough time and not enough friends for games. Boys who used to spend recess throwing a Nerf football as hard as they could at each other now pelt each other with jokes and insults. Sometimes Jimmy plays tetherball, winner stands, with the hand that hits the ball tucked inside his long sleeve. "I play Jimmy even if he loses," the next boy in line says, "because he's bad."

Jimmy's parents make him play one team sport each season, and occasionally he shoots baskets or zooms around the cul-de-sac on his bike, but for the most part, as with many boys his age, inactive hobbies have replaced play and movement. For the dream bedroom he designs for a geometry project, Jimmy includes a DVD player, GameCube, VCR, and flat-screen Phillips television. Unfortunately, the Schissels only have the kind of cable that makes your reception better, not the kind that brings you the Cartoon Network, so during the week Jimmy mostly watches the cartoons on PBS, which he knows are babyish, but still. He's not allowed to watch his favorite show, *The Simpsons*, and, besides, almost every kid in school, whether or not he will admit it, still kind of likes PBS. At a recent assembly, a teacher started singing the theme song to *Blue's Clues*, and every kid in the sixth grade joined in, heartily—the only time during the year they did something in unison. Jimmy doesn't watch *Pokemon* anymore, but he still watches *Digimon*. He's critical of commercials; he knows their tricks. What if kids with mental disabilities decide they can do back flips just because they wear Gap jeans?

As for movies, he likes *The Matrix* and the old Bond films that come on Saturday nights, and ever since he watched a documentary about asteroids he thinks that *Deep Impact* and *Armageddon* might be more realistic than you'd think. He gets to see PG-13 now, but he yearns for R. "I'm not a baby anymore," he says. "I know not to see movies with a lot of bad language." Anyway, he figures, he hears those words in school all the time. Though Jimmy has read all the Harry Potter books and can parse them emphatically, when his friends talk about how excited they are for the movie, he says, "It's stupid. I have to take my cousin."

Though he still sneaks into the living room to check out his Christmas presents using a Fisher-Price stethoscope and occasionally plays with his Star Wars Legos, Jimmy has started to think toys are boring. He barely touches the seventy Beanie Babies hanging in plastic on his bedroom door, except for a battle he stages every blue moon before bed. He and his friends have crafted origami planes and weapons and even a terrain for a fantasy game called Warhammer, but they haven't played it yet, and never will. More than anything, Jimmy—like all his male classmates—is obsessed with video games. He could probably play eight hours in a row if nobody stopped him, cross-legged, feet over knees, or lying his stomach. Jimmy can win at Super Smash Bros. even when he chooses the weakest character, Pikachu, and has paged through his game primers so much that the ink has begun to rub off.

Jimmy has always been curious, an active thinker. Inside his head sits a store of vivid memories, all in black and white, of things that happened when he was exactly three: He fell down the stairs. He left a chocolate bar in the car for a year. He spilled eggs on his sister's tent during a camping trip. He zoomed around the family room delivering toys from a cart, saying "I'm the mailman!" until he ran into his mother, making her spill hot tea down his arm, for which he went to the hospital. Three, Jimmy says, is when he first became good at vocabulary.

Used to be, Jimmy would sit up and wonder about how we had night and day, or whether Adolf Hitler might still be alive—or perhaps he has an equally evil twin none of us knows about. In the fall, a new invention is revealed, the Segway, a stabilized motorized scooter. This fascinates Jimmy; he also thinks magnetic sidewalks and jetpacks might be a good idea. He has concluded that Bill Clinton was a good president except that he lied about Monica Lewinsky and highway tolls. "He said he was going to lower them," Jimmy says, "but he highered them." He still wishes he had voted for Ralph Nader instead of Al Gore in last year's mock election, because of the environment, which he prioritizes right up there with sports and almost as high as video games. For a Chesapeake Bay conservation project, Jimmy and his father raise and study three thousand oysters out where they keep their boat, and cultivate bay grasses in a plastic tub on the family-room hearth. When he grows up he wants to work in 3-D animation or with lizards. In a cage in the kitchen live two green anoles, which eat crickets that chirp through dinner.

Boys and girls going through puberty swing madly from energetic to exhausted, and never get enough sleep to sate them. It's become more difficult lately. Jimmy is supposed to go to bed at ten, but often he's not tired—it's not known exactly why, but around age ten the circadian clock pushes back, keeping kids awake when they should be feeling sleepy. Experts have found that for preteens a good night of sleep doesn't just help the next day's learning but reinforces the previous day's lessons, and they recommend nine hours. Most kids never get that much, since they can't fall asleep when they're supposed to, even if they were exhausted all day, and the bus comes at seven-fifteen, whether or not you've had time to dry your hair. Sometimes Jimmy is on a sugar high from the candy he stashes near his trundle bed. With the sheets tangled and the mattress pad exposed from last night's tornado of sleep, Jimmy will stay up reading

Calvin and Hobbes for two hours. This makes him feel out of sync with this world, like a comic he once saw that said, "My internal clock is on Tokyo time." No problem getting up Saturday mornings for cartoons, but getting out of bed for school is another story.

Jimmy gets nightmares, too. The day before sixth grade started, he dreamed that he was going to get detention for being late and on top of that wasn't wearing underwear. Before September 11, he dreamed that a plane crashed into a skyscraper, there were screams, then everything went dim. After September 11, he dreamed that he was on top of a tall building, there was an explosion, then the building collapsed. His recurring nightmare, which makes him sweat, is this: He is hiding under his bed when a werewolf peeks into the room. The werewolf leaves, and reappears through a trapdoor in the floor. To escape, Jimmy skis down a mountain.

Then he falls off the edge.

chapter six

there's always next quarter

"Middle-school kids," Ms. Thomas says, "have to move around. They have to be able to talk, they want to be engaged in what they're learning, and you really can't do anything in the classroom for more than fifteen or twenty minutes without losing the class." A teacher learns at a middle-school seminar to divide his class into four segments: the teacher speaking, the students speaking, the students working alone, the students working in groups. When the teacher doesn't make movement a priority, the students fidget. They tap their feet. They sprawl. If you're Jimmy, "Sean, please stop tapping" doesn't have anything to do with whether you personally are barred from tapping. In class Jimmy makes origami cranes and arachnids and planes, the tinier the better. On the other side of the school, Eric drums with his pencil, hums, plays guessing games with the clock. What time will it be when he looks up? He always overshoots. If you say a word in your head enough times in a row, he discovers one day during class, it doesn't sound like a word anymore. *Accurate. Accurate. Accurate. Accurate?* When he can get away with it he studies the sheet of paper he carries everywhere, a printout from sk8house.com of the Rollerblades he wants for Christmas.

By preadolescence the brain has become quite adept at emotion, but the parts devoted to organizational skills—as well as reasoning and judgment—mature more slowly. The disorganization can be appalling. In sixth grade kids are enchanted by the orderly and proprietary cubbiness of their lockers; by eighth grade many, like Eric, stack their books on top of the lockers, wherever's convenient, science book in one place and binder in another. "Somebody stole my agenda," they tell Ms. Thomas when they lose it, as if this is an item with potential black-market value. Sixth graders' agendas are usually carefully tended, pages folded into shapes after each date has passed, boxes filled in dutifully. By eighth grade many agendas are, like Eric's in only the second month, a mess—pages gone, pages empty, except for notes like, "Dear Ms. Epps, NO homework rec'd Geography of the Americas pgs. 36–44." They leave their names off papers. Why use an eraser or Wite-Out when you can cross out with a mess of marks? By the second day of school Eric's book covers are scrunched; by the second week they are missing.

He pulls the school directory out of his bag, crumples it, tosses it in the trash. His binder, instead of being divided into classes and subdivided into Warm-Ups and Vocab and Notes and Graded Papers, has become a sloppy heap of materials that matter to Eric (Grand Theft Auto 3 cheat codes, a printout of the blue Supra he wants) and missed opportunities: A permission slip to be on the leadership council for the aquarium club, which he would have liked to do, but he forgot to turn it in. Half-finished worksheets of scientific nomenclature. Entire folders of assignments he completed but didn't hand in.

If Eric doesn't hear the homework announced, he says, he won't stay after class to find out what it is, because then he'll be late for his next class, which means twenty minutes' time-out during the upcoming dance and an automatic detention. Except that Eric doesn't like the dance—and every teacher at Wilde Lake writes the next day's homework on the blackboard before class even starts.

Eric has taken an orange highlighter to a reading called "Instant Study Skills," which says to find a fixed place in your home for nothing but studying. Where he studies—the living-room sofa—is also where he watches TV, plays video games, eats fried rice from the Hunan Wok and chicken patties from the freezer, and sleeps, under a sleeping bag but without sheets. The room is small, square, dark. The venetian blinds, like his neighbors', always remain shut. Thomas's stereo is distracting, but Eric doesn't ask him to turn it down because he figures he wouldn't. His best stuff is in a storage shed off Route 99. Above the television is a painting of Jesus, flanked by Ms. Beulah's high-school diploma and his dad's GED. There is a framed poem titled "Don't Quit" on the wall, a shelf packed with the Grolier's Encyclopedia, and, all over the place, in plastic cracked frames and nice glass ones, studio shots and candids of Beulah's family and a few of Eric's two brothers. Eric appears in none of them.

"I don't care," he says. "Well, I used to. It's pictures, man. I wished they cared, but pictures is pictures."

Feels like he's living in someone else's home. Even though sometimes she makes him chicken, gives him thirty dollars for a hockey stick, Eric decides Ms. Beulah is snappish, the way she tells him to do chores, the way she spends so much time upstairs in the bedroom, the way she walks in and grunts "Fine" to his question "How are you, Ms. Beulah?"

Aside from his choice in women, Eric worships his father. When William told Eric that eating raw onion cures a cold, he carried one around school in his pocket, stinking up science class. Eric practices playing "In a Sentimental Mood" on the sax for the wedding in October. He loves to hit the road with his father in his truck, not just for the father-son time but because "I know there's more up there than I learn in social studies." He can tell you why Wisconsin is boring and how to read a map and which truckers are retiring and how his dad got the handle Frosty because of a runny nose during a winter freeze.

William is on the road most of the time. That Eric doesn't see his father every day isn't unusual, but most kids who don't at least see their moms. Eric misses his, painfully. She moved to Columbia because she didn't want her kids going to school in Baltimore, and she doesn't want him back there now. Especially since she saw that commercial, the one that says a sixth grader knows a roach as a bug and a seventh grader knows a roach as marijuana. When Eric lived in Baltimore, before fifth grade, he knew that you could get weed on the corner of Barclay and Greenhurst for twenty bucks. A child in the city knows too much.

A parent in the city, or the country, or Columbia, Maryland, doesn't know enough. The truth of a child's situation is generally one step worse than parents perceive. Or more: One study showed that middle schoolers were at least ten times as likely to engage in risky behaviors—drinking, having sex, attempting suicide, smoking—as parents thought. If you're fairly certain she's tried a cigarette, it's likely she's smoked several; if you know he hid his last F on a math test, there's a good chance he's forged a progress report, too. Eric watches his Wilde Lake friends smoke pot all the time in the corner of an empty ball field. But he has no interest in trying it himself. Because marijuana's a pure plant, Eric doesn't think it can hurt you bad—not like cigarettes, the rat poison he's heard they put in there, the urea, the tar, the ammonia—but he knows Tenacious would cut his lips off. "My family," he says, "we don't do that."

Sometimes he thinks about asking to move in with his godparents, where his mom is, but he figures there's not room and he doesn't feel like imposing. "I don't ask for anyone's help," Eric says, "unless it's mad critical." Eric learned this self-reliance—an admirable trait, perhaps, for an adult, but a lamentable one for a thirteen-year-old—from his mother. "All my life, I hear from people, 'Remember that time I helped you?' and they throw it all back in her face."

Tenacious was raised as an only child by foster parents. She always waited, in vain, for her mother to appear magically at important moments: graduation, the birth of her sons. Because of that, she always promised she'd never leave her boys. The separation slays her. She can't hug Eric as much as she wants. She picks him up for school most mornings but doesn't see much of his work in those short snippets of time. A few days she initialed his assignments in his agenda, but then her brakes failed and she couldn't get to Columbia. Tenacious feels like this is a turning point for Eric; she sees his interest in school fading.

When their children reach this age many parents, mothers especially, figure this is their chance to work more, since their kids can dress themselves, let themselves in the door, get themselves a snack. This is exactly the opposite of what psychologists and educators say should happen. Teachers as a whole would choose more active parents combined with better-behaved kids, over higher salaries. While "active parents" is narrowly understood as those who help out at school, study after study has proved what teachers' intuition already told them: that the true measure of involvement, for families of all incomes or backgrounds, is something much more. It's tutoring one's children at home. Setting an example by turning off the television and reading for pleasure. Finding out when the newsletter comes each week and insisting it be dug out of the backpack. Setting high expectations and talking about college. Family "connectedness," feeling your parents care for you, improves academic achievement and protects against nearly every possible middle-school health risk and behavioral problem. Flunking, smoking, depression—to avoid these, merely spending time with your child is necessary but not sufficient; a family must participate in activities together and show warmth and love, every single day. Organizations across the country—and an entire office of the federal Department of Education—have been set up to help schools help parents help their children. "Being a whole family unit" is the way Ms. Thomas puts it, emphatically, to concerned parents, "and it has to start early."

Tenacious knows this, instinctively. She doesn't know what to do about it.

"I could lose him," she says.

"I feel inadequate."

Halfway to his second-quarter report card, in October, Eric gets his interim report. A D in reading and C's in academic enrichment, social studies, and English, for missing assignments. He doesn't know how he's going to make it through the year in social studies. "It's up and down in her class," he says. "You're doing things one minute that everybody's into, then you go back to doing the gay crap." Wars, he likes. Anything that can be tied to September 11.

"Why were the British after the Sons of Liberty?" Mrs. Conroy asks as the class corrects a true-false quiz on the Coercive Acts.

"They were the head of all the protests and things."

"Think about today—are we looking for the leaders of something?"

"Bin Laden!" The questions pile on: "Why don't they just kill him?" "Wouldn't there be more terrorism than ever if they killed him?" "Isn't it true that if Bush doesn't catch Bin Laden he won't get elected again?"

"The election's in three years," Mrs. Conroy says. "It's hard to know what effect that would have."

Eric says, "If they came over and did more terrorism, wouldn't that threaten Bin Laden—wouldn't we kill him?"

"The U.S. is a democracy," Mrs. Conroy says, "and we think people have certain rights. Okay. We're moving back to colonial times."

Bev Conroy knows the diversions perk the students up and teach them something, too. Maybe she could indulge more of them if she had

more time, if there were fewer standardized tests to prepare for, if students did the assigned reading at night, if there weren't so many inter-
ruptions for kids to go to guidance or the library or wherever. If they
were used to reading and tuned in to the world—each year fewer kids
raise their hands when she asks whose families take the newspaper. If they
didn't need their hands held so much these days. The teachers who have
been around a while say today's children show up with less of an independent work ethic than their predecessors. They are the beneficiaries
and victims of a new era of shortcuts: fancy calculators, spell check, years
of typing on computers that have precluded their cursive from ever becoming legible. They won't read the instructions even when they need
to.

All this and a county curriculum to get through. Some teachers feel
like they're pushing new knowledge too fast, instead of making sure the
kids have better mastery of a smaller amount of information. But you
can't risk sending kids on to the next class without covering the last two
units.

So back to colonial times.

"If you give me, like, the Bill of Rights and crap like that—man,"
Eric says later. "We're just sitting there, reading up the book, hearing,
'Class, c'mon now.' How you gonna be a kid, only thirteen years old, and
sit there in the class and listen to a teacher talk about nothing?"

"Nothing" means, for instance, Paul Revere. When Mrs. Conroy asks
what he was famous for before the British were coming, one girl says he
was "known for beautiful, elegant silver work." Mrs. Conroy corrects
her: "He was a talented silversmith and engraver."

This is one of the things Eric hates most—how some teachers look
for one right answer and only that answer. In science the other day, the
drill asked, "Charlie Chromedome went for a walk without an umbrella.
He did not wear a hat and he did not take refuge under a shelter: yet, not
one hair on his head got wet. How was that possible?" Eric doesn't know
why his answer—"He was wearing a hood"—or Robert's answer—"He
was bald"—was not just as right as "It wasn't raining." Who cares that
Paul Revere made tea sets and silverware anyway? At this point Eric's
head is buried in his shirt, to emerge only when Mrs. Conroy tells the
class that Paul Revere made false teeth, too.

In reading, Eric is supposed to have turned in journal entries for his research project on street racing cars. The first bit of writing flowed so well, all off the top of his head, that he couldn't believe how much was on the page—"What so great about its power is that it has 320 hp and 290 ft lbs of torque and that's good for racing because if the car has a faster start than the Shelby, the Shelby will catch the car and it pass the other car." Mrs. Cook wanted the completed journal Monday, but Eric didn't hand in any more than he had written in class.

In academic enrichment, Mrs. Cook urges the class to "transcend from elementary to approaching high school. You can tell the scholars, who use teachers as role models, *ex*ceed and *suc*ceed and *ex*cel. Look around. Not all of these people will be your classmates in ninth grade. As the teacher sets the example, so will you follow. Very traditional—it will last a lifetime." Eric doesn't understand any of what Mrs. Cook puts on the overhead. "Objectives: To develop representational thinking. To develop flexibility and plasticity by rapid transition from one perspective to another. To use several sources of information simultaneously to arrive at a conclusion." For practically the whole period they do a fancy connect-the-dots exercise, then fill out a "Take Time to Reflect" worksheet that prompts, "Today I learned." Eric fills in: "Nothing." Still, if he had to choose teachers to hug, Mrs. Cook would be one of the possibles.

He hates doing the homework in English but feels cozy there. Sometimes Mrs. Brown lets him use television shows instead of books for his homework, so he draws a character web of SpongeBob SquarePants ("Helpful—will listen to what people have to say. Funny—his shoes squeak when he walks") and describes why Dragonball Z illustrates suspense ("because Goku and Vegeta finally got to fight for real then they restarted the series. That shows suspense because want to know who win."). Eric likes writing the journal entries Mrs. Brown assigns each day.

> If I could buy anything I would buy a Toyota Supra—2002 white backs, loud pipes, high spoiler, 18 inch rims chrome, tinted windows, nitrus combustion kit, turbo kit, glowing chasis, glowing logo, racing sticker, lab top, big system, taz air freshener, waterproof seats, racing style seatbelts, hydrolics, twin turbo engine, with 430 hp, 4,300 rpm for tourque. 6 gear transmission, and fire breathing exhaust system. And a nice 3 room, 2 bathrooms, big basement, a yard and a brick kitchen and a half

pipe.

I love winter because I can relax and stay to myself. I drink hot
chocolate with marshmallows that gooze from the heat. I have
snowball fights and after play video games and go snowboarding
with my friend James just chill.

Mrs. Brown has Eric read this one aloud and praises the sensory images, the detail. Eric likes hearing other people's entries, too, how Lena's
brother is annoying but a policeman, how Max fasts during Ramadan,
how Talia's friend was shot and recovered, then was hit by a drunk driver
and died. Mrs. Brown tries to get the quiet smart people to speak up—
"Sandi, I know you're around verbal people, but you have to fight for it,"
she'll say, or "Let's listen to Sue. She talks softly and has a lot to say." She
has an orderly system of awarding points for participation, and Eric likes
to see the checkmarks accumulate next to his name on the overhead.
Once Mrs. Brown called his house. "Am I in trouble?" Eric asked. "No,"
she said, "I just wanted to tell your parents how hard you're working in
English." Eric was amazed a teacher would phone for a good thing, and
disappointed his father wasn't home.

Excellent in PE, excellent in band, of course. Eric's got a hundred in
math and a B in science, because, even when he doesn't get his homework problems correct, both teachers give full credit for trying. There are
some days in math where he has grasped the algebraic expression so well
that he gets to explain it to the rest of the class, step by step. "Yes!" he
says when this happens. "I was right! You know what you should do? Just
look closely at the parentheses next time."

He blames the bad grades on his lack of glasses, the way, when he
reads small print, a zingy pain shoots from the back of his head straight
out his eyes. Also, he says, it's because of the wedding, the day of school
he had to miss plus all that time picking out and practicing the song.
"Now that this wedding crap is over," Eric declares, "I'll get straight
A's."

Not exactly. When he opens the envelope on November 9, the wedding
long past and glasses living on Eric's nightstand, he has A's in music and

gym, D's in health and science, and C's in everything else. "But I'm awe-some in science!" he says. The immaturity of middle schoolers' frontal lobes causes a disregard for consequences, along with the impulsive be-havior. No surprise they often think grades fall from the sky. There they were on the spreadsheet all quarter, two F's on tests, a bunch of zeros on homeworks that brought down the hundreds, and then they ask, "Why did you give me a D?"

"Well, that's the most A's I ever had in this school," Eric says. "Oh well, there's always next quarter. Hopefully there's no distractions for second quarter. Hopefully."

After school he gets shrimp fried rice at the village center, then comes home, where Ms. Beulah, who works the very early shift, is asleep upstairs, and calls his mom. When he tells her about the D's, she is exas-perated.

"Health?" Tenacious teaches inmates about health and is studying to be a nurse. That her son blows this stuff off drives her crazy. "You've got to do better in that class. Eric, you're not even putting forth the effort to learn, and learning is free. Why should I put down a hundred dollars for a paintball gun for two D's?" He rolls his eyes. Beyond that, she cannot muster more punishment, since she is not there to enforce it. "It's not the best report card in the world," she tells him, "but we'll do better next time."

Eric sits on the sofa and watches television all afternoon—cartoons, the new Busta Rhymes video, extreme sports, Emeril, an obstacle-course show. He gets a ride to the skating rink, where the cashier lets him in for free even though he forgot his ID card. Eric's charming that way. When he gets home, he says he's tired and tries to slip upstairs to the bathroom. His father asks to see his report card.

"You know you have to do better," William says. "I'm going to start checking your homework."

Over the RA a few days later, Eric is called into Ms. Thomas's office, where she meets one by one with every student with so much as one D. Eric sits in the chair in front of her desk and says, "I've only been in here two times."

"Hi, Eric. You probably know I've been seeing kids for grades this week. What did you think of your report card?"

"It's not as good as I thought it would be, but I know I can do better."

She asks about the D's.

"In science, I missed a lot of days and she wouldn't let me make up the work. In health, I'm just not interested, and when I'm not interested, I don't do the work."

"So you prefer D's."

"I don't prefer them, but when I'm bored, I don't do the work. I used to hand in homework, but with classwork, she would be collecting it and I would always be skipped because I sat in back, and I would call out for her to collect mine but she didn't listen. So then I just stopped trying."

"When I listen to you, you know what I hear? 'It's everybody's fault but mine.' "

"It *is* my fault."

"What do you have for related arts now?"

"Tech ed."

"You bored in there?"

"No, I'm close up in there, not just reading a book." This week he made a wooden lamp and sanded it smooth. "I need to have activities, not just reading a book. Because, if I'm bored, I disrupt class, I tap on my desk. But I don't want to be in GT classes, because that's too much homework."

"Are you that lazy, Eric?"

"Yep."

Eric hears all the time that he's smart enough for gifted and talented, that it would be more interesting for him. Every year he grabs the form for GT projects, thinking he'll show how to soup up cars, but he never fills it out. Too hard. "And I don't have the time," says the boy who spends at least three hours a day in front of the television.

Typically for his age, Eric often starts things he doesn't finish. At the end of September he got a new little notebook with colored paper, dated the first page, and wrote about going with his mom to Boston Market and the Laundromat and helping each other put quarters in the machines. "This day may not seem like a lot to others, but it ment alot to me." He doesn't write in it again. He plans to build a snowboard in tech ed, but the class ends and the snowboard never happens.

Getting a boy like Eric to follow through, meet his potential, is a constant struggle for Ms. Thomas and the teachers at Wilde Lake. There are plenty of kids who are thrilled to be moved into GT, where learning tends to be less rote, projects and field trips more common, discussion richer. But just as often, when teachers plead with a parent to move a student up the child doesn't want to, and the parent doesn't force it. It's particularly frustrating for Ms. Thomas with a black boy like Eric. Her late husband was black, her son is half black, and it tore her up when he worked below potential because that's what his friends did. The last thing she wants is a class you can tell is GT because it's filled only with white faces.

Schools have been tracking—assigning students to classes based on ability—for a century. Between one-half and two-thirds of middle schools have some form of tracking, under the theory that kids this age are at such different places intellectually and cognitively that to lump them in the same classes does a disservice. A teacher with a homogeneous group of kids can teach at exactly the pace she needs to; there is less chance for boredom with the quicker kids, less chance for frustration with the slower ones. And kids who have an inkling to excel won't be held back among classmates who ridicule them for that.

Critics contend that tracking gives the best experiences, and often the best teachers, to the students who already have the most advantages, that it denies kids valuable role models: each other. They say it perpetuates lesser expectations for certain children, way before they are fully formed. They say getting shunted into a lower track is demoralizing, a self-fulfilling prophecy, the way Harry Potter's classmates whom the Sorting Hat sends to Gryffindor are slated for great things, while Slytherin kids are doomed to a life of malfeasance.

But for Ms. Thomas, the reality is that if a kid doesn't have GT at Wilde Lake he'll never get it in high school, and he'll never have the edge on the SAT. If he blows math in eighth grade, unless he plays a lot of catch-up he's blown his SAT scores totally, because, as Ms. Thomas puts it, "they're looking at math you're not going to be able to do. It's so sequential, but kids really don't understand that."

She says to Eric, "You have a lot of checks here for not coming prepared for class."

"I'm always losing pencils. I have a hole in my pencil case, so I have to keep them in my pocket. Here, I have them in my pocket right now."

"What are your goals for this year, Eric?"

"My goal is passing."

"That's a very minimal goal. You are capable of much more than that."

"Let's raise the stakes?"

"Yep. You're a very smart kid."

"I get bored and then I start tapping with my pencil . . ."

"I've seen it, and I'm not wild about that."

"Neither is my mom."

"The teachers will have to start making recommendations for high school very soon, the level courses you'll be at. And your teachers don't know you very well yet, do they?"

"Nope."

"So what can you do to let them know what you can do?"

"Study for tests. Do more homework, because that will prepare me for the tests. I should take my time more and focus more. I don't like to do homework, because it's no fun."

"Most people, if they were being honest, would say they don't like to do homework either. But in life there are always things we have to do that we don't want to do. In high school there are different tracks—GT, honors, on grade level, and review, which is below grade level. Where do you see yourself?"

"Probably on or above grade level. I'm going to get all B's."

"Do you want to go to college?"

"Yep, I want to go to Tennessee University. I want to be a Volunteer." Eric has seen the Tennessee Volunteers play football, heard they have a good culinary program.

"There are all sorts of things that happen soon that impact the university's decision to select you. SATs, PSATs, they look at the level of your classes, the activities you've been in—sports and band and even maybe student government—when they're considering what you can handle. I would like to see you taking honors-level classes."

"The work ain't hard."

"Not 'ain't.' We're not saying 'ain't.' " They laugh.

"My mom is my only motivation. No one else cares besides my mom, and my dad."

"Why are we sitting here? Do you think I care?"

"Yes."

"I care very much. You are a very smart boy. You are also a typical thirteen-year-old boy. You don't understand that what you do today affects your future. You don't have very long to show what you're capable of." She looks at his report card. "There are not many A's and B's here, and there should be. Next marking period I want you on the honor roll. That list outside on that wall should say 'Eric Ellis.' So what are you going to do about that?"

"When I go home, I usually turn on the TV, but instead I'll put on the radio, because that helps me concentrate. And I'll do my homework nice and neat and accurate—instead of rushed, like I normally do. And I'll buy a new pencil case."

"Yes, don't go into class without what you need."

"Yes, ma'am."

"If you need supplies, ask me. I always have some extra around here."

"All right."

If Eric were *really* screwed up—if he were blowing most of his classes instead of a couple, if he weren't such a "good kid," as everyone calls him, if his mother never showed up at school—maybe there would be a more thorough, more meaningful intervention to keep Eric from crumbling. But this one ends here.

"Got anything else to say?" Ms. Thomas asks.

"Thank you for . . . Thanks for . . ." He collects his thoughts. "Thank you for saying that I'm a good student. At least I know that somebody cares." Eric gets up to leave. "Do you want this chair pushed back closer to the desk?"

"Oh, that's okay," Ms. Thomas tells Eric, and he heads back to class, still for a moment meaning what he said.

chapter seven

it's not you it's me

Days after the girl and boys fooled around in the bathroom, posters fill the Wilde Lake hallways, decorated by the sixth-grade health class with teary-eyed stick-figures.

> Sexual Harassment! What it really is! Unwelcome conduct of a sexual nature that interferes with a student's ability to learn, work, study, achieve or participate in school activities!

> Ways to stop sexual harassment: Tell harasser how you feel—file complaint—talk to teacher/principal—write letter to harasser!

"Dear Mr. Harasser," the kids mock, "could you please stop harassing me? It makes me uncomfortable." They gather in the library, one class at a time, for a lesson on what constitutes harassment. Each group of six discusses a different form, and Jackie's gets Verbal. They watch a video they find hilarious, in which boys grab girls' butts, and decide if examples listed on a card are flirting or harassment.

The number of schools that educate students about harassment has increased greatly over the last decade. But incidents of harassment—comments and gestures in the hallway, flashing, groping—show few signs of abating. They're commonplace in schools even when they're hard to see, and they have an impact on what goes on in the classroom, where girls and boys who have been harassed have a harder time paying attention or participating.

At Wilde Lake, the kids come away from the library session with a few ideas: First, it can be harassment if two people are making out in front of you and you're uncomfortable. Leslie, whose favorite T-shirt is adorned with a glittered Playboy Bunny, does this on the bus with an eighth grader. Sitting behind them, Jackie says, "Stop making out and just hold hands," but the boys yell, "Kiss her again!" Second, the lines are hazy. "What if a little kid runs home and says, 'I'm gay,'" Jackie asks, "and someone hears? That could be sexual harassment." Third: "If you like it, it's not harassment." As for Lauren and the bathroom incident, Jackie now says, "No one really likes her."

The whole school takes an anonymous survey in homeroom asking if they've been harassed, or harassed anyone. Even though Jackie and her friends have all wound up on one boy's list of People Who Would Take Off Their Clothes for Money, all been grabbed—including Jackie, whose butt has come under increased attention from Adam—none of them check Yes. The boys write that they haven't harassed. At lunch they discuss the survey. Sometimes being grabbed bugs Kristina, sometimes it feels like her body is the only reason boys talk to her, and she's tried to stop it by ignoring, or getting mad, or at the very least not flirting in response. But she likes the attention—so does that count as harassment? Leslie figures she might just as well fudge on the survey. "Why not?" she says. "They'll just do it again." Then she leans on Adam's shoulder. "Right? You'd do it again?" Jackie approaches the table with her lunch tray. Kevin has stolen her chair, so she wallops him on the head with a carton of milk. "You got three boobs," he responds, and reaches toward one of them.

Jackie's parents would be horrified by such behavior; her father's response might well involve a baseball bat. Parents like them can be attentive (which they are), can model healthy patterns of sexuality (which they do), but they can't control their daughter's longings, they can't control the boys' boldness, they can't, as social scientists point out, infuse disgrace back into activities that are portrayed shamelessly on MTV. Nor, for that matter, can the teachers. And none of them can control what they don't know exists.

When it comes down to it, Jackie insists what happens at school is no big deal, even though she would never want her parents to find out about Adam grabbing her butt several times a day at recess, one hand on each cheek. She knows this is supposed to anger her, but she thinks, "Big deal, it's a *butt*." In a way, she's flattered, but "I wouldn't go out with Adam, because he likes too many girls."

Jay Starr, Jackie says immediately after Halloween, "is a fag. He stopped being perverted. He's not like, 'Hey, babe,' anymore. He doesn't even say hi to me anymore." She washes his name off her hand and writes instead, "*HippieBabe629*." "That's my screen name. My uncle says we're really close to getting the Internet." Now she is fixated fully on Anton, the "A" of "J-A-B." In the middle-teen years, social scientists have found, kids choose their mates based on more individual preferences, but at Jackie's age it's because the guy is someone her friends would approve of. For now, it's mostly about the superficial stuff: He's got the right look, he's got the right clothes. Jackie attempts her own explanation: "Anton's funny and—I can't explain it. He's not necessarily shy but he acts really—" Often she can't find the right word. "It's cute."

Jackie isn't sure how grown-up relationships start. "They wouldn't say, like, 'Do you want to go out with me?' like a little preppy person. I've always wondered that. What do they do?" In her world, the asking out and dumping are done through intermediaries, so at school, the first Friday in November, Kristina tells Anton that Jackie likes him and would he ask her out? He says yes. So they're going out, which is a concept that Jackie previously explained to Sara ("I'm not belittling you," she had told her daughter, "I just don't know what that means") as talking more to someone at school and on the phone. "It's just like saying, 'She likes him, he likes her.' They're just better friends." It's not like romantic status really changes anything, since the skating rink isn't cool at the moment and she's not allowed alone at the movies and without the Internet she can't even IM anyone. Jackie and Anton don't go anywhere together. They don't talk much, on the phone or at school. Mainly their relationship means Jackie checks herself in the bathroom every day after lunch and runs around Anton on the playground, except when she carefully ignores him.

He is pleased with her attentions but doesn't turn away those of other girls. Jackie and Anton are assigned to different days for the harbor field trip that week, so Celia sits with him on the bus, playing keep-away with his Red Sox hat and trying to snap the rubber bands on his wrist.

"You are the biggest flirt I've ever seen," says Martin, sitting across from them.

"I'm not," Celia says. "Anton's my best friend. I just like to annoy him. Anton is gonna keep me from falling off the boat. Anton calls me and never has anything to say. Look, Ravens Stadium!" She yanks his arm.

Martin tells Anton, "If I were you, I'd change seats right now."

"Somebody's gotta hold my hand so I don't get run over by a car." This is the girl writers like Mary Pipher and Peggy Orenstein explain, someone who tries to appear helpless around the guys she crushes on, submerging herself to make others feel bigger, better. You only have to meet Jackie to see this isn't always the case; if a boy doesn't want her bossy, brassy self, that's his problem. But even though twenty-first-century girls are supposed to be all about "empowerment," their self-esteem hasn't kept pace with expectations. And besides—this says as much about the boys as it does about the girls—baby talk works.

"You don't want me to get run over by a car, do you, Anton?"

"Why do you want to sit with Celia? Don't you already have a girl-friend?" Martin asks.

"I have, like, twenty girlfriends," says Adam.

"Yeah," says Martin, "whose names all end in at-aol-dot-com."

"Anton," Celia says, "you have a girlfriend."

Anton finally speaks. "So?"

"He goes out with Jackie," Jay says, and turns toward the window. "That's gross. Look, Gay Street!"

"Jay Starr," Celia announces, "is a homophobe."

"What's a homophobe?" he asks.

"Someone who hates gays and lesbians."

"But I don't hate *you*."

The boat ride captivates the seventh graders, who sit up in awe as their boat passes under a container ship and the largest cranes in the world scooping up coal. They steer the boat. They measure oysters to determine their health, and translate distances on a nautical map. They make tinfoil-and-Popsicle-stick vessels that are set in a tank of water and laden one by one with sinkers, to see which is most durable.

Walking up the pier to the bus at day's end, someone announces, "It smells like hamburgers." Jay says, "It smells like Anton's girlfriend." On the boat Anton was glad to be away from the taunting; now he is reluctant to get back on the bus. He thinks Jackie is nice, and funny, and he likes her, simple as that. They are, he says, "good friends."

The next day, Jackie, Lily, Mia, and sixty other kids stay after school to try out for *Peter Pan*. Jackie practices by herself in the hallway. Lily and Mia and five friends practice in a group outside the music room, tapping their white-stockinged feet, crowing through their rolled-up score sheets. They rub each other's heads, right above the ponytails, for luck. Lily is nervous and Mia is not. "I'm going to be real weird," she says.

At Jackie's turn in front of the teachers, she sings sweetly and does little movements she made up to match the lyrics. Jonathan flusters mid-song and leaves the room crying. Mia sings to the crowd, squawking goofily at the "I gotta CROW" part, and bounds into her chair when she's done. Then—Lily's turn. Even though she has a lovely voice and performs in ballet and shows off to everyone in the neighborhood how she can pedal her bike with one foot and may very well have to sing for millions at the Miss America Pageant, this is a different kind of performance: Her friends are watching. Just like she wouldn't dare raise her hand in class, she feels stupid here too. She keeps her eyes from the judges, tugs at the hem of her lavender T-shirt, forgets a line, sings softly, laughs uncomfortably. "I was horrible," she says later, when everyone compares how badly they did.

Back in the cafeteria, a few seventh-grade girls tell Mia, "Did you know Matt Grant likes you?" A group of boys appear on the other side of the room, the girls flock, and Mia and Lily roll their eyes: "Seventh graders." With Mia, Lily does cartwheels. Jonathan sits on a chair in the middle of the room, his head down. Jackie listens to her Discman, until Mrs. Bloom takes it away, announcing to the whole cafeteria that she's not allowed to have it here, even after school. Jackie didn't know.

She heads to the lobby and sees her dad's car idling outside. But she's not up for gymnastics. She doesn't think she auditioned well, she's stressed, she can't get her Discman back. She stews and glances at the car for fifteen minutes before heading out. Five days later, Jackie still hasn't gotten the Discman back, because a parent has to pick it up, and she hasn't mustered the courage to tell either of them. Sara will find a note on her dresser. It starts, "I got in trouble for no reason."

And Jackie doesn't get a part, not even a tiny one. The judges eyes' were down, she's certain, when she was doing her cute movements. And besides, "Ms. Drumm doesn't like me." Jonathan, despite his meltdown, is cast as a pirate. Mia is the only sixth grader to get a main part, little Michael, and Lily is the only other sixth-grade girl to make it in. She will play a Lost Boy.

Normally she would not be at all pleased to play a boy, she explains, "but the Lost Boys sit with Michael some of the time!"

"You'll do the 'freak' conversation?" Mr. West asks Ms. Thomas this November morning, hours from the first dance of the year. He's worked in elementary schools most of his career; it's strange for him to deal with such sexual stuff. So Ms. Thomas takes the mike at lunch and says: "I have a serious announcement. I need everybody tuned in here, everyone looking at me. We will wait." And she waits.

The freaking has been going on for several years with older teens and on MTV, and finally has crept down to middle school. Kids don't dance face to face anymore. A boy approaches a girl from behind and grinds his groin against her butt. At school and church dances the chaperones act as freak cops. But at teen dance clubs like the one a half-hour away in suburban Baltimore where a few Wilde Lake kids have gone, to the envy of several of Jackie's friends, children as young as eleven simulate sex on the dance floor as rappers bleat about oral gratification. (The lyrics made great use of the fact that "motherfucker" and "dick sucker" rhyme.) A mother may think her daughter is sleeping at a friend's house; that girl's father drops them off and thinks the place is okay, since kids are frisked at the door and no booze is sold. What they don't see is the security guard playfully slapping pleathered bottoms, girls bent at the waist with their heads nuzzling boys' crotches, girls not sure if they want these guys they don't know grinding fast as a coin-fed motel-room bed against their behinds, but what can they do?

At least Ms. Thomas can do something.

"We have had dances during the school day at Wilde Lake for almost twenty years," she tells the seventh graders. "We want to reward you, and we do it because very rarely do we have kids who don't know how to behave appropriately. Some people in this school almost ended this tradition two years ago by dancing inappropriately. When I go into that gym, I better not see one person dancing that way." Laughter. "You know exactly what I mean. I don't think it's funny. This is the grade I worry about most being able to handle this activity, and you are proving me exactly right."

Ms. Thomas and Mr. West aren't so worried about the sixth graders, who haven't coupled up yet. When the sixth graders on the playground talk about whom they're "going to the dance" with, Lily says Beth, the sweet girl whose locker is on the other side of her from Abigail Werner. They've become friendly. Someone asks Jonathan, who is sitting against the wall with three other boys, whom he's taking.

"Brittany."

"She just told us she's not going with you."

"She said sure. She said sure."

"Do you like her?"

"I like Melissa Marsh. I just need someone to walk in with me."

During recess, the seventh graders run wild. Middle schoolers, particularly on a big day like this, step on each other, shove each other—boys shove girls, and girls shove boys, and they all shove each other. For some kids it hurts, for others it doesn't; you can't always tell which. Everything has force, everything makes noise. Jackie organizes a game of duck-duck-goose. The girls, breathless and loud, hold cartwheel contests, and Jackie madly weaves in and out of groups of kids standing around talking. Some boys follow her, knocking everyone down. Others kick the soccer ball onto the roof, play three-on-three, give each other the finger every time someone makes a basket. Farther out on the field, the boys who like to throw trash have found trash to throw. Adam is wrestling, his pants to his knees, butt showing through thin white Hanes. Mrs. Brodian comes up to the group and says, "No pushing. Though I'm sure as soon as my back is turned you'll start again."

At twelve-thirty-five the students are released one grade at a time from the classes where they can no longer pay attention to the gym, where lights flash and music plays and fog spills across the floor. The sixth graders are excited about their first middle-school dance and enter the room slowly, unsurely. The seventh graders are excited to freak, or to see who else freaks, or at the very least to see their friends and request their songs. The eighth graders act like they aren't excited about anything. "Everyone cool has time-out," one says.

For the first twenty minutes, everybody clumps in groups and watches, moving almost imperceptibly to the music, lip-gloss wands emerging for duty. One fat boy break-dances and everyone laughs at his jiggle. In the corner, eight-grade boys stand around a chair and look down on it. They swear it is moving by itself. Then the DJ calls out, "How many of you know the Booty Call?" Ah, the line dance: the perfect dance for middle school, since the Law of Preteen Dancing mandates that you cannot move your limbs in any way differently from everyone else. Here the steps and their exact-sameness are laid out for you.

The seventh-grade boys start a brief, hyper conga line. The Electric Slide gets just about everybody dancing. At "Clint Eastwood," things get slow, and six couples are urged together by their friends. They clutch each other awkwardly, boys shorter than girls, one bold enough to pet his partner's back. Nearly everyone else leaves the room, because "it's a gay song." There are rap songs that send all the white kids to the cafeteria, and power-pop songs that send all the black kids to the cafeteria; there are a few songs, like DMX's "Party Up," that hold everybody's attention, get them bouncing, get a few of them freaking. One bold person, usually a boy, goes for it: He grinds his butt into the behind of whatever girl is handy, or maybe he jokingly freaks his guy friend, or humps the floor. A few kids join in. A circle grows around the dancers, to protect them from the teachers who stream through the gym, sniffing out inappropriateness. But the teachers are swift at getting right in the middle of it, nipping the freak in the bud.

Eric watches from the gym mats against the wall, except for when he tries to cool down a bunch of his friends who are stalking each other and verging on fights (for dancing with another's girl's boyfriend, for degrading skateboarding skills, and so on).

Elizabeth's friends teach her to dance to "Take It to the House," which essentially means jumping up and down, until the "Barney" song comes on, which she sings.

Lily's gang goes back and forth. In the gym, a bunch of them bounce to Blink 182 and sway to 'N Sync's "Gone," holding up silver barrettes like cigarette lighters, as Lily and Beth tentatively tap their feet. In the cafeteria, ten of them pose for group Polaroids they each buy for a dollar. Half the girls look goofy. Mia is front and center; part of Lily's face peeks from behind her.

Jonathan spends the dance in the classroom where *Shrek* is showing. Next door, the kids in time-out fill pages of paper: "Knowing full well chewing gum is against school rules, I will refrain from doing so in the future. Knowing full well chewing gum is against school rules, I will refrain from doing so in the future." Celia buys a heart tattoo that says "Love" and plants it at the top of her breast, visible down her tank top.

Jimmy occasionally comes into the gym to listen to a song, but since he can't dance, he spends most of his time at a corner table in the cafeteria, where a group of sixth-grade boys eat snacks and fold origami. They talk about Game Boy. They jump up and down with the idea that when they're off the ground they're farther from China. His friend John does a Russian dance with his fingers, and the other boys copy him. When the movie is done, Jonathan runs over, hiding from two seventh-grade girls he says want to dance with him, and the boys continue bragging, and interrupting, and arguing (as usual) about who's smarter and better.

"I can play saxophone better than you."

"I can play piano better than you."

"I can play trumpet better that you."

"That's because I can't even spell 'trumpet.' "

"Yes, you can."

"No, I can't. T-R-O-U-M-P-E-T-T."

"Exactly."

"No, I spelled 'troumpett.' "

"Exactly."

"I didn't spell 'exactly.' I spelled 'troumpett.' "

Jimmy tells Daniel a complicated fishing/cat joke that ends with the punch line, "If the fly drops four inches, there's bound to be a pussy involved." Daniel's freckled face is blank, his eyes scrunched behind his glasses, and Jimmy repeats the punch line. Ten seconds later, Daniel says,

"I get it," which he either does or doesn't.

On a Saturday in early December, at Jackie's thirteenth-birthday party, six girls in various forms of bikini—from Jackie's tankini that barely shows her belly, to Kristina's and Celia's revealing strings—carry Jay and Brad through the water at the humid swimming-pool bubble. The girls calls the boys babies and treat them as such, touching Jay's feet, holding him from behind, passing him around, dunking him. Sure, he likes being touched, but this is annoying. Jackie is cold and sits huddled into herself on the edge of the pool, near a group of seven-year-olds tossing a beach ball.

They get out to wait in line for the diving board, and Kristina rests her hands on Jay's shoulders. So do Meghan, Leslie, and Celia, who mock-strip for him. As this goes on, Jackie heads up the stairs to the top of the water slide, splashes down in front of them, and shouts, "Guys! Guys! I went down the tube backwards!" Her lips purple, she stands in line for the rope swing while the others disappear.

Over hot dogs and Pepsi, Leslie, whose hair is splotched violet, says, "I'm getting my eyebrow pierced next year, my belly button pierced the year after, and my lip pierced the year after that." Kelly says to Kristina, "If your mom was my mom, I'd have my eyebrow pierced already, but she's not, and my mom's a fag." Kristina says, "Anton says I'm going to hell," and "Anton says Celia's going to hell," and Leslie hears only a bit of this and says, "Where are you going? I want to go, too."

Jackie's lips are still purple as she opens her presents. "Watch me!" Jay gives Jackie a flowery card from his mom's drawer. She gets cash, fifteen dollars at a time, fruity glitter lotions and sprays, and a bunch of CDs. Her friends sing "Happy Birthday" but they're doing it off-key, on purpose, so Jackie says, "Shut up!"

When Jackie wrote invitations for her birthday party, she didn't have Anton's address, so she didn't invite him. A month after they started going out, they are still a couple, in a fashion. They don't hang out; they do write notes. "I'm not going out with u just for the hell of it," Anton writes, "I'm going out wit u cause I love you!!" The exclamation marks are punctuated at the bottom by a smiley face. Jackie is not so sure. He didn't ask her to dance at school, she's gotten ambivalent, going out with him has started to feel like a job: "You have to keep your eye on him all the time." Like how Celia told Jackie that Anton told her that he likes her instead. So, when Jackie sleeps over at the house of a friend who's on the Internet, she instant-messages him:

I can't go out with you anymore. It's not you it's me.
Anton responds,
WHY???
A pause, then he adds,
Fine. Be that way.

"It's not you it's me"? It *was* him, but Jackie doesn't want to be mean. "There's no point," she explains. "It's like revenge." She is, in a way, relieved—especially the next day, when Leslie passes her a note: "I'm glad u don go out w/Anton he was hitten on me online LOL." Jackie still has to sit next to him in social studies, and every time he opens his mouth she digs a little. When they have to pick Middle Ages personae Anton says, "I'm going to be a knight." Jackie snaps back: "More like you're gonna be *working* at night, as a blacksmith."

winter

why is it that when we are mad at someone we tend to wait right by the phone for them to call and tell us that they are ok but they never call and you mad at them and you

i can't make her do anything

By this evening seventh grade has been going on for three months, but still Mr. Shifflett, waiting in the front hall for his next conference, is stumped. "Elizabeth Ginsburg," he murmurs to the gym teacher. "Elizabeth Ginsburg. I have to remember what she's like in class. I have no idea."

Joseph and Ellen never get too much out of conferences. Teachers always say they want parents to show up even when their children are doing fine, but what's there to say? They come anyway, searching the bulletin boards and teachers' recollections for clues, however small, into their daughter's psyche. Once in a while is there a surprise, like when they hear about this jokey sense of humor Elizabeth supposedly has.

"We'd like to know Elizabeth's strengths and weaknesses," Joseph says once they're seated in a rectangle of desks—Joseph, Elizabeth, and Ellen on one side, and Mr. Shifflett and Ms. Hammond, the math teacher, on the other.

"Okay," Mr. Shifflett says. "Liz is an absolutely a stellar student in science. She had a ninety-seven percent this quarter, she's particularly well prepared, she gets right to work. For groups she picks people who will help her, and not those who she has to carry along." He asks Elizabeth, "What do you think your strengths are?" No answer. "Weaknesses?" She tucks her head into the crook of her arm.

"Look how red she is," Ellen says to Joseph. Elizabeth is in some ways easygoing, but also easily mortified. For example, her parents are the only people on earth who know she wears headgear at night. When Mr. West comes up to her lunch table and asks, "How you girls doing?" she starts giggling and can't stop. When she raises her hand in class, she tucks her fist into her sleeve and gives the answer in a mumble just this side of baby talk.

Ellen reaches over and rubs Elizabeth's shoulder, then quickly pulls away. Mr. Shifflett says he can't think of any weaknesses. "Have you caught her humor?" Joseph asks.

In math Elizabeth is doing ninth-grade algebra. If the problems aren't exactly like the examples in the book, Ellen can't help. Joseph grasps it—"It all just goes back to a = mx + b, distance equals rate times time, regression analysis"—but Elizabeth won't ask him for help. "I'll tell you," he says to Ellen, "and you tell her." Too shy to ask questions in class, when Elizabeth had problems she stayed after school with Ms. Hammond until she got it. She aced the test, best score in the class.

"You did a great job helping her," Ellen tells the teacher. "It was getting beyond where I could help."

"She did that by herself," Joseph says.

"What do you think about that?" he says proudly as they walk down the hall, hoping Elizabeth will share his enthusiasm. She does, inside. But she answers, "I don't know."

The next afternoon Joseph sits at a round table in the music room, across from Miss Colyer. Elizabeth got a B, she says, because she didn't practice enough—one week only twenty minutes, instead of the prescribed two hours. Other than that, she just says she enjoys having Elizabeth in class. That's not what Joseph wants to get at.

"Like I told you when I met you at Back to School Night," he says, "Elizabeth's the kind of kid who interacts with teachers. I don't think she's experiencing you the way you experience her. She says she's not having fun."

For soft-spoken Miss Colyer, this is the first year of teaching, the first year sitting across the table from discontented parents. "I tried to connect with her," she tells Joseph. "I'd love to do a better job, but I'm not sure how."

Miss Colyer asks for specifics, but all Joseph has is that one day Elizabeth came home in a tiff, saying she had had a fight with a teacher. She wouldn't say more.

"There was one day she had a small problem with another student," Miss Colyer explains. "It got worked out the best it could." Danielle had stolen Elizabeth's chair, they started yelling at each other and had to sit in the hall during lunch and write up behavior plans, but Miss Colyer stays short on detail.

"I hate to have her drop strings," Joseph says, rubbing his beard. "The dynamics in the class might be set. It's just something to be aware of. Sometimes she gets the sense you're not listening to her. Maybe it's the competition with other kids for attention."

"I can understand her feeling like I'm not paying attention. That class is a tough class."

"Why's it tough?"

"There are a lot of behavioral problems in that class. It's a lot of kids thrown together who don't mix well."

"Maybe that's what she's feeling. Isn't this class an elective in a sense? It should be fun. She should want to do it."

"I'm working on it."

"Sounds like you are. Basically, what I should tell her is she's doing a great job?"

"I know that there are certain disagreements. I can ask her if there's a way to talk about it without her feeling embarrassed."

"I just don't know. Her feelings are hurt easily. She's at the age she's not telling us much."

Joseph leaves the school with a feel for the class dynamics but no more feel for his daughter. He can't get her to practice viola. He can't get her to let him help with math. He can't get her to open up to him. Is this what he signed up for, twelve and a half years ago?

"I can't make her do anything," he says as he opens the door of his Celica. "I feel like a third wheel sometimes. I really want to help her do things, instead of just being a chauffeur."

Joseph and Ellen spend more time driving their daughter to various lessons—synchro three times a week, speed swimming once, Bat Mitzvah class, math tutor, Hebrew school—than they spend with her anywhere else. They shell out for the quickly outgrown swimsuits, including the tuxedo one with a fake red bow tie. Ellen applies Knox gelatin to Elizabeth's hair the nights before synchro meets so it stays glued in its bun, and carefully smooths it. Joseph and Ellen sit through long, steamy meets and cheer all Elizabeth's synchronicity while wearing their purple swim-team polos.

At speed practice Elizabeth cuts through the water on her back, doing a butterfly kick. Her body is graceful, grown, womanly almost. In her purple swim cap, her hair is a bubble of grape Bubble Yum. She uses this time, as she generally does, to think about problems at school and wonder why you don't choke when you open your mouth under water.

At seven o'clock, as a dozen girls swim laps around her, Elizabeth calls to her coach, "I want to go home."

"For that," he says, "you have to stay till seven-thirty-five."

"Nooooo!"

"I thought you wanted to be good."

"So?"

" 'So' is a child's answer."

"So?"

Children's sports are intense: In Elizabeth's grade there is a field-hockey player who runs two hours every morning so her coach won't move her from center forward, soccer players with chiropractors, swimmers with weekly massage appointments. Elizabeth wouldn't mind being in the Olympics but doesn't want to work too hard. At the speed meets, when she gets out of the pool with a time slower than the last, she does what kids her age do—with sports, with school, whatever. "That was the best I could do," she says, as if insisting she's happy with her performance means she doesn't have to be disappointed in herself. Ellen and Joseph don't like this, Elizabeth can tell. They don't congratulate her profusely enough, which she finds totally not right, especially since it's hard to swim fast with all this new *body*. It's not like Liz's parents want her to be an Olympian, or think she can, but if she's going to do competitive sports, she should be, well, competitive.

After practice, her wet hair as always soaking the back of her shirt, Elizabeth grabs her huge gym bag—stuffed with towels, affixed with key chains and laminated motivational quotes from her coaches—and gets in Ellen's waiting car. While looking at herself in the lighted vanity mirror (she will do this the whole drive home), she complains, "Katie Dean got to go in lane four and I had to go in three. Pat made me stay late." Ellen wishes Elizabeth were tougher; the complaints about coaches are getting to her. "If you're going to do it," she says later, "be focused and do it. She's perfectly capable. She's definitely capable of improving, and she really hasn't improved very much in two years."

Elizabeth's interests in general shift quickly. This is part of the process of the evolving brain's testing out which cells and connections to shed or to keep, but to an adult it looks a lot like lack of ambition. "When she says she wants to do something like be an artist or an actress or be whatever," Joseph says, "she's not taking steps to try to do that. We can offer her art camp or a play or whatever, and for some reason she doesn't want to do that." Sure, a twelve-year-old may just say these things to try them on, but the way Joseph sees it, she's not leaving them on long enough to see if they fit.

The balance between encouraging and overbearing is so hard to master. A kid thrives on your high expectations for her, but those same high expectations feel a lot like pressure. If Ellen and Joseph try to boost Elizabeth by suggesting she might make it to finals at synchro nationals, she wigs out. "That's really hard! Sometimes they expect me to do so good at everything, even though I'm not that good at everything." If Joseph says, "You're great," at a moment when Elizabeth doesn't agree, "it's sometimes annoying, because it's not always true!" If they skip a meet, she gives them grief. This weekend they're missing regionals for a blues festival.

"You like your friends better than my swimming."

"No," Joseph says, "I like my blues better. You could have come, but you didn't want to." She used to like that sort of event. He remembers taking Liz to the Folk Festival when she was little, and she stripped to her diaper and danced around; it's the kind of thing about which he says, "Don't you remember?" and she never does.

If the Wilde Lake principal could have one wish, it would be for parents and teachers to resist a distance that seems inevitable and draw nearer to their middle schoolers instead. With parents of preadolescents immersed in their own worries—the rate of children living in two-parent households is declining, for example, and more than three-quarters of children have mothers who work—it can be tempting to indulge the "Leave me alone."

But look close, Ms. Thomas says, and you'll see that these budding adolescents, for all their bluster, are still needy children. A better way to think of a preteen's changing relationship with her parents is as a reorganization, not a rejection. Wanting to be independent is not the same as wanting to be left alone. She wants to explore; she also wants a safe harbor. She will admit—not to her parents, of course—that hibernating into the bedroom isn't ideal for her either, not all the time. She enjoys helping shape the rules and having responsibilities around the house, especially those that show off her talents—just not so much that it's a burden. She needs some meaningful independence, and if she gets it at home, she won't seek it in inappropriate places. She wants to talk—but, please, not just about chores. She wants to talk *more* about her schoolwork, in fact, though not her grades. She likes to hear about her parents' past, and hers. She cares what they think of her; family is by far a middle schooler's greatest source of self-esteem. She wants role models. Their affection means tons to her, and she wouldn't mind cuddling once in a while. (No, not in *public*.)

It may not look like it, but a middle schooler wants to be told no. If she hears it from an early age, she'll be used to it when the stakes are raised. She wants rules—which sometimes get her out of situations she isn't comfortable being in anyway. Okay, maybe she doesn't *always* want rules, maybe sometimes she despises the rules. But psychologists insist parents should persist anyway, because, in ten, twenty, thirty years, secure, successful adults say they appreciate their childhoods rules, in retrospect. Even if the kids whose parents set strong, reasonable ethical and moral limits may experiment, they're likelier to drift back eventually within the standards their parents tried to enforce. They turn out better, simply put. Even if she resists them outwardly, a child with strong connections to adult authority figures becomes stronger herself, more in control. Kids whose parents have distanced themselves are far more susceptible to peer pressure and more likely to misbehave in school.

Elizabeth doesn't tell it to Joseph and Ellen much anymore, but she does love her parents. They may not hear it for decades, but she does want their help.

She still wants to be tucked in bed, she still wants to be able to let her guard down and be comforted during storms. She hated the time Joseph insisted, "Don't be scared, calm down," which didn't make any sense to her, because how can you decide not to be scared?

She wants to be taken care of. She's kind of insulted that Ellen stopped making her lunches this year, even though she prefers what the bag contains when there are no adults involved: a candy bar, malted-milk balls, Doritos, chocolate-chip yogurt. The kids whose parents make their lunches are proud of this, even prouder when their mothers use napkins not to remind them "Homework club today!" but to profess their love or, better yet, once a week to scribble a trivia question for the whole lunch table, answer revealed in tomorrow's brown sack.

She wants their company. She wants them home, as long as they don't bug her. Like most middle-school students, Elizabeth does her homework in the family room, not in the bedroom, so that her mother is nearby. "We bought her this desk," Ellen complains. "Does she use it?" When Ellen was in New England with her mother-in-law, Joseph taped *Buffy the Vampire Slayer* so that he and Elizabeth could watch it together, even though it bores him, and she slept in his bed because she was scared. She wishes he brought her to the office for Take Your Daughter to Work Day, instead of saying, "You'd be bored."

She wants their rituals. Even though neither Elizabeth nor her dad likes baseball, she cherishes their yearly Orioles game. (When the vendors only had square boxes left for her autographed ball, she said she wanted the round case with the stand and would wait till next year if she had to. Joseph thought, That is just like me. She likes the way her mother takes her to a five-thirty breakfast before summer swim team, and the way her parents treat her to golden rolls at Sushi King after good report cards, though she hates how Joseph sings "Sushi King, Sushi King" all week beforehand.

She wants her mom to be the swing vote when she can't decide between two pairs of jeans, and she wants her to shrink a few more T-shirts in the dryer so she can have them. She likes that Ellen is going to let her pick out her own clothes for Chanukah presents, because if her mom did the picking, "I think that, like, only half of it would be right, I guess, because she got these shorts and they were, like, white, and I liked the white part, but they had fireworks all over it and I didn't like that part."

She wants them to listen to her, sympathize with her, say how awful something is that she thinks is awful, not spaz out over it or try to solve it or anything, just say, "Oh, you poor thing," and mean it.

She wants her parents to pick up her hints that she cares. The only time she releases her pounds of curly dark hair from the braid in public is for school pictures, because she knows her parents like it that way. She carefully selects gifts—a fancy marble for him, hair clips for her—at the Chanukah bazaar. At the end of every phone call, and at the end of every silent twenty-minute drive to swimming, Elizabeth says, "I love you, Dad."

She wants them there forever. When she found out Will Meyer's mom died of a heart attack, Elizabeth thought for a week straight about her mom dying and couldn't imagine it. She knows she wouldn't be able to come to school like Will did. As it is, her mother has pneumonia for the second time and "bronchisimpatootie, I don't know." Elizabeth stays up at night and worries with each cough that storms through the wall.

As stingy as Elizabeth is about showing her parents affection, like many kids her age she clings to other adults. When her sixth-grade math teacher, Ms. Jones, visits from maternity leave like a rock star in purple sunglasses and a slick black trench coat, Elizabeth gets a pass out of strings to see her. They walk through the hallway holding hands as Ms. Jones says to the girls who pass, "How's my little mathematicians?" Elizabeth hugs her goodbye and says, "I got a cut on my finger from opening a calculator case. This wouldn't have happened if you hadn't put me in GT math."

The list of people to whom Elizabeth sends every sentimental chain e-mail she receives includes as many teachers, aunts, and coaches as it does peers. She embraces her synchro coach Lorraine unabashedly and calls her "Mommy" as a joke, ever since a waitress mistook them for mother and daughter. She likes to tell Lorraine all about school. "Guess what?" she'll say. "I think I failed." She always says this, but she never fails. Seems to Lorraine that Elizabeth's a lonely kid. "Sometimes she's *talk talk talk talk talk*"—Lorraine makes the gabby motion with her hand—"so I just have to shoo her away. I just want to talk with her about swimming."

At recess, Liz often wanders away from her friends toward whichever adult is monitoring the schoolyard. "Those boys took our court and they won't play half-court because they said they were here first," she tells Mr. Merrills, a guidance counselor. "And I'm scared of the ball." Mr. Merrills tells the boys to play half-court, then at the foul line tries to help Elizabeth conquer her fear. "I was hit in the stomach with a basketball when I was little," she explains. Her hands cover her face. She takes the ball and spins it, shoots. Shoots again. She's getting somewhere and then announces, "I'm scared of bees, too," and takes off. "The bees are attracted to you," Mr. Merrills calls, "because you're sweet. Your hair smells sweet."

"My hair doesn't smell sweet. It smells like chlorine. It's going to turn green."

Finally mature enough to deal in abstract thought, a kid like Elizabeth can see her parents as real, flawed people instead of mysterious, mythical characters. She can design in her mind the perfect parents—and determine that hers aren't it. She can compare them with whatever idealistic image she concocts in her head of the other adults in her life; not that she would trade, but, still, it kind of feels like she's outgrowing her mom and dad and needs to connect with other, less flawed adults who will treat her more like an equal, who don't know her baggage, who might give it to her straight. It's the same mechanism, child psychologists explain, that causes crushes on rock stars. It's healthy and normal—though more common among isolated children, and certainly among only children, who tend to be more comfortable with adults than with peers—unless the relationships become too thick with emotional attachment, turn into substitutes for those with parents and friends.

In this sense Elizabeth is on the edge. In some ways, the relationships she builds with grown-ups are a replacement for the relationships other kids her age have with their siblings or even their friends, when they're in tighter-knit friendship groups, or at least more dramatic ones. Elizabeth creates her own drama; she has a hard time rolling with the punches when she feels a chosen adult has let her down. She is trying to figure out who likes her and who doesn't, and, absent proof either way, she makes up the answers. For one, she is certain Miss Colyer has it in for her—with a seventh grader it is always, always personal; when you're twelve you're obsessed with justice—and therefore has engaged in a constant power struggle, a whining campaign that a teacher can shut down but never win. So, too, with Mrs. Rashid, the teacher who monitors lunch and always tells Elizabeth to stop playing with her food and get outside, which Elizabeth never wants to do, because it's cold and boring, or hot and boring.

"She singles me out," Elizabeth says. "She doesn't pick on anyone else the way she picks on me."

This is the unanimous complaint of middle schoolers, a scientific impossibility.

chapter nine

i barely ever have a chance to make fun of anyone

Dodgeball has been banned this year in the Howard County Public Schools—too violent, too humiliating. In a way, though, middle school is a game of dodgeball, except instead of a red ball you avoid annoying people. Nobody is immune: Jackie is teased for being short. Eric is teased for being fat. Elizabeth is teased for being Elizabeth. And so on.

Jimmy started sixth grade closely knit into his group of best friends from elementary school, boys who are clever, obedient, and not very popular. There's Daniel, who wants to be a band director like his dad and keeps a pen clipped to his shirt collar "because it's resourceful." There's John, who has secret stress stomachaches and natural, impeccable humor, a combination that makes it inevitable he'll quit premed one day to write sitcoms. And there's Will, who plans to apply to Harvard, Stanford, Yale, Princeton, MIT, and Caltech and become a biroboticist. For his eighth-grade science project, he wants to make an artificial hand.

The boys' favorite things to do together are play video games, talk about video games, and taunt each other. This sort of taunting is tolerable, a sign of affection almost, coming as it does from true friends. It's not unfathomable to Jimmy that when he grows up the nerdy guys will have become the cooler ones while the popular kids turn fat, bald, and boring. Maybe what adults say is true: Jimmy's type wins in the end. But that's not great comfort right now. "I'm not funny," he says. "I used to correct people too much, and I still do a little. It makes me feel better a little. I don't know what I like about myself. I don't like anything else."

Of the group, Will and Jimmy fight the most—practically all the time, it seems—mainly about friendship stuff. Girls' bickering gets most of the attention from teachers and parents and authors and so on, but they tend to deny their conflicts, let them fester under the surface. The sports and rule-based games boys choose are ripe for argument. So, in fact, boys actually report more conflict in their friendships than girls do. Jimmy keeps a framed photo of himself and Will in first grade on the shelf above his bed, the same photo Will has over his bed. Will is a loyal friend. But Jimmy hates the way Will makes him feel when he gets B's. And, concerned about Will's uncoolness, he is facing a common dilemma of the preteen years: balancing the benefits of a satisfying one-on-one friendship with the desire to negotiate a better place for yourself, popularity-wise. Deep inside, Jimmy thinks that maybe part of growing up is growing out of people, and perhaps Will will be the first.

The kids above their group socially act older, as if they have to be nasty to be popular. Will especially arrived at middle school worried about big mean kids, and it comes true when Chris Kopp lifts him up by his backpack on the bus, which chokes him and makes him cry. In telling the story, he mentions that Billy Mara saved him a seat on the bus. "Billy Mara? He's a geek," Jimmy says.

"I hate him," Will says, "but he saves me a seat."

You will never, all your life, forget the rank order of popularity in your sixth-grade class, or the rules of the middle-school food chain: You will prey upon anyone who appears remotely more vulnerable than you are. The people toward the bottom, rather than refrain from teasing because they know it is the single most painful thing about middle school, "get so mad they have to take it out on someone," Jimmy says. With nothing to lose, they make fun of everyone. They feel bad, but they feel good. Strong, kind of. For someone in the middle, like Jimmy, it's no use getting mad at the popular people, "because then a lot of people gang up on you."

"I barely ever have a chance to make fun of anyone," he says, "because they make fun of me."

By the time winter starts, though, he's getting his chance. He makes fun of Billy for keeping his school supplies in a Game Boy case around his neck. He makes fun of blue-haired Louis, turning around in science to call him an Oompah Loompah or say, "I finished three seconds ahead of you," or threatening to tattle when Louis hides in a banned cranny of the schoolyard. And he even has a seventh grader to make fun of.

At an after-school class called Engineering Challenge, Jimmy and his friends are building a shoe-size magnetic levitation racecar. Annoying Mitch, from seventh grade, is also on the team. "It's Engineering Challenge," John tells him, "not Engineering for the Challenged." As they use various instruments they find in the shop room—the vise, a string, a pencil—to shape foam for the car's body, they keep calling Mitch "M-Dog."

"That's not even funny," he says.

"The only not-funny thing here is your fricking face," says John. Mitch kicks the ground and stomps away. They call after him: "Girl! You're a girl!" Mitch can't stand it, collects his backpack, and leaves. "M-Dog got in trouble!" Jimmy says, and turns his attention to the pencil he's got in a vise. It heats up as he saws at it with a string. "Smell that. It smells like popcorn," Jimmy says, and smashes the pencil.

A little rejection isn't the worst thing—kids who are isolated in childhood tend to emerge as more self-sufficient adults, which might be why the coolest grown-ups were miserable in middle school. But there's a difference between rejection and humiliation, and teasing comes in degrees. On a scale from one to ten, Jimmy getting ribbed for missing a catch in gym class is maybe a four. It hurts, has a little truth to it, but is neither persistent nor insurmountable. Mitch in engineering club: more like an eight or a nine.

An adult who doesn't inspect extremely closely might never be able to figure out why certain kids merit the eights. For example, there is a sixth grader named Valerie who gets teased every day. Very few people want to be her friends. A grown-up would look at a lineup of middle schoolers and be unable to pick out this girl, who, despite a lack of physical defect or lisp or back brace, will elicit snickers and eye rolls no matter what she does or wears or says—the one whom classmates won't talk to, though they secretly wonder what would happen if they made her up like all the uncool-turned-cool kids in the movies. The adult would think,

"What a friendly girl. Those pigtails are adorable." To the kids it's obvious but hard to explain.

Something about how her bright-pink nail polish is always partially chewed off.

Something about how, when she's called on to read aloud, she orates.

Something about how she wears a Mickey Mouse T-shirt the day she presents her biography poster of Walt Disney.

Something about how she writes your name on her binder in milky pen as if you signed it yourself, when you're not even her friend.

Something about how you'll be talking at recess and she'll come and say, "Hi guys. What do you want to do?"

"Stand here and talk."

"Pick on people, or just talk?"

Something about how during the culture presentation in social studies she says she likes *Amelia* books and *American Girl* magazine, as if she were ten. "For transportation," she announces loud and clear, "I put a van. I'd like to have a van one day, when I have children." The idea of Valerie having children sends several kids into snickers.

"Valerie," a girl asks during health class, "do you know what a D-I-C-K is?"

"I know what it is."

"What is it?"

"I'll tell you later."

"We want to know if you know what it is."

Valerie mumbles.

"We can't hear you."

"Fine, I'll tell you what it is. It's the front part of the woman's—"

"No, it's a man's you-know."

"I knew that all along."

One time in art, Abigail tosses a crumpled paper towel in Valerie's face and says, "Oops, sorry, thought you were the trash can." The next period, her class searches reference books in the library to fill in various facts on a worksheet. One of Valerie's braids has come out of its pin, and dangles. Two boys and two girls sit at a table staring at her instead of at the books spread in front of them.

"Look at the back of her head when she walks," one boy says, loudly.

Valerie drops some books from the shelf and they laugh. The look on her face is half defiant, half scared. "You're a retard," the boy says. "*You're* a retard," she replies. Mrs. Stokes intervenes: "I thought I told you two to stop talking to each other. One more word and you're both going to the reinforcement room." The teacher walks away and the kids at the table laugh. The boy says, "Retard."

Back at her table, Valerie wonders what the crime is in self-defense. "I'm trying to protect myself," she mumbles. " 'If you say one more word.' I know I'm not a little kid."

Teasing, if some people had their way, would become a federal crime. Brightly colored pamphlets tout efforts like the National Education Association's National Bullying Awareness Campaign; "bullyproofing" schools is debated on the floors of Congress, with the idea that bullying is why angry teens turn guns on their classmates; Miss America takes it up as her platform. Just like with sexual harassment, schools teach prevention. In health class, Ms. Rouiller gives the middle schoolers "effective strategies" against bullying; in academic enrichment, Mrs. Stokes says you can choose not to give a bully the power to make you afraid. She teaches an acronym: CUE. "Check it out, Use your strategies, Evaluate." Ignore them, she recommends.

These trendy awareness programs, the laws and lawsuits, are predicated on a false, almost quaint notion: that the "them," the bullies standing ready to take your lunch money and your dignity, are a minority, vultures who can be ignored or disciplined into quiescence. In fact, though, the primary form of bullying in middle school is not shoving or threatening but excluding from the group. The bullied are the small number (usually the aggressive, or the withdrawn) and the bullies nearly everyone else, who—empowered by groupthink, tinged by guilt over abandoning their Do Unto Others values but not so much so as to trump the overwhelming desire to belong—poke and prod these chosen victims more often than not in subtle, gossipy, tiny ways, ways impossible to legislate away or even, often, to notice.

Besides, "ignore them" doesn't make you feel any better when you learn Andrew only asked you out because he was paid twenty dollars, when everyone laughs because you're fat and collide into the hurdle, when you hear a boy in gym class saying, not quietly at all, "That's ugly. She dyed her hair. She has a pointy nose. Point point," or when one of the popular kids' instant-message profile announces "RICH . . . YOUR A LOOSER . . . YOU THINK UR COOL BUT UR NOT, UR A FAGGET . . . UR SO FUCKING GAY."

Gay. Used to describe an activity, say, or a book, it's a simple synonym for "lame." Used to describe a person, it's the biggest insult in the male middle-school lexicon. If someone called you gay, a boy this age figures, it would be even more upsetting than if he spied on you in the shower or pulled your pants down or even made you touch him. A boy knows he can't deviate or he's a "fag." Not being a fag preoccupies him. Being normal preoccupies him. But there are no guidelines for whether you're normal or not. So he and his friends identify freaks at school, outliers, oddballs, to define themselves against. You can't know if you're normal, but if you've established that these other guys are freaky, you definitely have an edge on the competition.

Many of the kids at Wilde Lake think Jack is hilarious on *Will & Grace*, many have a gay aunt or uncle or cousin they enjoy, many would say they support gay rights, if asked, and many surely are curious about the whole thing. None of this, however, diminishes the horror, in their minds, of homosexuality encroaching on their own lives. Eric, for example, professes to be a huge proponent of the "live and let live" school of thought. But every time a certain mysterious boy shows up at the skating rink wearing his striped rugby shirt and knit scarf—it's unclear if this kid is actually homosexual or just enjoys the trauma pretending to be so creates—Eric and his friends spend the whole evening strategizing about how to avoid him.

"He's so faggy," Eric's friend says. "I asked if he was gay and he said, 'Yessssss.' "

"We gotta watch each other's back," says Eric. "One skates forward, one backward, and one sideways. All gays should go to the moon or something. I mean, no offense, but that is nasty."

"If I so much as smell his breath."

One boy the sixth graders have decided is gay—not to mention "Donkey," "Four Eyes," and "Metalmouth"—is Jeff Graff. His main crimes are whining, "Can I play with you? Can I play with you?" nonstop at recess, growing a little tail of hair down the back of his neck, and bringing an Icee to lunch one day after a doctor's appointment. Everybody likes Icees, but because Jeff has one, it is proclaimed a stupid thing to bring to lunch. In health class, Ms. Rouiller makes groups by drawing names from a box, and when the first group is completed without Jeff's name called, there are "phew"s.

"If you have a problem with who is in your group and make it verbal," Ms. Rouiller says, "you will work alone." Then she calls a group with his name.

"Oof."

"Ow."

"Ha!"

Ms. Rouiller freezes. This is her pet peeve. "Jeff, go ahead to the media center and start your work. The rest of you stay." He leaves the room. "Do you know why I let him go ahead and had the rest of you stay?"

Silence.

"Because he was the only one who wasn't talking?"

"That's not exactly it."

"Because people were making fun of him?"

You can hear the lights buzz. "How would you like to be the person singled out and laughed at?" Ms. Rouiller pauses long between sentences. "Do you think it feels good? I don't. Hopefully, he didn't hear what people were saying, because he was sitting in the front." Jimmy looks at his purple pen. "How do *you* feel? Do you feel bad? You should feel bad. I don't know what is allowed in the rest of the school, but this does not happen in my classroom. It does not happen in *your* classroom. What do you think I should do?"

"You should have us apologize to him?"

"What else?"

"You could call our parents if anyone makes fun of him again?"

"That's more what I was thinking. I'm not going to have you apologize, because if he didn't hear what was going on and then we apologize, he'll know. But if this happens again, I'll call in your parents and you can work it out then. If you can't work in a group with him, have your parents call me. Have them write me a note."

What would that note look like?

Dear Ms. Rouiller,

My son can't work with Jeff because he has a tail, and might be gay. Not like he has sex with other boys, just that my son knows he is supposed to dislike Jeff and can't articulate it any better. He isn't comfortable with himself, he thinks he might be kind of unpopular, but as long as he can make fun of Jeff he feels a little better about himself. At least he's not that *bad.*

Most often when you're teased there's no Ms. Rouiller to defend you. Another boy pegged as gay is a seventh grader named Petey, definitely show-offy and nasal and his jeans are all wrong, but he is kind and bright. He has friends, though they don't defend him, and are often the ones torturing him. Toward the back of the field-trip bus he is told, "I would have voted for no one for homeroom rep before I voted for you." The boys stone him with insults.

"If he were hit with a crowbar, fifteen minutes later he'd say 'Ow.' "

"You don't want to hire Petey for a freak show because he'd scare away all the freaks."

"Your momma's so dumb she climbed over a glass wall to see what's on the other side."

"Your momma's like a TV—even a two-year-old could turn her on." *Check it out.*

The insults are swiped straight from a crappy dollar-store joke book. Petey rolls his eyes at how lame they are, but still it hurts bad.

Use your strategies.

Petey tries to ignore his tormentors. He slouches and looks out the window, can't block it out. He tries clever sparring. "You don't even know what 'E equals MC-squared' stands for."

"Oooh."

"You just sit there. You three, no one listens to you, so you can say what you want."

Evaluate.

"Find one person here who hates me who's not on crack."

Several hands go in the air.

chapter ten

but what does this actually have to do with real life?

For the second day in a row, Eric refuses to do his work during math. He hums, hard. A4 is Ms. Adams's nightmare class, and Eric is usually a leader—raising his hand, telling the other kids to be quiet. She needs him for that. But at the beginning of the period he and David were throwing cookies at each other and one hit a girl. Even though David threw that particular cookie, and even though a few minutes before that she was throwing paper, and even though she was smiling and the cookie didn't mess up her shirt or anything, she blamed Eric, whom Ms. Adams threatened to send to the office. So—humming.

The humming drives the teacher crazy, it drives the kids crazy, and the louder the class gets, the louder Eric hums. Ms. Adams tells him to stop and he says, "I don't care. I don't care about any of this stuff. This is stupid." She squats next to his desk and speaks steady and slow, looking him in the eyes, which look elsewhere. "Do you hear me, Eric? You know, Eric, what you want to do is your choice. If you sit and tune me out, that's your choice. If you're disruptive, I'll have to ask you to leave. If you're disrespectful, you'll have to go to the office. Do you hear me? Eric, if you don't acknowledge me, I can't be responsible for you. Eric, you're not responding to me."

Eric doesn't bother talking—doesn't seem like anyone listens to him anymore anyway. "Why am I the only one she ever picks on?" he thinks.

He gets up and heads for the door. "Stop! What are you doing?" He goes right out of the room. She follows, and yells so the other teachers can hear, "Eric, stop! Stop!" He walks down the hall.

When Eric leaves school he doesn't have his homework and has no intention of asking Ms. Adams for it. If someone in his class were standing right in front of him, he'd ask for the assignment. But nobody is, so he heads home.

For the first two-thirds of the twentieth century, where junior-high schools existed they were seen mainly as dehumanizing, anonymous institutions in need of defrosting. They comprised seventh, eighth, and sometimes ninth grades and were, in essence, miniature high schools: the same content-divided structure, the same content-oriented teachers. By the time the midcentury baby boom had settled, elementary schools were crowded and adolescence had sneaked earlier. In response, a new model emerged in the 1960s, in which sixth grade was moved up, and the name was changed, to "middle school."

Often the name and grades were all that distinguished this new school from the old junior high. But educators had developed a philosophy for middle school, based on the idea that brains change substantially during early adolescence. The human brain has two major growth spurts: in infancy and preadolescence. Though it's nearly full-size by this age, it is no longer thought to be fully formed. In fact, there is still enormous capacity for development. Right before puberty, brain cells grow extra connections far more than are needed, like trees wildly putting out extra roots, twigs, and branches. This growth in the frontal cortex peaks at age eleven for girls and twelve for boys; the cells then fight it out for survival. The ones that are being used prevail. The rest will be shed.

Thus, it has been acknowledged, only during these years when the brain is so amazingly adaptable is it neither too early nor too late to fill the mind with its most important frameworks of ethics and knowledge. What a child learns and does at this point is crucial—sports, languages, typing, whatever—because those connections can last forever. And preteens are finally able to get themselves around the abstract as well as the concrete. They begin to see—in fact, need to see—the relationship between the self and the world the self lives in; they are unsatisfied simply to hold a fact in their heads. They have to know *why*.

So, in the ideal middle-school class, the theory goes, students would be challenged to use their newly acquired cognitive skills, with "Why" and "What if" questions that they might not have been able to tackle just a year ago, that don't have only one correct response, whose answers begin, "I think . . ." They would work collaboratively, and debate. Fact-finding would be emphasized over fact-memorizing. To overcome twelve-year-olds' fickle attention spans, information would be relevant to life as they see it, and the presentation hands-on. To address the vast diversity children display at this age, the curriculum would let students progress at different rates and to different depths, and explore their own interests. The kids would have some say in what happens at school.

There was also a consensus among educators that at this hormone-roaring point in children's lives—when they are searching for their selves, when moods swing wildly, when tossing a cookie leads to storming out of class in three minutes flat—they need more nurturing at school. Students at the ideal middle school would have a daily "advisory" period, so a specific adult checks in with each of them and teaches various coping skills. Teachers would team by grade rather than content area, so they could share knowledge about shared students and plan lessons that cross academic subjects. Schools would be better connected with their communities, the way elementary and high schools are.

Above all, middle-school teachers would be trained specifically to teach middle-school students, so they would deeply understand who these kids are—their mood swings on the one hand, their curiosity on the other.

"The great thing about kids this age," says Ms. Thomas, who taught social studies in high school for eight years and middle school for ten, "is that they're not jaded. They'll try different ways of looking at problems, and they can be very creative and out of the box. When I taught high school, the kids were just basically walking into the classroom and waiting for me to teach. Whereas these kids can be much more active learners—if they're tapped by the right teachers and right materials."

Several Wilde Lake teachers have mastered the perfect combination of serious and light; they know when to treat their students like adults and when to treat them like children. Group work is common. ("Can we work with partners?" is heard every day, in every class. Partners of their choosing, they mean, since preteens would rather clean latrines with their friends than ride roller coasters with people assigned to them.) When a girl is elected student-council president, some teachers notice, and joke, "Do I have to bow to you now?" One takes a role in the school play that includes crawling on the ground; another chants raps to help students remember math formulas.

The best middle-school teachers set high expectations and stick with them. They point out the good things a student does as much as—or more than—the bad ones. They can tell a child is having a cruddy day just by the cant of his shoulders. They hand back work promptly. (If not, kids bristle at the hypocrisy.) They explain why the right answer is right, and why it matters. They indulge questions about how banks work when the lesson is actually on the specific formulas for principal and interest, instead of saying, "Does anyone have any real questions?"

The right material is connected to students' culture and interests and lives. When one teacher surveys her class about what would help them write better, none of them say learning more mnemonic devices like CUPS (Capitalization Usage Punctuation Spelling) and ACE (Answer all parts, Cite all evidence, give Examples); most check "Writing about things that interest me." In the science fair, eighth graders studiously determine whether music affects your heartbeat (yes) and which type of pitch falls the most in inches (curveball) and which gum lasts the longest (Original Bubblelicious). Whenever kids relate history to something they've watched, there's one teacher who always says, "Remember, don't use movies for reference, because they're only for your amusement." But to teach probability, Mrs. Bloom brings up the Showcase Showdown wheel on *The Price Is Right*, and Ms. Knighten has her sixth graders create their own carnival games, which they play for prizes. For percentages they go to fast-food restaurants and calculate how much of a value the value meals are. She likes to say, "No matter what you're doing, it seems like math," and activities like these make the kids believe it. Mrs. Rashid's seventh graders create clever political cartoons: "Osama," one says, "I think we're losing Taliban support." "What makes you say that?" And there is a series of signs outside the hideout: OSAMA THIS WAY. To explain electrical charges, Mrs. Harris talks about static when you pull clothes out of the dryer, what lightning really is, how Saran Wrap works, and this makes sense.

The right material allows students to solve problems. In science seventh graders determine which teacher committed a murder by studying hair samples under a microscope, and in English they interview the principal and secretaries for a newspaper article about a fake anthrax scare. At outdoor ed the sixth graders figure out how to fit seven people on an eighteen-inch square by holding hands across and stepping on each other's feet, and keep the music teacher aloft on a wooden A-frame attached to red ropes like a Maypole. In science class, to show why bones are shaped the way they are, the kids experiment to see which shape of folded-up note card, rectangular prism or cylinder, will support more textbooks.

Middle-school reform has become its own industry, the subject of many research dollars and foundation studies, which all say this kind of learning is key. But it takes an unusual amount of determination and creativity to be able to turn the academic research—and the intuition each teacher has about what the kids really need—into connections strong enough to engage all students. The norm is lessons that fall flat. As it stands, according to one estimate, 70 percent of questions asked in middle-school classes are rote recall.

A large part of the problem is that most middle-school teachers learn what their students need only on the job, if at all. Even though educational researchers have concluded that middle schoolers learn best from those who were trained specifically to teach *them*, and in theory teachers should know as much about the students as they do about their subjects, very few teachers have had significant coursework on approaching young adolescents. Middle school was long neglected as a developmental phase unto itself, so at most universities students are turned into specialists in content with high-school certification or specialists in elementary education. And if you've heard enough horror stories about seventh graders, or remember your own, you're not apt to seek out the unmarked door for middle school.

The number that offer middle-school specialization is growing, and as of 2002, twenty-two states require specific middle-school certification. But in some states that certification is preceded by only three or so specialized courses, and anyway "require" is a loose term during a teacher shortage, when many desperate school systems hire faculty with no training at all.

If they take the opportunity, teachers can still read up on the pre-adolescent brain, or attend a seminar in "hands-on" teaching strategies. Many schools across the country have aligned their classrooms with the prevailing philosophy to at least some degree, and their students have been shown to have significant academic and other advantages. In reality, though, in most school systems curriculum is king, and cannot be discarded in the name of self-directed learning. Been there, done that, got really bad test scores. When many middle schools transformed into more nurturing places in the 1970s and 1980s, their mission to cultivate good people sometimes overtook their mission to educate them. Middle school, many educators thought, simply needed to be a place to do no harm, just get those crazy kids through. And it showed, academically.

But now the balance has shifted. State and locally mandated assessments often dictate what is taught and how fast, making flexibility nearly impossible. Much attention is being paid to the fact that standardized test scores stagnate in middle school—experts call it an "intellectual wasteland," in which Americans start to fall behind other countries—at the same time that middle school is thought to set the stage for how well students will do the rest of their academic careers and even their lives. It's a time considered particularly make-or-break for poor and minority children. The standards-and-accountability movement that has overtaken the country's schools in general, means that the academic demands on teachers and students are higher than ever. The push gives rise to tests about the tests:

The Form-Audience-Tone-Purpose (Fat-P) can be found where in the prompt?
   a. First paragraph only
   b. Last paragraph only
   c. Middle paragraph only
   d. First and third paragraphs
   e. Second and third paragraphs

The Maryland Writing Test includes which of the following:
   a. Narrative composition
   b. Explanatory composition
   c. Objective test

d. All of the above

e. A and B only

In an attempt to beef up a middle-school education that was considered too soft and nurturing, the pendulum has swung the other way, disturbing even those who agree that achievement should be measured, and must improve. "We're going backward thirty years," is how the head of the National Middle School Association puts it. The group work, "why" questions, and exploration too often fall victim to the quest for content, to the drive to get everything covered before the assessments, instead of serving to make the content all the more learnable, and real. Content versus compassion is a false debate: Both are necessary, and getting one right necessarily makes the other easier.

Teachers, however, are human; they differ in their ability to be interesting, to mediate debate, to manage a roomful of kids who aren't silent, to understand what is relevant, much less make it so. Students, Ms. Thomas says, "are never going to be in a situation where they have nine different teachers, and every single one of them is dynamic and thought-provoking. That just doesn't exist. Maybe it does exist in some places, but I've never seen it." So, in algebra, when one seventh-grade class is introduced to matrices, the example on the overhead is about how many boys and how many girls take various classes at fictional Kelly and Glenn middle schools.

"But what does this actually have to do with real life?"

"Okay, listen. I'm showing you the basics, and then I'll explain why information is sometimes organized this way."

"Today?"

"I'm going to add a homework problem for every time I get interrupted."

The teacher explains that Ms. Thomas presented the school's state test scores to the Board of Education in a matrix, and the kids would rather see *that* matrix, find out if the boys scored higher than the girls or the other way around, than figure out the enrollment for each class if the number of students at Kelly Middle School—wherever that is—triples.

Jimmy is annoyed when his science teacher says there's not enough room in school actually to fly paper airplanes, and instead they learn whether construction paper or notebook paper flies farther by copying data off the overhead. Jackie wonders why in home ec she has to plan for a randomly assigned career as photographer, instead of a fashion designer, her real-life goal of the moment. Elizabeth enjoys taste-testing cocoa cereals but wonders why they write To Whom It May Concern letters to the companies of the cereals they liked best. Who ever writes a letter that says, "Your cereal was the best bargain and surprisingly had the taste I liked the best"? Wouldn't you write to the one you liked least? Eric is happy to eat Snickerdoodle dough but wonders why they assemble the recipe from ingredients a girl has already measured and placed at their work stations. If he's going to be a chef, he figures, shouldn't he create dishes from his head?

Eric knows his teachers care. Then again, caring is necessary but not sufficient. Eric will tell you what the rest of the equation is: Understanding kids his age. Knowing how to control a roomful of unruly kids. Making the material interesting. Avoiding the touchy-feely goal-setting and "What I Have Learned" crap that just feels to him like a fat waste of time. When those pieces converge, he experiences the joy of discovery. With any of those pieces missing, the teacher's heart can be irrelevant. In science, Eric thinks a lot about Mr. Shifflett, like the way he turned a tragedy into a perfect project last year. When someone knocked over the dead little shark he keeps in a jar, "instead of fussing around, talking about 'Nyah nyah nyah, everybody has extra homework,' he actually dissected the shark and let us look at the insides. 'Cause he was in love with that shark. Instead of getting mad, he made it into a project, where we had a packet, we filled out the different information about the certain parts of the shark."

"Ms. Drakes, she goes directly by the curriculum." He doesn't like her idea of "cooperative learning," in which pairs of students fill out a worksheet ("What is an ionic bond? What is chemical bonding?") and then switch partners for the next set of questions. It's not really a two-heads-are-better-than-one thing, because each kid just digs through the textbook for half the answers, then they swap. Eric works by himself, bored but productive.

And then there are the problems that no studies of effective teaching or organizational reform can solve: the problems that take place at home.

They assume particularly great significance at this age, when the brain's emotional and logical control centers are engaged in a tug-of-war. The frontal lobes managing memory and learning also manage emotion, which, being the more developed skill at this point, wins this battle every time. If you're sad that you rarely see your mom or dad, those emotions literally shrink the space available for your science test.

After talking with Ms. Thomas in October, Eric got the pencil case, for a while even put the radio on during homework instead of the TV. When he told her he wanted to do better, he wasn't lying. "I really like to do well," he admits. Chris, who taunted Eric for going to the Most Improved party last year in seventh grade, is thrilled because, for the first time in his life, he is getting all A's and B's. His mom is so happy, his dad is so happy, and Chris himself never had any idea *good grades* could make him this happy. Eric doesn't say so, but he's envious. "To tell you the truth, I may be like 'I don't care,' but sometimes I really do care."

He blames his teachers, but that's not really fair: If you pay attention and follow directions and attempt your homework, no matter how unintelligent you are, you will get at least B's in most middle schools. Eric, however, can't be bothered. He'll do his math in pen instead of pencil, and turn down an opportunity to copy it over: minus fifty. Absences to him mean no homework. When he lived in his last neighborhood, Tenacious wouldn't let him go outside until he finished his homework. Many of his friends had the same rule, and they'd come around and hurry each other up. After homework Eric would go to Liam's house and ride bikes and eat his mom's famous cookies and play games. His report cards had lots of B's and even A's back then. Even if he had that rule at his dad's, there's nothing to go outside for—those kids aren't his friends.

A teacher can give students a dozen opportunities to retake a quiz they bombed—Come in before school! At study hall! At lunch! After school!—and they won't, either because they forget or because their time is too important to them. A kid who is sick on the day review worksheets are handed out will neglect to get one the next day, then blame the teacher for his bad test grade. A child can be asked again and again how her social-studies project is coming, and she'll say it's done; then, the day before it's due, she asks for help.

Mrs. Conroy doesn't understand why Eric's class has 84 percent for homework. "You just have to try it and you'll get credit," she pleads.

"It's easy. It's easy to do well." Mrs. Brown, too, practically begs her students to do homework, so she won't have to drop the grade three points for lateness. One day, as she hands back the graded homework, she tells the class, "People say, 'Oh, it's so easy,' then you don't get one hundred percent. You say, 'It's so easy,' then you get six out of eight." Eric, who said, "It's so easy," and then got six out of eight, raises his hand.

"Is six out of eight good, though?"

In life, Eric has been told over and over, we all have to do things that are boring, simple as that. But Eric thinks he's smart and isn't convinced he should have to prove it. "If I got judged in math for the quality of my work and not for whether I did it or not," he says, "I'd get a hundred percent. It's not like I'm a bad student, I just don't like school. I know what I can do. I've seen what I can do."

Too bad they don't learn clairvoyance in teaching school. Because he's heading toward a D in English. And in science, he's on way to an F.

His very first F.

Tuesdays and Thursdays, Eric goes to after-school Homework Club. He gets to work right away and races through, according to his motto: Why do it good when you can do it fast? Occasionally, stopped up on an assignment, he will ask, "Anybody good in science here? Real good? Like teacher-good?" If someone can explain a concept one-on-one, he'll listen, and learn. If not, he writes down whatever.

"I don't care anymore," he says. "It's too hard not living with my real mom. My mom has just always been there. It just ain't the same. Everybody's 'Do this, do that.' " It feels like his brothers—one of whom is back from college and sharing the couch with Eric, and one of whom lives upstairs—think they're too cool to hang out with him. Close quarters in the four-room apartment are rubbing the luster off his father-worship. William's on the road half the time, and when he's back, it's never like, "Let's do something fun." He just goes upstairs and hangs out with his wife. Eric tells his teachers that he got a fifteen out of fifteen on a geometry worksheet but Ms. Beulah wouldn't let him put it on the refrigerator, which is decorated with advertising magnets and a chore list, because it looks junky. "She's a witch," he tells them.

Worst of all, they're talking about having a baby. That can't happen—all that poop and crying. "Why are they going to have another kid? He don't have time for this one. He's not even home long enough to make a pot of beans. Not canned beans, but his homemade beans. Man, I love beans. I'll strangle the kid if it keeps me up." Eric's opposition isn't just logistical: "*I'm* the baby. But she's his wife, and what she wants, she gets." Tenacious suggested the baby idea recently, when her friend gave birth to the cutest little girl. Eric said, "Mom, I'm the baby," and that was that. He wishes his mother were married because she'd be happy, but, then again, "She wouldn't be all mine."

Eric still has goals—culinary school, the automotive program at Lincoln Tech, racing his own car, and running his own restaurant and jazz club in California called ETT (for Eric Thomas Tim), where he will take surveys to find out what people want to eat and drink. Sometimes Eric feels like, Hey, success is possible, I can always do better in high school. But more often these days he feels as if it's too late: The teachers will see his old report cards and say, "He doesn't look like a hardworking student."

What is success, anyway? Eric doesn't really know what it looks like; he doesn't feel he knows anyone settled, with a good job, who has what he wants and what he needs. The one day Eric spends in downtown Washington, he goes to the ninth floor of a building, sees all the office people on the sidewalks, and wonders if neckties hurt. He feels like this is as high as he'll ever get.

Tenacious feels Eric's depression, his drastic change in attitude. He's withdrawing from her, too. He still answers "Great" to the question "How's school?" but she knows it's not. She doesn't see everything, but she did see that sheisty book report he did for Mrs. Cook, and wonders when the teachers will call.

When he tells her Ms. Thomas wanted him in GT but he didn't want to, her skin crawls. His relatives always say, "Go go go, do do do. Do good, don't do what I did." His brother Tim always says, "Why settle for Lincoln Tech when you could go to MIT?" Sometimes Eric agrees. An MIT grad doesn't wind up with kids early and nothing to settle on, but a Lincoln Tech grad might, and if his dad had been more ambitious they'd have a house already. But sometimes he feels like he just wants to be ordinary, and ordinary, as far as he has seen, means being a mechanic or a truck driver, and Eric tells Tenacious he'd be content with that.

"Without truck drivers," Eric says, "you wouldn't have clothes, you wouldn't have food."

"Is that a copout for not working hard, not applying yourself? You're telling me you'd rather be mediocre than be extraordinary? It's okay to be ordinary," she tells her boy. "But it's also okay to be extraordinary."

"I don't get it," she says later. "I just don't get it."

When Eric walks out, Ms. Adams is frustrated and desperate, too. She doesn't know what to do about fourth period. "How do you remove the fact that they hate math because they did bad before because they didn't have the skills and they still don't have the skills? My mentor says, 'You're behind in the curriculum. Go faster.' Okay. I'll go faster, so they can hate math more, so they can hate me more, so I can hate teaching more, so I can hate kids more."

She can't find the right balance to let her students talk a little bit without getting wild. She incorporates their interests into classwork, like when they learn proportions by resizing Garfield and Boondocks comics and making scale drawings of skateboards, but at test time the grades are still low. She knows she is supposed to set high expectations, but how can kids meet them who can barely multiply? She tries the interactive teaching methods she learned in school. Once she paired off the kids to tutor each other, and Eric, who was a tutor, whispered in her ear, "Ms. Adams, this is great. Everyone gets to do things." But more often when she tries to do supposedly engaging activities like a math game show, all of a sudden a quarter of the class is going over to Malik to check on his latest bruise, a quarter is talking about how even if you don't like your dad it's okay seeing him on the weekends if he buys you stuff, a quarter is arguing about who spat on whom. A quarter is sitting there ready to go, ready to learn, ready to play, but Ms. Adams is so fed up she just makes the whole class sit and copy definitions from the book instead.

At the start of the quarter she'd announced new policies to the class: no late homework, no credit if you don't show your work, the whole class stays after if anyone is disruptive. And an incentive: homemade funnel cakes if there are no more than six D's or F's on a test. "It's your choice now—you're in a new quarter. It's your chance to shine. Many of you have shown great ability in the past, and I know you can do it."

But four weeks in, Ms. Adams doesn't see any difference. For the life of her she can't control the class. Eric feels for her; he wants to say to the kids around him, Stop talking, maybe you'll learn something. "Her bogus rules make it worse," he says. "She's just making good kids go bad." They don't get things the way Ms. Adams explains them, so they goof off instead, which results in her perpetual chant: "Please listen. Please listen. Please please please listen."

At first it saddened Ms. Adams. Now it just angers her—working hard all week preparing students for the quiz, pulling them out of study hall, e-mailing and calling at home to ask, "Are you doing your homework? Should we go over any problems?" Then eight kids do okay, and the rest just finish. One girl can remember exactly what page in her agenda the multiplication tables are on. Why can't she transfer that brainpower to remembering the actual multiplication?

"You can't teach," a kid told her once.

You can't learn! she thought.

And the funnel-cake bribe doesn't work: On one quiz most of the class get eight out of twenty; Eric gets thirteen, a D-minus.

"I'm surprised and confused," Ms. Adams says as she hands back the papers. "There is a correlation between homework and the grades you get on tests and quizzes. Homework is practice. When I go to run a race, do I sit on my sofa first all day and eat bonbons? No, I practice. I run, even when I don't feel like running. Are you perfect the first time you Rollerblade, the first time you do sports, the first time you draw?"

"Yeah," Eric blurts, "the first time I played Tony Hawk, my high score was forty."

"Some of you think, 'I can do this, but I'm lazy.' When you go to apply for a job, I'll give you a hint. Don't put on there, 'I'm lazy.' Lazy is not a quality that's admirable. This is a sixth-grade quiz. You're laughing. It's not a joke. You will be here this summer. You will be here next year. You're mature outside of class, social, kind, for the most part smart. But you are terrible students, because you're lazy."

"Why you blow up my self-esteem?"

"Don't talk about self-esteem or how you feel, because it's your choice." Eric is typing on his fancy calculator, which has letters as well as numbers. "You have the ability. I don't understand why you're choosing to fail. Shannon, if I may, has chosen to do her homework, and she got one of the highest grades on the quiz. Last quarter, what was your grade?"

"An F," Shannon says.

"Did you do your homework last quarter?"

"No."

"That book is pretty heavy," the girl next to her complains.

"You know how you only have PE a few quarters? Well, carrying the book is your exercise the rest of the time."

"Were we close to getting funnel cakes?"

"Not even close."

"Can we just have some of the powder?" one girl asks.

"Who invented funnel cakes?" asks another.

Teachers know that Tenacious Epps cares, that she comes when called, and the day after Eric walks out of class she sits for forty-five minutes with him and Ms. Adams. That Eric refuses to show his work or use pencil, doesn't raise his hand anymore, copies homework answers—this hurts. Who is this child?

"Eric, what's going on?"

"Nothing. I don't know."

They go back and forth, gently, as Ms. Adams thinks, They're friends.

"Why don't you show your work?"

"I don't know why I have to. I can do it in my head."

"You have to show your work. How do you think she knows how you got your answer? You could have cheated. You could have guessed. Eeny-meeny-miney-moe."

To Tenacious, Ms. Adams says Eric is one of her brightest students. To Eric, she says, "I cried when you left class yesterday. I care about your learning."

"Ms. Adams, I'm sorry I did that in class. I'll be more helpful from now on."

"I need you to be a leader," she tells Eric, and squeezes his big shoulder.

chapter eleven

purple. is that close enough?

Of course everyone has seen *Snow Day* already, but it's still irritating that the girls dangling their legs from the side table won't shut up. It's the day before winter break, Holiday Activity Day, and Lily sits between Mia and Beth in the front row of Mrs. Stokes's dark room. Between Mia and Beth is Lily's new favorite place to be. Beth, a girl with looks like Lily's and a manner just as serene, is Lily's new second-best friend. She joined her at the last church dance when Mia wouldn't, and empathizes about Abigail Werner taking so long at the lockers, and might take gymnastics with Lily next month, and is the only girl she really, truly likes in PE and health. It's nice to have a friend in health class, with all the stress induced by the laminated line drawings of sex organs that make Lily gasp and whose names you have to actually *say*, and the boys who shoot rubber bands and pretend to smoke their pen caps when Ms. Rouiller is in the hall. When Beth shows off her newly decorated binder or a new hairstyle, Lily says, "You rock, girlfriend!" In her locker Lily has stashed two long tubes of neon-green lights, Christmas gifts for Mia and Beth.

You may think friendships get more stable as kids get older, but at this age they're not. A preteen has become more cognitively able to see the problems in her existing friendships and envision the potential for new ones. When you are eleven, the new is alluring, idealism is very powerful. This next friend will be better than the last—perfect, perhaps!

During the movie Alexandra sits with the talky girls, limbs entangled, and Lily's glad for the distance. "It's always me and Mia," Lily has explained, "and then Alexandra butts in. Alexandra more than anyone else, she has to be the number-one friend of Mia. We could be walking down the hall, and all of a sudden I'm in the back. And Alexandra's there talking with Mia. She used to seem kind, but then she started to get, I guess she started to realize me and Mia were closer than me and her were, so then she got snobby to me, and bratty and rude."

Alexandra and Lily are both wearing metal bangle bracelets from Mia. She asked Lily to wear hers today so that Alexandra will think it's the main Christmas gift she's giving out, when in fact she bought Lily a felt pencil case and glitter nail polish. Why should she get Alexandra a real gift with the way she's acting lately? When Alexandra's other friends are around, Mia says, "she acts like I'm trash, and then, when it's just her alone, she says, 'What's up, Mia?'—all friendly." This kind of thing didn't happen in elementary school, and Mia doesn't say anything about it, because what can you say? "Do you still like me?"

Alexandra is oblivious to this. In true eleven-year-old fashion, Lily and Mia tell each other she is rude but never say anything to Alexandra, who is just happy to have more friends. The black people tell her she shouldn't hang out with the white girls so much—now, that doesn't make sense to her. The children of Wilde Lake have grown up steeped in Columbia's multicultural sensibility, and whether they get along with each other has little to do with race. In high school, interracial dating is common and black kids and white kids both are elected to Homecoming Court. But most Wilde Lake Middle kids grew up on streets or in buildings that were largely either black or white, and when it comes to choosing cafeteria tables in middle school, they stick with what, and whom, they know.

Research has always shown that race is one source of attraction to friends. Hanging more with the other black girls in middle school is a natural part of growing up, not born of prejudice but, rather, because in middle school race and income and all sorts of differences come into sharp focus and a child seeks out peers she can identify with on at least these basic levels. An eleven-year-old cares more about similarity than an eight-year old, and her views on what makes people different or similar can be superficial, unnuanced.

One day Alexandra arrives at school with glitter still stuck to her cheeks from a cheerleading party, and talks about how, because her squad won the last tournament, the coach gave out red, black, and white roses and made a toast over sparkling cider. Lily goes to one of Alexandra's tournaments and enjoys it, but she and her mom are both glad she quit the squad, what with the cute but sadistic coach who made them do push-ups and repeat the entrance eight times, until nobody turned her head, and the fake smiles, and the real tears, and the mothers on the sidelines who petted their Shih Tzus and chewed gum to calm their nerves and loud-whispered about the girls, things like, "She's got issues. She thinks she's in a beauty pageant."

The way Alexandra sees it, she acts the same with everyone. She likes being part of different groups. She still thinks Lily is a good friend, and Mia her best friend. Alexandra's been telling this to people, and when they relay it to Mia on the bus—where she sits with Lily every day—she says, "Lily's my best friend." This reassurance is especially important since Mia didn't agree to the double birthday party.

"Alexandra's in a different world now," Lily thinks, "but that's okay. I'm the one Mia calls her best friend."

Over winter break, Lily dances as a lovely Snow Angel in *The Nutcracker*, eyes slathered in blue eye shadow and glitter. One night she falls during the curtain call, but she is not embarrassed. If that happened in the cafeteria, she'd die. She goes to Beth's, where they play with her baby sister, and Beth comes over to Lily's, where they play Outburst Jr. and model and dance. They put up a sign on her bedroom door offering free massages and makeovers: "Ask about it. You'll look cool in no time." A light-up mirror sits on a little table in the corner of the room, which is newly painted lime green. A pom-pom hangs from the mirror. Curlers from her Southern-belle days sit on the top bookshelf; propped on the shelf below are three picture frames and a paper on which she's written in bubble letters "Friends and Best Friends." In the center of a fuzzy star-shaped frame, Mia smiles with her lips closed, and Lily leans on her shoulder in the bottom right of the frame, a bigger smile. The other frames are empty.

When it comes time for Christmas services, Lily gets out of the bath and can't find her special red cardigan in the closet. She insisted on wearing it to a birthday party with no shirt underneath, even though her mother warned it would get dirty. Lily insists she put it in the laundry hamper. Boy, is she getting to be a pain, Avy and Jack think. When they tell her to do something, instead of saying "Yes, ma'am," she might say, "No, not right now," or "I don't think so." They wonder if her friends are making her this way. "Sometimes I think she was put on God's green earth to drive me crazy," Avy says as Lily searches the house for the sweater.

She eventually finds it in her bureau. For some reason this, like everything, is her mother's fault. "She's so stupid," Lily says, brushing out her wet hair.

The instant soulmate is a hallmark of middle school, and a month later Lily gets one, a third-best friend. After opening night of *Peter Pan*, Lily rides with Mia to Bennigan's for the cast party. With Ashley Schwartz, the bubbly seventh grader who plays Peter Pan, they squish into two chairs at the long, crammed table. Ashley took a big-sister interest in the girls during the play, and all of a sudden, as they share chicken fingers, Lily feels like she has a new lifelong friend and wonders if it's too late to invite her to her birthday party Friday. She rolls her eyes in the right places when Ashley tells about how a secret-admirer note for her fell out of a boy's pocket and then he denied he wrote it, and the three decide right then and there the world will end if they don't go to camp together. Ashley says they have to find a camp for less than three hundred dollars. "Maybe bowling camp or ice-skating. I'll think about it," Lily says, and she will, for several days.

"Are you friends with Katherine?" Ashley asks.

Lily is tentative, not knowing the right answer. "Sort of."

"Me, too."

Phew.

They talk about favorite colors.

"Pink," says Ashley.

"Pink, too," says Mia.

"Purple," says Lily. "Is that close enough?"

Six days later, on Lily's birthday, her parents take her, Mia, Beth, Ashley, Lily's sister, Gabrielle, and a girl named Nina to Port Discovery in Baltimore. There they solve mysteries about Egypt and spelunk through a giant model of a house's plumbing and race around an indoor play-ground. At Hard Rock Cafe, the waiters put Mia and Lily up on chairs—Mia's birthday is tomorrow—and the whole restaurant shouts "Happy birthday!"

Ashley sort of has fun, except that these girls still laugh at dumb stuff like farts, and her three best friends went to see *A Walk to Remember* without her. Also, it feels to her like Lily ignores everyone else in favor of Mia, who in turn treats Lily as if she were her daughter, as opposed to an equal. Beth is polite but a little gossipy for Lily's parents' taste, whereas they are impressed that Ashley includes everyone and nudges the conversation away from anything nasty. Of course they wouldn't tell Lily how much they like Ashley, because that might ruin it. Ashley gives Lily a Build-a-Bear, Beth gives her a shirt and socks, Nina gives her a CD, and Mia gives her a shirt and eye shadow. Mia's party is coming up in three weeks, and her gift sends Lily into an intense mental quandary on how she'll ever reciprocate, when her mother has set the birthday-present limit at fifteen dollars.

Even though Lily thinks *The Diary of Anne Frank* should be banned because Anne wants her best friend "to be her girlfriend!"—she says this with eyes wide open and mouth scrunched tight—and, like all her friends, she signs yearbooks "LYLAS" ("Love You Like a Sister") instead of simply "Love," lest someone mistake her for a lesbian, the only way to describe Lily's affection for her own best friend is as a crush. It's a common though rarely studied phenomenon among girls this age: They crush on other girls, as much as on boys. Though there's no sexual component it's a real romance, an attraction, a feeling that everything is better, brighter, warmer when this person is around.

Lily, like practically all the other sixth graders at Wilde Lake, thinks Mia is cool, kind, and brave. In fifth grade, popularity corresponded to athletic aptitude, mainly soccer and lacrosse. The middle-school formula hasn't been worked out yet, but it's clear Mia tops the list, and she is that one girl in every grade who has achieved popularity without being mean. When someone's binder comes apart during recess and papers fly all over the schoolyard, Mia chases them down as the other girls watch, and grabs sheets from the hands of boys who want to rip them. When she pats her hair at her locker and the boy next to her says, "Who puts a mirror in her locker?" Mia says, "Me. You got a problem with it?" Lots of boys want to go out with her, and to Lily's dismay she finally says yes to one of them, a gymnast named Ricky.

At game time in study hall, Mia and two other girls make a dollhouse out of Jenga blocks. Mia and Ashley make people for the house, and Abby makes the furniture, and all the other girls, barred from participating, lean in and observe. Mia is the first to embrace designer Paul Frank's monkey T-shirts. Within weeks, everybody tries to draw the monkey, Julius. "Julius is the coolest," their binders say. Mia shows up with a shoelace tied in her hair, and for one day, every girl wishes she'd thought of that, although, of course, if any of them had thought of it, it wouldn't be impressive at all. Once, in Mia's absence, the girls are talking about soft shirts, and one girl says that when Mia has fluff on her sweater they blow it off their fingers. "Mia?" asks Anna, as if this sweater-fluff girl has no claim to her. Before gym, Mia and Anna play with a purple nylon book cover, swatting it at each other and putting it on their heads. Three girls look on, wishing for the intimacy.

When school is out one January conference day, Lily and Mia eat cereal out of the box in Lily's kitchen and try to choose between ice-skating and bowling. They decide to vote, but Lily won't until she hears what Mia wants. She is totally hyper—now and until Mia leaves—dancing all over the floor. She occasionally reaches to touch Mia, or bumps into her. Lily tears slips of paper for the vote. Mia writes, "I would like to go ice-skating *and* bowling because it seems fun." Lily doesn't write anything.

They wind up at the rink, and though Mia hasn't skated much, she's a natural. Lily lags behind. "Mia!" "Mia!" "Mia, watch this!" Mia figures Lily says "Mia" a million times a day.

"No, I only say it three times a day. Except today."

"I only say 'Lily' three times a day."

They make up a dance routine. Lily keeps falling into Mia. She pats her butt—just kidding! Mia tries to teach Lily to spin, but she can't really let herself go.

Back home, Lily asks Mia to sleep over and Mia says yes. When the adults go to sleep, the kids go down to the basement and make up a skit. Mia sings, and Lily, with unbelievable energy, dances to S Club 7 on the boom box. She crawls on Mia—just kidding!

Her little brother shouts, "Shake your thing, Lily!"

And she does. She has no inhibitions. She is having a blast.

Mia is having fun, but she's a little weirded out, too. She knows she wouldn't get much sympathy complaining about the downside of popularity, but "it kind of freaks me out," she says, the way girls go and buy *her shoes*, the way she never knows who likes her for her popularity and who likes her for her, the way people sometimes get into fights in her name when she just wants everyone to get along, the way Lily talks to other friends about Mia this and Mia that, the way she always has to be so close to her, clingy even. It can feel threatening, invasive.

It's not like Mia's this supersocial dynamo anyway—over break, when Lily was hanging out with Beth, Mia mostly redecorated her bedroom, and the one time she had plans, to meet some elementary-school pals at the mall, they switched the time without telling her, and Mia found herself all alone. So—to be, supposedly, the object of everyone's affection? Mia, who thinks of herself as a big dork, doesn't really get it.

chapter twelve

i don't care about the
snack pass

At seventh-grade lunch, Elizabeth isn't wiping the cafeteria tables well enough to please Mrs. Rashid, who tells her so. Elizabeth swings her fat braid and protests in her grinding whine, which turns one word of each sentence into a weapon:

"I *waaaaashed* that one already. I did it *gooood*!"

"Elizabeth, you're not washing this one well either." Mrs. Rashid points to a wet spot. "It's not going to be dry there."

"Yes, it *wiiiilll*! I'm giving it time to *dryyy*."

They go back, they go forth, until Mrs. Rashid says, "Well, if you're not going to wash the tables, then just go outside and don't get a snack pass."

An hour later, heading to English and thinking about the lunch table, Elizabeth all of a sudden breaks down—absolutely breaks down. With every other Wilde Lake student walking to class around her, she slumps her newly grown body to the ground underneath the awards bulletin board, right beneath a slip of paper announcing, "Elizabeth Ginsburg was caught helping out Mrs. Rashid!" She wails, and only if you have a clue what's on her mind can you decipher what she's wailing: "I hate Ms. *Raaaaashid*!!!" Two teachers bend down to try to talk with her, and Eric, walking by, asks, "What's her problem? Is she having a nervous breakdown?" This makes Liz cry louder. Mr. West helps her up and into his office to calm down. Middle schoolers wear their hearts on their sleeves, and this surfeit of emotion is what so many of their teachers love about them. But it's also what drives them mad. Elizabeth sits at Mr. West's table with her head on her binder for fifteen minutes, sobbing and snuffling. He tries to coax her out of her misery, saying he'll get her a snack pass, but finally she breathes in deep enough to speak:

"I don't care about the snack pass."

It's not about the snack pass. It's never about the snack pass. It's about practicing her Torah and Haftarah portions every day with the tape recorder so she can chant in front of hundreds of people in just two months, and about the thing she said about a girl at synchro that got back to her so now everyone's acting all weird, and about Elizabeth's dad obsessing about every little thing for the upcoming Bat Mitzvah, and her mom obsessing about every little thing for the upcoming swim meet, and though her parents wouldn't call it fighting, more like discussing in naturally loud voices, that's what it sounds like to Elizabeth.

It's about how, even though she was nice for a while, now Miss Colyer's "poopy," as Elizabeth puts it, making her lower her music stand even though she likes being eye-level with the music; making her cut her fingernails, which Elizabeth likes to keep long, especially the pinky; telling Elizabeth she might have to go to the principal's office when Liz swears all she did was get a tissue; announcing that she and Molly can't sit together "for the rest of the year—understood?" When Elizabeth is the only one who has the pizzicato down pat, why does Miss Colyer have to say, "Whoa, *some people* have been practicing very well," instead of naming her specifically? The injustice infuriates Elizabeth so much that she vents in Spanish class, where Mrs. Bloom yells at her for talking.

It's about how Elizabeth never remembers the good dreams and never forgets the bad ones, like when her math teacher dropped the ring from *Lord of the Rings* and turned evil, or when she had to leave in a rush for synchro nationals and forgot to pack her clothes. Fortunately, the car turned into her bedroom, so all the clothes were there, but she left her toothbrush and hairbrush behind, and it was very stressful in the meantime.

It's about Mitch teasing her in social studies, when maybe she'd like him back if he were half as annoying, and homework that seems as if it never ends, and this self-induced quest for not just straight A's but also perfect attendance, which is hard when you have a sore throat.

And it's about one of her least favorite things in the world: being told she didn't do something well that she's sure she did.

When her mother gets home and asks what happened at school today, Elizabeth says, "Nothing."

When her father gets home and asks what happened at school today, Elizabeth says, "Nothing."

And then it storms. Used to be, on nights when Elizabeth was scared from the thunder that boomed through her window and the witch who scowled in her dreams, stressed out about schoolwork, or sad about an argument, she'd crawl into her parents' bed. Their room is in the back of the house, protected by trees, and because they have a waterbed, nestling in the middle is particularly snug.

She considers telling her parents about Mrs. Rashid, but lately when worries spill into her nights, instead of climbing in bed with her parents—instead of mentioning her problems to her parents at all—Liz writes.

> now i hate ms. rashid and shes sssssssssssssooooooooooooo annoying so thats y i cryed and i didn't like her that much b4 anyway. i felt stupid it was stupid to cry like that about something like that its just she hurt my feelings she told me i was acting like a brat and stuff and i just felt really bad and all this stuff is happening

Then Elizabeth lies under a pile of old blankets, resting her head on the soft, worn butt of her doll Rebecca, and wondering how she'll face all those kids who saw her crying, until she finally falls asleep.

Ellen used to think it was her job to sniff out the source of every one of Elizabeth's bad moods. If she asked the right question, maybe she'd find the problem, and solve it. Now, she's decided, Elizabeth's bad moods are her own. Her daughter often holds the secret that's upsetting her like a little gold nugget and at bedtime is generous enough to share it before she goes to sleep.

"It'll be like nothing—'Hanna looked at me funny' or something—

so I've learned not to panic. She'll tell me when she wants."

When she wants, it's usually the little things, which they connect about comfortably in the car, or on the rare afternoons Elizabeth stays downstairs to talk with Ellen instead of heading right up to instant-message the friends she left twenty minutes before.

"How was school?" Ellen asks one day as she sits down on the couch, arm around her daughter's shoulder.

Elizabeth takes her binder from her backpack. That's kind of a hard question to answer—the specific ones usually work better. "Boring. I missed the strings picture."

Ellen looks at the worksheet. "You're learning how to tell time? Is this advanced math? Oh, Spanish. Do you have any tests before the end of the marking period?"

"No."

"No projects? I ordered your Bat Mitzvah invitation."

"But I wanted to see it! We played a game in math. Can I see it sometime? I don't remember what it looks like."

"It's just like the one in the book. We can see it on the Internet. There's a response card, too, and a separate invitation that says the party's at seven. And there's thank-you notes that say Elizabeth Nicole."

"Did you do the thing with the Hebrew name? 'Cause Dad was like 'Nyah nyah nyah.' "

"No, I didn't think you'd want that. I forgot to bring Fuzzy home." He's the guinea pig at the preschool where Ellen teaches.

"I want to see Fuzzy. I miss him."

"We can bring Fuzzy home for the weekend. So you'll have your nice thank-you notes so you'll be motivated to write them. Everything cost extra. The lining, changing the ink color."

"How much does it cost?"

"Guess."

"A thousand dollars?"

"No, three seventy-five."

"Three thousand seventy-five?"

"That would be an expensive invitation. No, three hundred seventy-five. We were going to put the brunch invitation and the directions in there, but we knocked off almost two hundred dollars—we decided to go to Giant and get cards for that. Nancy from swim team can do the calligraphy for the envelopes. She charges a dollar an envelope. Or we can find a nice font on the computer, if we can figure out how to feed the envelopes."

"Calligraphy—I want to do that."

Elizabeth starts her math.

"You woulda had fun today," Ellen says. She often shares quotidian details she knows won't be boring to a kid. "A kid threw up. Remember when you threw up?"

"Yeah, Danielle walked on it. I want cookies."

"I'll get you some. I'll be nice. Do you want one or two?" She brings back a Keebler elf. "So are you done with sex ed? Because I haven't been signing anything lately."

"Mmmmm."

"You don't know?"

"Mmmmm." Elizabeth nods, and returns to her Spanish worksheet. "Mommy, do you think 'leaving for school' would be what time I leave for the bus stop or what time I get on the bus?"

"What time you leave the house, probably."

"What time do I do my homework? It's different on different nights. This is hard."

"Liz, you can make up a time. No one's gonna come over and check."

"Mommy, what time do I watch TV?"

"Nine."

"I'm not even supposed to watch TV."

"What do you want for dinner?"

"Sketti. Do I go to bed at ten or ten-thirty?"

"Liz, why don't you know what time you do all these things? We learned about different types of learners today. You're an interpersonal-intelligent learner. You like to do things in groups and discuss them."

"I do? How do you know? I have to call Becky."

"That's how I know. You call Becky every day."

"Oh, I got a hundred on my math quiz!" Elizabeth says, and pulls it out to show her.

When Joseph comes home, Ellen tells him about the quiz. He asks Elizabeth, "Aren't you going to show me your math?"

"Show him," Ellen commands. Elizabeth puts the quiz under his nose and flicks it back. He wants to look at the equations. She gives him two seconds: "One. Two."

"That's great! Congratulations!"

There must be, Joseph thinks, some vast conversational world Elizabeth shares with her friends. If he eavesdropped at lunch, however, he'd hear the girls talk about how cold the cafeteria is, which is their favorite Powerpuff Girl, how stale the taco shells are, and how if you go to the nurse she always just says, "I can't do anything for you." Not that Joseph wouldn't take those scraps, were they offered.

"When did you get that coat?" she asks him on the way to swim practice.

"Last year. You like it?"

"Yeah. I don't remember it."

"I got it when you got that other stuff that time."

Pause.

"You want to have your Hebrew name on your invitation?"

"I don't care. It doesn't make that big a difference."

"The scrolls have to stay blue."

"Why?"

"She said the lettering can change. Between the scrolls you can have your Hebrew name on the top."

"I don't care."

Elizabeth puts her elbow on the armrest and leans her head on her hand and turns up the radio.

Joseph looks at his daughter. He has an idea for a Bat Mitzvah gift, passing on the thirteen silver dollars his grandfather gave him on his thirteenth birthday. "She won't understand," Ellen has warned—not that she thinks it's a bad idea, she just doesn't want Joseph to be disappointed if Liz is ambivalent. It didn't use to be like this; he used to know what she wanted, she used to tell him things. Car time is valuable time, Joseph knows, Quality Time. If he had an idea what he was doing, he could use these trips to instill some values in his daughter; if things had turned out the way he imagined, they'd spend this time talking about blues or photography.

Instead there's silence for the next fifteen minutes.

They pull up to the swim center, and as Elizabeth gets out she says, "Love you, Dad."

At least he has that.

While Elizabeth swims, Joseph drives back to school for a School Improvement Team meeting. Plied with Snapples, the parents and students on the committee page through packets that explain, for one, the difference between "milestone" and "benchmark," watch a PowerPoint presentation about standardized test scores, hear that office referrals have gone down but the seriousness of offenses has gone up, and learn that school-improvement goals should be Specific, Measurable, Attainable, Results-Oriented, and Timebound (SMART!).

When he picks Elizabeth up at eight-thirty, she asks, "How was the meeting?"

"Better than when Ms. Thomas goes on and on."

"Ms. Thomas is annoying."

"What about her?"

"I don't know. She's just annoying."

"Is there anyone there you like?"

"You mean, like, a teacher?"

"Yeah. We have to get Ms. Jones's address. Do any of your friends have her address?"

"Noooo."

Ten minutes later: "Wanna go to Subway?"

Elizabeth nods. "What did you do at the meeting?"

"Listened to Ms. Thomas talk. They seem to be doing better with discipline, academically. It's all about goals, goals, goals. Do you have to write complete sentences in each class? Read and understand? They're having someone come do experiments in the fish tanks. They're getting more computers, PCs for the eighth graders."

"We had to do a survey about computers."

"About what exactly?"

"Computers," Elizabeth says, and escapes the car in search of dinner.

Once, when Liz was two, Joseph told her Mommy was out running. Wearing only a diaper, Elizabeth toddled unnoticed out the front door, through the parking lot, down the path, and to the curb on Columbia

Road, where she stood watching cars whiz by. When a frantic Joseph finally found her, she wasn't scared at all. In her two-year-old way, she said she knew he would come get her.

Now being rescued is not so simple.

Joseph has been expending a lot of energy trying to assure Elizabeth's happiness in strings, a task that's become more difficult. Elizabeth dreads the class. She fights with the other viola players and laughs in the middle of her scales; she is dawdly; Molly makes raspberry noises, borrows her viola, and breaks a string on the bow. Elizabeth talks back, which is new. She's always asking her reading teacher, "Don't you have more work for me? Isn't there something I could do for you next period?"

"You have a hundred-five average," the teacher says. "Go to strings."

Joseph and Miss Colyer have talked on the phone regularly these last two weeks, and they're no closer to solving the mystery. Some days Elizabeth's fine, and some days she's not.

"That probably means she really likes you and wants the attention," Joseph says.

"That's what I'm assuming."

In one call Miss Colyer tells Elizabeth's father that she has been making weird noises, sighing, asking, "Why do we have to *dooo* this?" Maybe, she says, it's because they switched to a boring practice book.

"She's under a lot of pressure," Joseph says.

One day Elizabeth doesn't play because Molly says she's messing her up, and the next day she doesn't play because Molly borrows her music.

"Is there a reason you're not playing?"

"I don't have my music."

"Share with Stu and Karen, then." But Elizabeth hates sharing. Miss Colyer e-mails Joseph: "Today Elizabeth didn't play, she just sat there." Joseph and Ellen don't tell Elizabeth about the e-mail—they figure they'll give it another week—but Elizabeth sees it anyway while playing on the computer. Excuse me? This is my life you're whispering about.

That night Joseph and Ellen ask Elizabeth if she's too stressed, if she wants to give up swimming until the Bat Mitzvah is over, but she says no, and stomps upstairs to the computer.

"You're not in trouble now," Ellen calls after her, "but get it together."

Later she sees another e-mail, about the "weird noises," and doesn't think she did that. "It's not fair. She didn't ask me about it. She didn't even know what was going on. Stu plays all the time, Molly talks, and she never gets mad at them. If she's going to call my parents, she could tell me." Joseph has taken notes on the computer from a phone call: "Liz is not following directions (slow to get started?)." "Oh my gosh, I hate her. That is so not true."

Ellen suggests that Elizabeth have a talk with Miss Colyer, but she won't. Joseph suggests Miss Colyer go to the source. She sends an e-mail.

Hi Elizabeth,
I noticed that you seemed upset today in class. Are you doing ok? Are you frustrated with Stu or is it something else? Sorry I didn't get a chance to ask you today after class. See you tomorrow.
Miss Colyer

hi
well its just that molly said she was squished and she had more room then me also i'm always at the end and really far over and a lot of things have been going on and i have been very annoyed and frustrated and upset and mad etc. lately so . . . . .
elizabeth

Once, when Elizabeth looks particularly upset, Miss Colyer tries to talk with her after class. She ticks off a list of things Elizabeth might be mad about, and Elizabeth shakes her head no to each. Finally, "Are you stressed?" A shrug, then "Yes," "Friends? School?" Elizabeth won't elaborate. "Sometimes," Miss Colyer says, "when I'm stressed, I journal," so Elizabeth does that in Miss Colyer's office for twenty minutes, well into English time. "Is it me?" Miss Colyer asks, and Elizabeth shrugs. Miss Colyer trusts Elizabeth to be open with her and figures that if she's not saying the problem is her it isn't.

In general, teachers, particularly the more experienced ones, don't allow themselves to be drawn into their students' moods; they have learned that power struggles are unwinnable, whining unanswerable. But Liz's way of developing relationships with adults sometimes sucks in the unwary.

Miss Colyer wants to figure out how to please Elizabeth. Just as much, she wants to figure out how to end the tension, tiny but nagging. She tells Elizabeth that she knows she has problems with some of the kids in the class but that "you have to compromise, too."

Why doesn't she see that it's bigger than that?

Elizabeth is sick of Miss Colyer calling her parents. She is sick of Miss Colyer. She is sick of being this character in a novel like the ones she has to read in school, except her parents are the students, talking about her in the third person and figuring out symbolism in her every move and finding interesting ways to discuss her inner struggles.

Elizabeth is scared of getting in trouble. She wonders if her parents will make the situation worse, or better.

She instant-messages a swimming friend about how mad she is.

tell ur teacher.
NOOOOOOOO.
CHICKEN!
its scary. y dont u try, FRUITCAKE
if you dont tell her how u feel itll just get worse
u dont no that so there. anyway i cant
wwwwhyyy
bbbeecauuuse im scared ☹
then write a note Shes just trying to help you
i know but thats annoying
then tell yr parents to do something
no its scary
LIZ, if u dont tell and make up the escuse that it is scary then i don't want to ever hear u complain about a teacher!
i will . . . later . . . maybe.
i don't understand u i mean i would tell!!!
yeah rite i bet and ud b as scared as me just meet her. u can tell her 4 me. i g2g!!!!
fine
bye
bye be strong
whatever

Chapter thirteen

not much just chillin'

In the nineteenth century people came calling, in the twentieth century they phoned, and now preteens communicate on the Internet. They type to each other fast as thirty-dollar-an-hour secretaries (except that secretaries can spell), one instant-message box on the screen for each conversation.

Wus ∧.
NMJC.

What's up? Not much just chillin'. If not much is up and they're just chilling, you wonder why they don't have time to type out the words. But anyway. Parents have become familiar with the sounds of IM, the arpeggios of acceptance twinkling every time the person on the other end of the line has something to say.

Or nothing to say:

Starlett89:..........
KT2001: ....
Starlett89: dont copy me! find ur own system of dots!
KT2001: no thanks
BABExox: go bonguesha!

BABExox: LMAO*

Starlett89: ROTFLMAO†

Starlett89: ah! somethings under my desk!

KT2001: is there a reason for me to be here?

Starlett89: oh, its just my shoe...

BABExox: cause we know who u are..but u don't know who we are

KT2001: yes i do

KT2001: catherine

BABExox: WRONG!

Starlett89: do u know her?! r u her mother?!

Starlett89: i think not!

KT2001: no but i no her

BABExox: no you don't

KT2001: and i wasnt tlkaing to u so fuck off

Starlett89: fuck urself

BABExox: ...your better at it

BABExox: haha

KT2001: okay bye

BABExox: isn't this such a nice conversation?

Starlett89: extremely!

BABExox: damn, i wish kelsey was here

Today's calling card is the IM profile, a box you click on to read a kid's explanation of himself, updated every possible moment. The moment a girl returns from an event, she uses her profile to evaluate it:

Hiya this is Traci! I just got back from the best dance in my life! CHA CHA SLIDE!!!!!!! and the booty call..... (put your butt in it!) I had the best time slow dancing with Andrew (he didn't .go for the butt) The CHICKEN DANCE! Well thanks to Jen, Jen, Cubby, Dina, MM, and Dave for making this the best dance of my life!

**Laughing my ass off

†Rolling on the floor laughing my ass off

Boys make lists like "Whos most likely 2 suck dick rite now" and announce their favorite phrases ("Bonermobile," "chillin shit!," "poo fuck!") and their favorite sports teams and their least favorite teachers ("dont u just wanna kill mrs weinstein i mean bitch") and their philosophies ("Remember it takes 42 muscles in the face to frown but only 4 in your arm to bitchslap that asshole who pissed you off"). Kids create quizzes about themselves: "What is my favorite sk8? What is my favorite color? What is my dog's name?" They self-publish:

why is it that when we are mad at someone we tend to wait right by the phone for them to call us tell us that they are ok but they never call and you get mad at them and you worry about them and you start to fall in love with them and you realize that they dont love you back and you are so sad and angry and you want to cry and cry until they see you curled up into a corner crying and you just sit there and wait for him to say its ok and for him/her to put there arm around you and then you feel better like there is a god like someone is up there praying for you and that is the best feeling you can ever have in the whole world

~Leslie

Each of the swim-team girls has her own Web site (the introduction on one: "Hi I'm Eileen. I am 11 and single") and they have a collective site:

Dolphins Gossip! Ex-tra Ex-tra! Read all about it!
More good news has arrived! The couples still out there:
** Sarah & Kendall
** Lia & Peter (maybe/almost. if you want to vote about this go to the mini quiz)
** Abby heard that Henry likes Dale! But Dale does NOT like Henry back (she is not trying to be mean she just doesn't like him).
** At the dance, Noel asked Tina to slow dance! And guess what she said! NO WAY!!! You won't believe this, NOEL LOVES TINA!

Middle school is when most kids start to truly immerse themselves in the twin worlds of culture and consumerism—the Internet is only the latest manifestation. Fads—short-lived, by definition—have always been a big part of being eleven: Twenty years ago at Wilde Lake girls affixed safety pins to their Docksiders, last year they simultaneously fished glittery plastic kindergarten barrettes from their bathroom drawers, this year they stick rhinestones on their upper arms and pass out rubber bands they've popped from their braces so everyone can chew on them.

But even spheres that have always interested the preteen have become more and more centered on them. Now the promoters of popular culture—like *CosmoGIRL!* and the Delia's catalogue and ABC Family Channel—focus to an overwhelming degree on a girl like Lily, whose every penny spent is the result of a calculated decision about what CD or shirt or lip gloss will help her fit in. What they watch on television, whether they drink, what they want to be when they grow up—for preteens, parents influence these decisions more than any other source. But for music and clothes, the biggest influence is friends. Lily's ballet and sewing skills don't matter so much as these things, because at this age children define themselves by what they have. Or what they don't: What agony when the girls arrange themselves on the schoolyard according to shirt color—purple, white, purple, white—and Lily's wearing a black vest.

Middle-school kids no longer crib their older siblings' cultural identity—they've got their own—and retailers are seizing on this like never before. It's partly because the preteen population is growing so fast. It's partly because kids, beneficiaries of a flush economy and victims of busy-or-otherwise-guilty-thus-indulgent parents just have so much money to blow. (Someone between twelve and fifteen spends, on average, fifty-nine dollars a week, about one-third on clothes, the bulk of the rest on entertainment. And that doesn't even count what their parents spend on them.) It's partly because kids are growing up faster. And it's partly because retailers, having saturated every small town, every other market, simply have nowhere else to go. So they aim downward.

Thus there are more teen magazines on the newsstand than ever, more teen lines of adult clothing brands. One by one, grown-up retailers in the Columbia Mall are closing, replaced by stores or entire wings for preteens and teenagers, with Skinmarket and Limited Too and Aeropostale and Journeys and the Piercing Pagoda and Viktor Viktoria and

PacSun and Stickerz. Parents drop their kids off a little jealous. When they were that age, there weren't any stores for them—just the kids' department, which you couldn't wait to get out of. But they're also a little wary: The styles have grown up. This year the small of the back is everywhere, as shirts for girls stop short of the belly and make announcements across the chest: "Trouble," or "How Hot Am I." The jeans ride tight and low, real low, so flowered cotton underpants—these are still children, after all—bunch up above the belt loops. The boys wear pants low, of course, and baggy, and the girls like to mock the way this forces them to run, grabbing their waistbands and bowing their legs out, a waddle almost.

The consumerism that is such a big part of young adolescence these days is, truly, a big pain for parents, many of whom reasonably think those pants look stupid. But they can, and should, pay attention to the school dress codes and exercise some control at the mall, even when they hear, "But it's *my* money!" Giving in is easier in the short run, but a kid who gets used to hearing "no" might stop fighting it after a while.

Insensitivity to the importance of fitting in, however, is unforgivable. By all means, a boy in the year 2001 should not be made to wear snug slacks. But he *can* be denied any jeans where a basketball could pass through the leg. A girl who wants a message to crawl across her chest? A mother can tell her which messages are too slutty and why, and let her choose from among the others.

A parent's control is limited—nothing's changed on that score. An aspiring punk-rocker might be forbidden from wearing that raggedy skull wristband, but he will keep it in his backpack and put it on at school. A girl whose parents ban eyeliner applies it, shakily, on the bus. That doesn't mean parents shouldn't forbid what they truly feel is untoward. They should, however, think carefully about just how dangerous that ratty wristband really is. Because growing up, after all, is in large part about creating a style.

Or, rather, choosing from among a small range of options.

It's one of the biggest contradictions of preteenagerhood: The kids see clothes and music as their chance to shape their own personae, but that identity needs to be as much as possible like everyone else's. That's why stores like Hot Topic and Urban Outfitters, meccas for nonconformist conformists, are so popular. Or clothing stores that are a socially safe brand but offer enough choices and accessories so that kids can feel they're creating their own look. At American Eagle Outfitters, for example, you can customize the jeans you buy with rhinestones and studs. They're your very own creation—but they're still American Eagle, so you're okay. Your phone has a pink faceplate nobody else's does—but it's still a Nokia, so you're okay. You've concocted your own gold-glitter Supersmooch Lip Gloss at Club Libby Lu—but you're still wearing lip gloss, so you're okay.

Middle-school kids have their own sitcoms, at once treacly and ironic, usually starring the Olson twins or some facsimile. The music industry, too, has begun to capitalize on the vast buying power of preteens, who used to listen to their older siblings' records (or even their parents'!) but now have genres all to themselves. They are sick of hearing their baby-boom parents brag about how great their music was. They are sick of what they listened to last week, and thank goodness, because, with the music-production process sped up, there's always something new right around the corner. They begin to realize music can be their own and at the same time a way to connect with their friends, which means they all like the same stuff, give or take. Jimmy started the year listening to his sister's boy bands, but by the middle of the year he has developed his own favorite groups and written their names in silver pen on his backpack: "Blink 182. Kid Rock." Bands with an attitude go over well with middle schoolers, bands that they consider "outsider" and "punk" and "underground" but that the music industry considers pop. "When a band becomes popular, they get shallow," one eighth grader puts it, without realizing that once Good Charlotte's music has made it way to the thirteen-year-olds in Columbia, Maryland, it's no longer "outsider," and its first album went quickly gold, what with every other girl just like her at every other school in the country feeling the same way.

chapter fourteen

it's the jackie show!

The night after Christmas, just after his first birthday, Kyle Taylor has a fever. Sara gives him baby Tylenol in the living room, and moments later he throws it up, aspirates on the vomit, stops breathing. Jackie watches as her father carries the purple-lipped baby like a big fish to the kitchen table and begins CPR. To her mother Jackie says, though she's not sure why, "I'm sorry. I'm sorry." Her mind goes blank; she goes to her room and can't cry but prays, a prayer that mostly goes, "Oh my God. Oh my God. Oh my God." Her baby brother, whose poops, cries, and giggles she jokingly charts on the computer, whose noises she's listed ("argglgle," "hahhahooo"), whose cuteness she is certain he gets from her even though he looks exactly like his dad and she like her mom, whose peanut allergies she carefully tends, whose crawling body she crabwalks over as he laughs, looks like he's dying. Jackie's sure that he's dying.

But he does not die.

Kyle is breathing again as the ambulance wails to a stop in front of the house. On his way into the house one of the paramedics says to Jackie, "How you doing today?"

She doesn't know what else to say but "Fine."

Preadolescent passion flits. Just when you think a child will never detach from an obsession, her attentions take off and alight elsewhere. For Jackie, her brother's crisis is the first gust that lifts her off the rock she was sitting on, thinking of boys. Crushes slip to number five on her priority list, or even six, as Jackie lands firm-footed on a new fixation: identity. She will spend the rest of the winter immersed in the vital preteen exercise of figuring out and then creating the Jackie Taylor *she* wants to be. This is common for a thirteen-year-old, to pause for a moment to question her values, her life-style, her hobbies, her wardrobe. Jackie wants to grow up but knows she's not going to do it by fooling around with boys, breaking rules. So she looks elsewhere.

The first stop on her inner journey is religion. Her mother is Jewish and her father Lutheran; her religious practice mostly consists of holiday dinners and gifts, but with everything happening in Israel it feels like she should go to synagogue. Maybe, if enough people talk to God at the same time, it will help. So her mother takes her, four Friday nights in a row, until Jackie decides she'd rather have friends over. In temple Jackie looks up at the stained glass, listens to the beautiful songs she doesn't understand, feels safe. As well, she writes letters for her mother to deliver to the cemetery, where her grandfather has been buried two years. "I miss you Grandpa. I love you. Love, Jackie." He was her biggest fan and gave her a gymnastics jacket that makes her think of him every time she puts it on.

Jackie has been spending a lot of time in the basement playing Sims, a massively popular computer game in which the players create characters and decorate their homes and find them jobs and control their levels of comfort and hygiene and energy and so on. It pretends to simulate real life, except that in real life bragging doesn't always cause couples to like each other more and you can't earn spending money simply by typing shift-control-C and then !;!;!;!;. Jackie likes to be in charge of her own world of characters, which never happens otherwise. She and her neighbor Jenny have created the Sexy family and the Pimp family (their mansion is P-shaped, a swimming pool tucked into the hole in the P), the Lovers' Castle, the J Squared House, and a Japanese pagoda where the band members from System of a Down live.

Beyond Sims, Jackie is sick of everything there is to do in her house and, able to do some serious imagining, has begun to wonder incessantly why she doesn't have a cooler life, the life her mental Jackie Taylor—hipper, older, freer—is entitled to. "My life is so boring. If we had cable my life would be so much better," she says. "We'd be watching MTV right now." There are no stricter adherents to the grass-is-always-greener conviction than thirteen-year-olds; Jackie is certain all her friends have more exciting lives. But when she tests her theory with a phone survey one day, three girls, all of whom have cable, are doing chores, and the fourth is visiting her grandma.

Sometimes, it seems to Jackie, life is just a collection of things she cannot do or have. Mr. Acie won't let her sit at the back of the bus anymore, because he said she was bouncing when she really wasn't, and Jackie wants her mom to get him fired for this and other grave injustices, but Sara points out that Mr. Acie probably has a family, and do you really want to put him out of a job, and besides, she likes to hear he's strict and doesn't let the kids dangle their limbs out the window.

Already Jackie is bargaining for a car in three years. You pay for the car and insurance, Jackie offers, and I'll pay for the gas. Sara suggests the opposite. If Jackie were the mother, she would let her kid walk to Giant in the daytime with friends she knew and trusted. "I'm just like, 'Why can't I do this?' and they're like, 'Because I said so.' The thing that gets on my nerves—it plucks my last nerve—is when my mom says, 'I'm the parent, you're the child.' "

A reason, *please*.

She thinks that her dad is so laid-back that if he made all the decisions she could go wherever she wanted, especially Giant, but she is wrong.

Jackie can never pass notes in math, because, even though Ms. Hammond once overlooked a spin-the-binder game in the corner during study hall, she knows a note's a note, wherever in the room she's standing, whatever work she's immersed in. A hawk, that woman is, and there's just something unconstitutional about it. Doesn't she know that a seventh-grade girl's need to communicate with her friends is as fundamental as her need to breathe and bathe? In English, Mrs. Gayle, however, thinks that when they toss crumpled paper across the room they're just trying to hit each other, so, as the class does a worksheet about the

characters in "The Monsters Are Due on Maple Street," Jackie passes a
note back to Stephen:

> *wassup? do you like any 1? (i dont know y, do you wanna pass*
> *notes?)*
> *Stephen's wiggling the black Bic in his mouth, squiggling in his*
> *seat.*
> *i don't know why but i wanna. yes i like someone actually i like*
> *3 people!*
> *3! tell me 1. or 3.*
> *okay i'll tell you 2 but u gon tell . . . please don tell. [He hides*
> *the note under his worksheet as he writes.]*
> *i promise on my grandfathers grave i wont tell*
> *i sorta like Kristina. i think Ann is hot.*
> *i know you ass wipe.*
> *who do you like*
> *you have to tell me the 3rd person because i already know the*
> *other 2 and never talk to me again like that. Bonge moi pat garcon.*

For some reason, Jackie thinks this means "Bite me, dough boy."

She turns around and asks, "Kate?"
"She's ugly! You and Ben. You and Eugene."
"That's nasty."
"You and Dante."
"That's nastier. Why are you picking on me? Because I'm short?"
Stephen writes another note:

> *lets talk about something else. i read the note you gave 2 Leslie*
> *on friday.*
> *what note? how did u get it?*
> *that said you might have cancer.*

Jackie is going to explain that the cancer thing was a joke on Leslie—
who got quite pissed about it—but instead she crumples the paper.
"Jackie. Jackie. Write back."
But Jackie is finishing her worksheet. "What's that word, a small
word, one little thing that's wrong with you? It starts with an 'f.' " She

looks in the glossary. "It's not in here." And then the thesaurus: "Flaw! That was it! I feel better now. I feel complete." Jackie loves thesauruses, the way they take you from mad to angry to infuriated, or nettled, or splenetic. Stephen wants another note. "I'm trying to do my work," Jackie tells him. "I'm sorta trying to pass this class"—she bounces her head from side to side and smiles—"even though I have a ninety-six-point-one."

Jackie knows she's a good scholar, so she figures New Jackie should play on Old Jackie's strengths. In reading, she's been raising her hand so much, ramrod-straight, almost always with the right answer, that the teacher announces, "It's the Jackie show!" In math, they're graphing in-equalities, which she loves. In science, Jackie watches the crabs mate and does all her experiments with Leslie. Jackie has seen this salinity experiment before on *Zoom*, where you pour three candy colors of orange, blue, and green water into a beaker to see how they layer. "You put the one with less salt in first," she says. Jackie likes *Zoom*, although ("not to be clique-racist") she doubts any of the kids on that show are popular. Jackie draws the beakers on the worksheet and shows Leslie how. She tells Mr. Shifflett that the orange on top is fresh water, the green is brackish, and the blue is salt water. She sets up beakers with different water levels and taps them to play "When the Saints Go Marching In."

Science is so easy that sometimes Jackie wants to move into GT, which her mother would love. Sara has always envisioned her daughter in an outdoor, exploratory kind of job, though she hopes not Greenpeace. But Jackie doesn't want her grade to go down. Also, she figures Leslie would get a C without her around. Jackie is selected to go on a field trip with other girls who are good at science, to a place where computer chips are made. She looks at a display of how the chips have gotten smaller over the years, and puts on a spacesuit and booties and gloves to enter the disinfectant chamber. She keeps the gloves.

It sounds corny, she knows, but Jackie really enjoys school right now. Not just the seeing-your-friends part, but the work. The surge in enthusiasm is due in part to her brand-new career goal, one she thinks good grades might make possible, one shared by Lily and Elizabeth and probably half their peers: Jackie now wants to be an actress when she grows up. That way she can buy a yellow convertible Dodge Viper and be remembered after she dies. She hasn't told her mom, who would suggest something more practical, and she hasn't told her dad, who would say it's not realistic. But Jackie knows it can happen—"TV, movies, commercials, whatever I can get my hands on." Though she often imagines herself a Casey or an Elissa, she's not going to change her name, because it's a pain to redo all those documents and she's already practiced her signature. She zips "Jackie Taylor" across the page, over and over, like she used to do two months ago with "Jackie Starr."

As for trampolining, Jackie wavers. Since she started at age eight, the tramp has gone a long way toward teaching Jackie how to take turns, sit still, focus. "A Mexican jumping bean," Sara calls her. At Gymnastics Plus, Jackie waits tidy and cross-legged on the mat. She loves the social part, goofing off with her teammates in between routines. When it's her turn for the double mini, she mouths "Watch me" across the gym to her mother, runs as if toward a vault, performs a series of tricks on two small tramps, and dismounts onto a mat. "I did back tuck back tuck!" When she jumps, with the thick practice harness or without it, her arms swing in the air, and at each bounce her left knee bends for momentum.

Jackie loves speed—when she was little, Mike had to wear roller skates to keep up with her Big Wheel—and as the Olympics play on television, she wonders if she should bobsled instead, or maybe figure-skate. She goes to the rink for the first time and is amazingly at ease. She teaches herself to do triple spins and pull her arms in fast. A man who used to teach skating tells her she is phenomenal, and a group of girls her age watch, looking impressed despite their best efforts not to be.

Right before trampoline sectionals there's a stretch when Jackie's not doing well on the double mini and she always complains before practice. On the way to the meet, Jackie, in her purple warm-up suit, keeps saying she's not going to do well. If she has that little confidence, Sara says, she can choose not to compete, just like that. Jackie goes ahead and warms up, but you can see from her hard face that she's miserable—she blew her new trick two practices in a row, and the equipment in this gym sucks, and she's going to screw up. Her coach comes up to Sara and says, "She's a headcase."

"She said she had a couple of bad days this week."

"She has fifteen bad days and one good day. She has twenty-five bad days and one good day. She convinces herself she can't do it, then she can't."

Jackie aces the double mini and the tramp and wins first place in both.

Looks-wise, Jackie's in a good groove these days. In sixth grade, when she didn't care what people thought, she wore a turtleneck with a vest. "Eww," she says, "I can't believe I wore that. I have no idea how I got so many boyfriends wearing that." Her look, she has decided, should be dark colors and black, though not Goth. She proudly coordinates tops and bottoms from different stores even though they're not made to go together. Her aunt bought her new shirts, all long-sleeved variations of navy blue, with messages of course: "Angel to Devil in 3.5 Seconds." "I Know I'm Cute So Keep Trying." "Samurai Princess." She's pleased with her new style, and if someone she admired criticized her favorite shirt, she'd keep wearing it. (If it was just something she got because it was on sale, though, she'd save it for weekends only.)

"All my neighbors think I'm beautiful," Jackie says. "They're like, 'Oh my God, she's so beautiful.' Then they look at Kyle and then nobody talks to me, but that's okay." Jackie wears a tiny bit of makeup, a little liner mostly, to frame her eyes, which she thinks are amazing, the way they change color. She has just started shaving the nearly invisible blondish hair on her legs. Aside from the tricky ankle area, she's doing pretty well. Though Jackie wishes she weren't so skinny and her legs not so bruised from gymnastics, she is proud of her abs, a baby six-pack. Her eyebrows she has started to find "thick and manly—I have one. I have *one*." So she asks, "Mommy, can I use your tweezers?" Sara approves of the action but not quite of the result: The brows are plucked so glamour-girl thin that Sara says they need to grow out so Jackie's grandma can fix them.

Jackie thinks Leslie is pretty, too, but is a little worried about (1) her style and (2) her family life, in which she argues with her mom and thinks her dad considers her an embarrassment to the family and only her cat really loves her and (3) her forwardness with boys. Jackie is totally in line with Leslie on checking out the guy across the street at the high school who rates a "Cole," the highest rating on their scale of hotness, named after the bad-boy character on *Charmed*. But she is creeped out by how many boys Leslie will "make out with." Kristina tells Leslie she's acting like a ho', changing who she likes every day, and Leslie says that she knows she can act a little ho-like sometimes but she'll try to change. "Everyone has a flaw," she says, "and that must be mine, I'm sorry." It's not like any of those guys are into her anyway, she's just seeing who likes her. She wonders, Is that acting like a ho'?

Although *YM* tells Jackie that a "forward Leo" wants to be her Valentine, on February 14—when the boys at her table eat candy hearts their moms put in their lunches, and the girls wear red and have hearts on their hands or pink stars glued to their eyelids or Valentines to pass out to friends (and other girls who ask for them, because what can you do, say, "You're not my friend"?)—Jackie shows no signs of holiday spirit. Maybe she doesn't need Valentine's Day. Maybe she doesn't need boys.

She goes that week to the skating rink, where as usual she rules on the car-racing video game and cannot resist the opportunity to not win a stuffed animal from the crane. As she skates around the rink, Dan Arnstein, her ex, watches from the penalty rink. As she passes, he says: "Dan likes you."

"Which Dan?"

"Dan Pryor."

Next time around the ice: "I heard you're going out with Adam."

"Which Adam?"

"Adam Buchman."

"No."

When she gets home, she says to Sara, "Dan Arnstein was there."

"Oh, he's such a cutie."

"No, he isn't."

"Sure he is. I think he's such a cutie."

"Mooooooom," Jackie says, and that's that.

Nobody's asked Jackie out since Anton, whom she is way over. On his IM profile he pays homage to the women of the world by posting the lyrics of Timbaland and Magoo's "All Y'all," in which the rappers feel "like a pimp," plump with cash and class and "a gat loaded for that ass."

This has never made sense to Jackie, the way rappers are, like, as she puts it, "I love you ba-a-by. I'll show it with a shotgun! Baby, I love you, but you're a BLEEP!" Celia doesn't mind it, and for a while goes out with Anton. But she grows tense from the instant-messages she gets from a girl in New York who calls her a bitch and says she stole Anton away from her; besides, she wants to be single, "because then you can have fun, and Stephen and I always like to put our arms around each other, and Anton would get all jealous, and also the whole school would know, since our school is so involved in everyone's relationships." So she breaks up with him at Kelly's Bat Mitzvah and then cries, because she still likes him. Jackie is glad she can enjoy the dancing at the party and not have to cry about anyone. For the record, the supposedly lesbian rabbi doesn't hit on anyone.

Jackie attributes her sudden ambivalence about boys in large part to her horrible pickiness. She will only eat Burger King fries, not McDonald's. It takes her forty-five minutes to choose one movie at Blockbuster. Even though it's a bad age for movies when you have a strict mom—everything is either too adult or too babyish—there are a thousand that would be acceptable. Jackie doesn't want any of them, especially if they were made before 2001. And the boys: "In sixth grade, you're like, 'Omigod, I'm in a new school, I'm so cool—ah!' You didn't know the people in sixth grade. But now that you know they're big butt-munchers and jerks, you're like, 'Eww, I don't want to go out with them.' I can't believe I went out with them."

She doesn't want anyone who likes her just for her looks—if someone asks her out, she makes him explain in a note or through a friend why he likes her, to make sure "funny" and "smart" are in there and not just "hot." Which pretty much rules out all the seventh-grade boys, she figures, because all they care about is big boobs. "They all just like Ann," Jackie says, "because she's hot and she can do a roundoff back handspring."

"Some people think they're, like, the most beautiful person in the world and they can go out with anybody, and they say it in front of the world: 'I want to go out with this person, I'm so beautiful and lovable, look at me.' Some people are just like, 'I'm so ugly, no one will want to go out with me.' And I'm just like, Okay, whatever. If someone likes me, that's cool.

"If you like somebody, think about it. If it's not going to happen, reality-check."

Even if she did like someone right now, she'd think twice before writing on her hand again. It's embarrassing if someone finds out you like him but he doesn't like you back. She would confide in Leslie only.

She is keeping that prospect open; it's not like she's joining a convent. Brad broke up with Mimi, and she'd go out with him if he wanted. There are a few others she'd consider, too. Plus, the last few months her horoscope has mentioned an "exuberant Aries who smiles a lot."

Who, Jackie wonders, could that be?

chapter fifteen

i'm not that curious anymore

Jimmy calls out his bedroom window into the clouds, "Do we need a notebook?"

"Three years we've been going to the oysters," his father says, slamming the trunk, "and you still ask that?"

Jimmy shuffles out on the cold driveway in his holey-toed socks, holding his boots, one pair of many. *Independence Day* was on last night, loud and intense, so he had trouble sleeping.

"Do you have a ruler? A pencil? The Game Boy is going in the trunk." Jimmy goes back upstairs, then downstairs, and finally they are off, toward Annapolis and the oysters they raise. At the pier next to the family sailboat, Paul lifts four metal baskets from under the dock with a long hook and hauls them dripping onto the wood. The three thousand oysters, small as poppy seeds, are crusted onto dead oyster shells. Jimmy hoses off the dirt and mud so the bacteria wash away and the oysters can grow. He absently wipes muck onto his jeans.

"Watch what you're doing here," Paul says, bending to pick something off the pier. "Those are your good boots."

"Dad, stop showing your underwear." Jimmy thinks nothing of embarrassing his parents in public, returning the favor. Over pasta and candlelight and a big loaf of crusty bread being passed at Will's house one recent night, Jimmy told his mother loudly, "You're wearing too much eye shadow."

Paul hitches up his jeans. "Jimmy, how's the oysters?"

"The thing I've really wanted to try all my life is giving an Alka-Seltzer tablet to a seagull to see if it really explodes."

"Is that how we treat living things?"

While the oysters dry in the sun and the flatworms on them die, Jimmy and Paul go for lunch in tourist Annapolis and browse the stores. At the Discovery Channel store, each next item Jimmy sees is the one he has to have. Back at the dock, Jimmy holds the oysters up to the ruler and calls out measurements: "Twenty millimeters. Forty-three. Sixty-four." He's really not into this anymore. There are four hundred things he'd rather be doing, but Paul always says, "No, Jimmy, you have to keep on going for years. It's a major job." If it's so important, Jimmy wants to say, why don't you do it yourself?

Just like that, Jimmy has stopped sitting up in bed wondering about the universe. "I'm not that curious anymore," he says. This, too, is part of the changes engulfing him as he enters adolescence. Though these changes take place in the brain, he has no more control over them than he does over the growth of his feet. And they happen so fast. All of a sudden Jimmy gets bored more easily, his temper slips from his grasp—full self-control won't come until the brain's frontal lobes are pruned—and, like Jackie, he is contemplating seriously whether maybe what made up the old Jimmy should not make up the new Jimmy. No longer is pleasing his parents a major factor in the equation of how to spend his time. Just the contrary: For reasons he cannot figure out even while it's happening—and not like he loves them any less—Jimmy, like his peers, finds great sport in contradicting his mother and father.

A preteen has plenty of interests, they just rarely sit still for long. Jimmy's theory is that school used to teach you less stuff, so you had to be curious on your own, but now, in sixth grade, the material is more interesting, so there's less room for extracurricular curiosity. Occasionally he digs up his backyard, where among the archaeological detritus of his childhood he might find something cool, like Jefferson salamanders. He looks up their habitat on the Internet and creates a home for them in his sister Brianna's old frog tank, but the next day he opens the lid and lets them disappear. Mostly he plays on the computer or GameCube. You could say he's a big reason the video-game industry has grown so massive in the last decade—except that his parents only let him own five games at a time. It's alluring, the totally captivating, passive, out-of-this-world experience of a video game, a place Jimmy can excel. Boys today can't image their counterparts three decades ago, who didn't have video games to play at home, who spent money on music (now downloadable right from PCs), who spent more time outside, when that was considered a safer option. Two decades ago home-video games became popular, Atari and the like, but even one decade ago they weren't nearly as big a deal as they are right now—new, better, faster, sexier games arriving on the shelves each week, easily accessible on the computer, affordable to kids with a whole different level of spending money.

Scientists have varying theories on the impact of so much gaming, but in general they're cautionary. "Hand-eye coordination," Jimmy protests, but he doesn't realize what's going on in his brain. Whatever brain cells he's using at this phase of his life are the ones that will survive. Video games may help you maneuver in a fast-paced, info-saturated society, but if you're perpetually playing them instead of something more physical, the development of your cerebellum may be delayed. And one theory posits that the rapid pace of video games triggers irrational fear responses, so out of line with how you should respond in the real world that the development of rational thought is at risk.

At school Jimmy has been spacing out a lot. He especially tunes out whenever the lesson revolves around reading the textbook (often) or filling out a worksheet (which takes up one-fourth of a middle schooler's classroom time) or anytime the overhead projector is turned on. God, how these kids hate copying from the overhead: definitions of the jobs required to put on a play ("director," "stage manager"), definitions from high school ("SAT," "elective," "graduation requirement"), definitions from the school mission statement ("community," "stimulating," "lifelong"). Jimmy likes learning new words but sometimes feels like only a vessel filling up with vocab, vocab, vocab.

He's playing with his calculator when Ms. Knighten says, "What's the principal, Jimmy? Page two seventy-four." "Plains and plateaus, Jimmy," Mrs. Graves tells him in social studies, but he's writing instead of following the textbook, and it takes a few seconds to focus, as air drones through the vents. He is flipping his miniature skateboard from one desk to another when the squeaky-voiced substitute in academic enrichment hands out a crossword puzzle. "I'll take that, please," she says. As everyone else copies the science answers from the overhead—"Magma cool slowly → called intrusive rocks. Ex: granite"—Jimmy doodles. The aide directs his head to his worksheet and pats his shoulders. He yawns, audibly. In music, when he's supposed to be underlining "aria," "duet," "quartet" in the reading, it's "Jimmy, put your chair down, please." Four second later, he leans back again.

"School is the worst thing that ever lasted six hours in a kid's life," Jimmy says. And homework is the worst thing that ever lasted three hours. It's an endless struggle between Jimmy and his parents.

Today, as soon as he gets home from school, he turns on the radio in the family room, plops on the rose-colored rug in front of the entertainment center, and starts playing Super Smash Bros. Melee. At three-thirty his dad looks in from the kitchen. "Homework, Jim."

"No."

"You made the choice to wait till the last day. You know the rule. Do I have to take the game away?"

Silence.

"The game is done."

"You promised me thirty minutes of free time! Good job, Dad."

Paul sets a kitchen timer for thirty minutes and places it on the floor between Jimmy and the television. "When this goes to zero, the game goes off."

God, Jimmy thinks, when will Dad get out of the house? Paul lost his job at a dot-bomb last year, the same time Marie was laid off from a telecom company. At first Jimmy was worried about the money, but Marie assured him there was plenty in the bank. He likes that his mom isn't working, that she's around more, that he doesn't have to worry every time she's on a plane or wait at the babysitter's for her two-hour commute to be over. For a child, one study posits, having a parent travel for work is as stressful as having a close relative die. Now it's just that his dad is around *all the time*.

Four-twenty. The timer beeped when Paul was upstairs, and when his mother comes home, Jimmy has just switched from GameCube to car-toons. "Jimmy, come on," Marie says. It feels like his parents call his name three hundred times a day.

"Only seven or ten minutes till *Dragon Tales* are over," he says, and she goes upstairs. Four minutes later she comes back down, and Jimmy is trying to download the Starship Troopers game from the Internet. "You can look up one more thing," she says from the kitchen, "and then it's homework time."

Four-twenty-seven. "Your show is over. TV off."

"I'm not turning it off. Brianna got to do her homework in front of the TV."

"Jimmy, I'd like to see you." Pause. "Jimmy, I'd like to see you. Now."

He switches the radio to 99.1, which his dad calls the "cussing, swearing station," for its profligate use of not just "hell" (which Jimmy doesn't consider a swear anyway) but also "bitch" and "f'ing."

"I wish to see you now." Pause. "I wish to see you now." Seven times she says it, until the phone rings and she answers. Jimmy can't get Star-ship Troopers to work. He finds three slices of cheese in the refrigerator and fills a bowl to the rim with Peanut Butter Crunch cereal and milk.

"You're stalling, Jimmy. Jimmy, I asked you to take the trash out. Please do so."

Four-fifty. "Homework, please?"

Four-fifty-six. The phone rings again. Jimmy changes the screen color on the computer.

Five-oh-four. He goes outside to check the birdhouse. He turns the latch, lowers the side, and peeks in: four or five babies snuggling up to a very fluffy mom. He goes back inside, gets the old cutting board he puts his papers on, and flops it onto the ground. The best time to get infor-mation from your child is when he is trying to procrastinate; Jimmy will talk about anything to avoid his work—the skunk in the neighbor's back-yard, how much he likes babka. "The baby birds are in there," he tells Marie. The television is still on.

"JIMMY!"

"Yes, I AM!"

"You show me you can get it done, and in a half-hour you'll have time for TV."

"What are you thinking? I'll finish and then I'll have no time for TV." He fetches a strawberry-cheesecake granola bar.

"Oh, I see, Jimmy. You're avoiding again?"

"I'm hungry."

"That's called avoiding. Jimmy, you're dawdling. Jimmy, you're dawdling. You may have one. That's it."

Five-oh-nine. He lies on his stomach on the rug, kicking up his left foot, staring into space, eating the granola bar. He takes his shoes off; his feet smell like old apple peels, or a filled garbage disposal left too long.

"Jimmy, go upstairs and change those socks RIGHT NOW."

"If I finish this, can we go to the mall to get a present for my communion?"

"Your father and I already got one."

"But I want Starship Troopers."

"We already picked something out, and maybe you'll get it, after the communion."

Five-eleven. He goes upstairs to change his socks and, while there, counts his money.

Five-sixteen. He goes back upstairs to get paper.

At five-twenty-three, Jimmy starts his homework. He cuts out a bookmark for reading class, and swirls a paper shred that came off onto the scissors.

"See what my parents do?" Jimmy says. "They overemphasize." The way his dad makes him go into "overtime" when he screws up homework problems, how before a quiz his mom makes him go over not just the sample questions but also the key concepts and definitions, how they don't understand that he can't make a drawing without his favorite mechanical pencil, how when he gets a C for the quarter they make him do extra credit, even though *that* quarter is over and he's doing fine in this one. When he gets a seventy-seven on a math quiz, he fears his father's reaction. "Don't tell him," a classmate says. "Say you got an A and Ms. Knighten kept it."

"He'll call her. He's strict."

At school the Schissels are known as intense parents, "Active" with a big fat "A." Jimmy doesn't mind having them around school or on field trips; he's glad when they drop off Chick-Fil-A or cookies in the cafeteria for special occasions. He likes it when they guide him on projects, and he was grateful for his dad's mnemonic device to remember the countries of Africa.

But their checking his homework so carefully every day aggravates him: "They look at the *one* thing I did wrong." Even if they didn't check, he says, "I would do it and all. If they laid back on it—like, did it every couple of days instead of every day—maybe I'd do better in school. It stresses me out." Don't they trust him? Would it kill them—would it kill *him*—if it was good enough, instead of perfect?

The homework fights have been leading to tantrums ever since fourth grade, ever since grammar got serious and math passed division. Two or three times a year, Jimmy gets too obstinate and the argument ends in a smack. Jimmy thinks a kid his age should be "old enough to take the pain" and tries to save the tears for things like thinking about his great-grandma, who died before he got to know her, or cutting himself when he was affixing aluminum-can pieces to his bike tires so it would sound like a motorcycle. Really, when you're a sixth-grade boy, you're not supposed to cry even if an inch-long splinter lodges in your finger or a hockey puck nails your crotch, because that's sissy, and sissy is gay. But when his dad hits him Jimmy always cries, half for the pain and half for the sadness.

Paul isn't proud of that; he blames himself. Like most middle schoolers, sometimes—much of the time—Jimmy can be so fun, so lovable. But, also like most middle schoolers, Jimmy has mood swings, and he can swap his lovableness, without warning, for something unimaginably frustrating. His tiny handwriting—you really do need a magnifying glass. The humming and whistling and singing ("Rudolph the Red-Nosed Reindeer" in March?) while he studies. His insistence on always using the exact long procedures he learned in class instead of his own logic, which might yield the same answer faster. When the instructions say to use resources from the worksheet, he won't accept Marie's suggestion to look on the Internet, too, because the instructions say "worksheet," not "Internet," duh. The way he can hear, over Paul clicking at the computer to his right and Marie slicing potatoes to his left, the faintest hint of music coming from Brianna's room. He marches to the stairs. "Brianna, turn it down!"

And above all when he completes his homework—they watch him finish—and it never makes it into the teacher's hand. The English assignment forgotten in between pages of the math book, the English assignment remembered in between pages of the English book but never passed up front: It is one of the largest mysteries of middle school. Solving it would have to merit some sort of Nobel, teachers figure. After Marie found out about five completed assignments never handed in, she bought Jimmy clear plastic sheets to organize his work in. It didn't make much difference, and she tries to pull back and concern herself with the important things: "Is he having fun? Is he happy? Is he learning? Is he increasing his vocabulary? Can he sustain an argument?" (An emphatic yes to that one.)

Marie is trying to get Jimmy out the door for the orthodontist, but he keeps playing piano, "Für Elise" and then "Star Wars." "He needs to listen to your mother," Brianna's friend says as the girls lie on the family room floor doing homework in front of cartoons. Jimmy grabs a twenty-ounce bottle of red Gatorade and downs it in the quarter-mile between the house and the orthodontist.

After one minute in the orthodontist's back chamber, Jimmy comes out and announces they've come on the wrong date. He takes a pack of chewy Jolly Ranchers from his pocket, unwraps one, and pops it in his mouth.

"We can take him anyway," the receptionist says.

"No, next week," Jimmy protests.

"He's already got candy in his mouth," Marie says.

"He's not supposed to do that," the receptionist says.

"The candy just turns up." It disappears at home; it appears from school. Jimmy and his friends all have this need these days, sugar every half-hour, or more. Marie found four Reese's Peanut Butter Cup wrappers in the bookshelf behind his bed the other day. Marie is glad Jimmy got braces at age eight, when he was too young to really fight it. He goes back to the chair, and she writes the check, eighty dollars for the month.

The receptionist pokes her head through the window to the waiting room. "Jimmy has a loose appliance today. This is his sixth. We start charging after five, but we won't count this one."

"This candy thing. He must have gotten it off the counter. I found it in a suitcase."

"He didn't get a star either. And I know he likes stars." The stars add up to prizes, but when your mouth literally waters for Jolly Ranchers, who can think of stars? All that effort Marie makes to follow the rules, cutting his apples into pieces. He doesn't understand that the candy does harm even when it doesn't pop out the bracket, that it bends the wires, pushes your teeth in directions they're not supposed to go.

Jimmy isn't even out the door when he pops in another Jolly Rancher.

"No candy."

"Just if I suck it! He said I can suck it."

"Jimmy."

"I'm not chewing!"

"What's the homework situation?"

"Some English, I have to finish these chapters, and math, some polynomials. They're easy."

"How many problems?"

Chewing sounds from the back seat of the Lexus.

"Give me the candy."

"I'm not chewing!"

"Give me the rest of the candy. I didn't put it on the counter so you could take it."

God, Jimmy thinks, it is like his parents are trying to rule his life. Jimmy is big into the concept of "my time," and he doesn't feel like he's getting a lot of it these days, what with the oysters and homework and his stupid teeth. He plays hoops with a neighbor in his driveway but otherwise doesn't see a lot of his friends anymore outside of school.

One afternoon a few days later, when Jimmy is supposed to stay after for aquarium club, Paul is surprised to see him walk in the door at three. Jimmy says he forgot about Aqua Havens, though really he just doesn't want to go. Paul gets mad, talks about honoring commitments, and drives him back to school. The next day Jimmy refuses to go to the Engineering Challenge contest. He doesn't give his reasons: that he doesn't want to give an oral report and, anyway, he's sure they'll lose. Then, the same week, Jimmy won't budge from the sofa as the clock ticks toward the time of his dentist appointment, then past it. What can I do, Marie thinks, carry him there?

It was embarrassing to call the engineering teacher and apologize, and call the receptionist and apologize, and he'll have to go to the dentist eventually, and now his dad is talking about the video games "being taken out of your life." Jimmy figured his pertinacity would result in all that fighting, but afterward he says his weeklong strike "was worth it one hundred percent. I know he'll get mad. I just have to take the risk." He had to show, just for a little bit, who is in charge of Jimmy and of Jimmy's time.

Besides, the magnetic levitation car only got sixty out of a hundred points.

"Ka. Boom. That. Is. What. You. Heard. On. October. Four. Teenth. Nineteen. Forty. Seven. If. You. Lived. Near. Mur. Oc. Army. Base." Today the students in English are presenting their biography posters. After Aaron finishes stuttering about Chuck Yeager and his cheeks cannot get any redder, it's Jimmy's turn. Going through old *Calvin and Hobbes* cartoons for a poster on Bill Watterson was fun, but reading aloud is misery. Jimmy's shirt is misbuttoned at the collar; his broad shoulders and eyes point almost at the side wall. The other kids gave their presentations out in the open, but Jimmy talks from behind the teacher's counter, rubbing a roll of masking tape, sure he'll blow it. Since he has no notes, the teacher's aide, who is holding his poster, prompts him. His eyes are scrunched a little, he looks down at the table and pauses big. He reluctantly puffs the words out of his mouth.

Last year Jimmy had little problem putting on a kilt and ruffled collar for the elementary-school production of *Macbeth*. Now he wonders if he was insane. Not even his bold classmates are immune from such nerves. Lily has been pleading with Mia to do an act together at the outdoor-ed talent show, and even though they did one last year, Mia says no way. "This is middle school," she says. "People look for the littlest thing to pick you apart."

Jimmy so hates getting up in front of people lately that he dreads his first communion, even though he doesn't have to say one word during the whole ceremony and only has to walk down the aisle in a line with the other kids. His parents held off on communion until Jimmy was old enough to really understand, but now everybody walking with him will be half his age and half his size, and he doesn't care about what it stands for anyway. Jimmy believes in God, whom he used to ask for a million dollars, but he doesn't feel like a churchy person. Maybe a private communion would be okay. "What happens if someone I know is there and doesn't like me very much and makes fun of me?"

At least, he says, he wants a sports jacket. Marie takes him to JCPenney, where, for the first time in his life, he doesn't fit into boys. Even the biggest size, twenty, is short in the torso. So they try the men's department. The men's department! A little old man takes one look at Jimmy and says, "Thirty-six short." And he's right.

The blazer is navy blue, with three smooth gold buttons at each wrist that Jimmy rubs with his thumbs as the priest speaks. The gray pants are a little tight, the blazer a little roomy, and the Looney Toons tie a little short, but Jimmy looks great. Throughout the service, he leans on his dad, bored, as his parents and sister sing out. He works on his cuticles. On his white felt banner, which hangs alongside the others on the platform of the interfaith center, the sun and goblet and host and cross are cut out perfectly, thanks to some help at home. He likes the wheat stalks the best, since they are real. For his sermon the priest goes into the aisle Oprah-style. He singles out Jimmy and asks what Jesus wanted them to learn. All he wanted was not to be embarrassed, and in front of the hundreds of parishioners he squeaks out, "I don't know."

As the parents sang "One Bread, One Body" and the children walked the aisle during rehearsal the other day, Jimmy slouched and studied the floor. When he was back on the plastic chair, feet in the aisle, leaning into his father's arm and neck, Paul told him, "Life's more interesting if you look up"; then they nuzzled, and he kissed Jimmy's head. They were the oldest parent-communicant combo, the tallest by far, and also the cuddliest. When the teacher asked, "Do you want try again?" all the little kids said yes, except for Jimmy, who said, "No!" This time, the real thing, Jimmy walks in a straight line, military corners, faster, head down— please, don't look. Though cameras have been banned during the service, everyone else is photographing, so Paul extends a lens the size of his forearm and shoots.

Jimmy grimaces at the wine in the chalice but toward the end of the service whispers to his mother, "It's a special occasion. Can we have Asti

Spumante tonight?" Though he'd rather go home and play his new Spider-Man game all night, he knows that's out of the question, so he approves an outing for barbecue. By night's end, his legs kill from all that sitting.

chapter sixteen

i love you more than words can say

For the first time in twelve years, Joseph oils the kitchen table, so it will look nice for the brunch the Ginsburgs are hosting the day after the Bat Mitzvah. He leaves the green turtle sandbox in the backyard, though, for another thirteen years perhaps, because he doesn't want to know what's under the plastic lid. Over the Internet he orders his favorite sour pickles from New Jersey. He hangs the photographs he used to take all the time, including one in the dining room called *Fire* that Elizabeth doesn't think looks like anything.

As long as Joseph is on this hanging kick, Elizabeth asks him to put up the crayon-shaped coat rack she made in tech ed. So he does, and while he's at it he putties the nail holes in the door and paints over them. This freaks Elizabeth out. He's not a professional! You can see streaks! They argue over whether repainting the door was part of her work request, leaving Elizabeth dreading the rest of the week. "I just know we're going to get into a big fight about something annoying," she says.

Ellen and Joseph sense Liz's stress, but they're stressed, too. Frenzied, even. At least the dress shopping goes fine: At Teens 'n Up Elizabeth picks out a lilac knee-length dress with a long matching coat that ties in front for the Bat Mitzvah service. For the party she gets a black dress with sparkly flowers and a zigzag hem. It's cocktail-length, Ellen tells her. Ellen and her neighbor Kay—their daughters are having their

Bat Mitzvah together—are making the centerpieces themselves, which seemed like a good idea, once.

Two weeks before the Bat Mitzvah, the Sterns come over for a wine tasting on the screened-in porch. As everyone sips from tiny Dixie cups, Laura says she's been studying every day.

"That's better than me," Elizabeth says.

"Aren't you supposed to practice two hours a day?" Ellen asks.

"No."

"Yes."

"No."

"Now I know the truth."

Elizabeth works on her Bat Mitzvah speech, but the part about her parents gives her trouble. Who knows what to say? She'll ask her Bat Mitzvah tutor. Then she works on her science. "Daddy, do you know what 'experimental group' and 'control group' means?"

Saturday morning before the Ginsburgs leave for synagogue, Joseph gives Elizabeth the silver dollars his grandfather gave him, which date as far back as 1878. There are nine tarnished ones plus, to replace those his father spent at the market long ago, four shinier ones. She shrugs and says "Thanks." In fact, she is touched; this is her favorite gift. Later Elizabeth tells this to Ellen. Ellen tells it to Joseph.

Liz has been a wreck all week, as nervous as they've ever seen her. In the rabbi's office before the service, he tells Joseph and Ellen that, while a lot of kids in the Bat Mitzvah class were disdainful of the whole thing, acting like it wasn't cool, Elizabeth showed enthusiasm. She took it seriously.

In the same room of the interfaith center where Jimmy had his communion, Elizabeth and Laura sit in chairs next to the bimah, so poised. Elizabeth has invited several teachers—though not Miss Colyer—to the service, and this is the first time they have seen her hair down, pounds of it spiraling down her back. Laura looks at ease but Elizabeth is shivering. Joseph is telling people where to sit. "This is the day she made me a man," he says. "Look at those shoes." They are black sandals, platform, they make a tall girl taller than her father.

Ellen is amazed at how her daughter looks. So grown up. So grown up and glorious. Times like these, Joseph feels a tiny bit of selfish pride: Except the nose, Elizabeth looks like him, everyone says that. He never thought he was beautiful, but there's no doubt she is, always has been. "Oh my God," he says as he looks at her. "I'm a little nervous." Ellen is concerned about the parade of the Torah: "Do I kiss, then touch—or touch, then kiss?"

"Mom, I'm scared," Elizabeth says.

But she reads Torah and Haftarah flawlessly; her baby voice morphs almost completely into something more teenager. At the point in the Torah where she reads, "You shall each revere his mother and father," she exchanges smiles with Joseph. When she parades the Torah by, navigating well in her heels, Ellen kisses it. Then she reaches for her daughter's hair, but Liz is gone.

Elizabeth looks at her nails as Laura gives her speech, which is thoughtful and well written. Then Elizabeth's turn. Hers is standard Bat Mitzvah speech issue, complete with the jolty transition from "what my Bat Mitzvah means to me" to the thank-yous.

> I would like to thank many people for helping me to achieve this day. First I would like to thank you, Mom and Dad. I would like to thank you for loving and caring for me and supporting me through the ups and downs of my life. You have not only helped me prepare for my Bat Mitzvah but you helped me with school, swim team, and becoming my own person. I love you more than words can say.

When she gets to the last line, Joseph and Ellen look relieved. They are relieved. As much as their daughter has grown apart from them in all the superficial ways, she is still theirs. They are still hers. Joseph's eyes are closed, and nearly teary. Much of it, including the "I love you more than words can say," was suggested by the Bat Mitzvah tutor. But Ellen and Joseph don't know this, and to two people who haven't been thanked for loving and caring for Elizabeth since that kindergarten proclamation, the speech is no less touching for being formulaic.

Elizabeth will say later that she screwed up, because of the one time she said "all" instead of "those," but to her parents she is perfect. After all her anxiety, they are shocked by her poise. It's magical. Thirteen years down, not bad, and a long time to go.

"I never had two such girls in all my life," the rabbi says.

Between the ceremony and the party, Joseph's car runs out of gas, and he trudges along the road until an uncle picks him up, but everything else runs perfectly. Under the party tent there's a buffet, and a kiosk where you can get your hand molded in rainbow-colored wax, and a disc jockey named Jumpin' John who orchestrates line dances and a mummy-wrapping contest to "Walk Like an Egyptian," which drives the thirteen-year-olds into a determined frenzy and wastes enough toilet paper to accommodate the bathroom needs of a moderately sized village for a week. Stu, one of the few boys there, works up the courage to ask Hanna to dance. He chucks bread at Elizabeth, and she sticks out her tongue. In a couple of days the routine will take over, the intense flash of love and pride from her parents will fade, it will become all about whether Elizabeth will ever sort her presents and write thank-you notes, the science project, getting to swim practice.

But for now her dress sparkles all night long.

chapter seventeen

sometimes i wanna say stuff, but i don't wanna say stuff

Tenacious shows up one morning before school and Eric has already left the house, after a fight with Tim. Another morning he introduces her to a rubber glove filled with water and knotted on the bottom, a face drawn on, his new friend Buddy. After work on New Year's Eve, Tenacious made it over with fifteen minutes to spare and Eric was fondling his Rollerblades, waiting with a bottle of sparkling grape juice as his dad and stepmom hung out upstairs in the bedroom.

"I feel like a bump on a log in here," he says one day.

"C'mon, Mr. Bump, let's go to school," Tenacious says, giving Eric a cheerful hug, wounded that a boy can feel like a bump on a log at his own father's house.

In middle school, who really feels like he fits in? Eric has seen one of the high schoolers flying through the parking lot with wavy blond hair and a skateboard. He's got on a maroon-plaid shirt and a red mismatched tie with his baggy cords. There's something about the guy that says Cool even though there is, probably, nobody else like him. Nothing about middle school makes Eric cool. Band doesn't make him cool. But Liam, who has older siblings, tells him that in high school band is more like a club, where all sorts of people can fit in. Popularity is flexible; there are far more niches in which to find acceptance. This, to Eric, is what high school is about.

It's not about the fat packets that sit on the desk in front of him, explaining the course options for ninth grade. They have to make a four-year plan. Pick honors classes, Mrs. Cook warns. The on-level classes, "they're a bunch of dummies. You go out there and cut the fool with the rest of them." Eric has been placed in Intro to Algebra and the Reading Acceleration Program and the rest on-level classes. No room for the Italian he wanted.

The high-school stuff brings Mrs. Cook to full form. "Try to keep your binder organized—that's a good sign of becoming a scholar." "This is just a dress rehearsal." "Knowledge is contagious." "They're not going to say how cute you are and give you a good grade. They'll say, 'Did you do the work? Did you do the work? Did you do the work?' " Teray is at the shut door: "You're late," Mrs. Cook tells him, and says that, just like in high school, he'll have to wait.

One boy asks, "In high school, failing is a D, right?"

"No, you pass unless you have an F."

"Whoo-hoo," Eric says, "I'm gonna make it!"

The guidance counselor comes to talk about how they can be kept in eighth grade if they don't have at least C's in all their core subjects, but how Ms. Thomas will consider whether they come to school each day, seek extra help, work to the best of their ability. She explains the mathematics of grade-point averages, which Eric can do in his head, and when she says that an F is below 0.75, Eric says, "You must be helluv stupid to get that." Fresh sheets of paper are handed out: Write your goals for fourth quarter and how you'll get there.

"My goal is to pass," Eric says, and writes nothing.

Mrs. Cook has invited three Wilde Lake High School boys to talk about clubs and sports. Eric raises his hand when they ask who's trying out for football and then takes out his calculator and types. He shifts in his chair and knocks his instructions on class scheduling to the floor, where they'll stay. "Anyone worried about high school?" the football captain asks. "Do you worry about getting stuffed in lockers?"

"I'll be stuffing people in lockers," Eric says to himself. He has heard about Freshman Fridays, when the upperclassmen beat on the ninth graders, and about the huge essay assigned the first day of school, but

Eric's not worried—the rumors about sixth grade didn't come true, did they?

The high schoolers give advice: Jog before showing up for fall sports, or else you might get a full-body cramp like this one guy who couldn't move and had to be taken to the hospital. Drink Gatorade before the game and water during. Don't turn in your permission form more than one day late. They tell about the kid who was the first to do band and football at the same time, and Eric says he'll be the second. The captain talks about what a blast spirit week and pep rallies are, and all the while Eric is typing, SCHOOL SUCKS SCHOOL SUCKS SCHOOL SUCKS SCHOOL SUCKS.

They head to the gym for an assembly, and while they are settling on the floor Eric hears the high-school marching band. "Hey, a euphonium! That's going to be me someday." He chants with the fight song: "Go, Wilde Lake! Go, Cats!" He smiles, hums along. For a small moment he is delighted. "That's the drum major. Man, I know that whole rotation. I've been listening to it four years in a row. Four years!" Liam is typing patterns of zeros and ones into Eric's calculator.

As the assistant principal talks about schedules and orientation, as model students talk about how much freedom there is in high school and how everything is handed to you on a silver platter freshman year and how to get into the Letterman Club, as the guidance counselor explains you need twenty-one credits to graduate and you can't be in activities if you get F's this year, Eric lies on his side and lah-dee-dahs.

"How many years of social studies do you need to take?" she calls out, hoarse but cheery, arm cocked to toss a foam Wildcat paw to the eighth grader who answers right.

"Three!"

"What do you think makes the difference between students who get A's and students who get F's?"

"Nerds," Eric mutters.

"My lizard's leg is rotting away," Liam says. "We're going to leave him outside when it's below freezing. He'll fall asleep and die. It's painless."

"Man, this is gay," Eric says.

Liam shows Eric the sign-language alphabet he made up. Chris raises his hand. "If there were a girls' football team, do you think they could beat our team?"

The counselor laughs. "Any other questions?"

"I have a question," Eric says, not so quietly. "When is this bullcrap over?"

"What is the one most important thing to succeed in high school?" Another foam paw at the ready.

"Popularity," says Eric.

"Homework," says the kid who gets the paw.

The next day, the girl on Eric's side in doubles Ping-Pong lets a lot of balls past, and his street clothes have somehow gotten wet, and there's a dollar missing from his pocket. He keeps his clothes in Mr. Jackson's office, a three-dollar lock being yet another thing he doesn't want to trouble his mother for.

To add to the misery, every other day for the next three months the whole band has to go to Mrs. Bloom's classroom to prepare for the state standardized tests—in math, English, social studies, and science—in May. The grade will count toward band—before today, Eric's only sure A. Last year's scores have just been released; they dropped significantly for Wilde Lake. The highest score in the county was seventy-eight ("those rich preppies," Eric says), and Wilde Lake's eighth graders had forty-nine, third from the bottom. Fine with them, as long as they beat Harpers Choice.

Teachers rarely explain why students have to take a given standardized test, what the scores mean, but in Eric's review session Mrs. Bloom does elaborate on the "rewards and opportunities" that come on testing week in May: no academic classes, no homework all week, daily treats like ice cream and doughnuts.

"You have to think on this test," she says, and the class groans loudly. She explains that it's "really, really, really important," and Eric has his head in his hands. Because all the feeder elementary schools have much higher grades than the middle school, it looks like Wilde Lake's teachers are doing something wrong, she says. *So this is about the teachers?* The Maryland School Performance Assessment Program gives scores for a whole grade, not for each kid, so the students know their personal performance is never evaluated. If it's the teachers being judged, who cares?

Mrs. Bloom tells them what they already know: "In elementary school, the teacher tells you something, you believe. In middle school, you start to make your own choices about these sorts of things."

Between the test prep and Ping-Pong and the gym clothes, Eric's in a really lousy mood when he gets to social studies. He's supposed to search the Constitution to see which chamber—House, Senate, or both—is granted each of the powers listed on the worksheet.

Eric hasn't been Horshak with the eagerly raised hand lately, but this is something else entirely. He's not moving at all. Mrs. Conroy makes it to the back corner of the room to check homework and asks him, "Do you have the terms?"

He shakes his head no.

"Why?"

"I didn't know we had to do it."

"Let me see your agenda." She points. "It's right there. I suspect you forgot to look." Tapping. Shrugging. "What are you going to write with? You've broken both your pencils. Want to sharpen one?" No response.

She moves on, and when she tells the class they can work with partners, Shawn comes over. "I could be in GT," Eric says while setting Shawn's watch. Shawn copies the worksheet into his notebook in case he loses one or the other. Ever since all the D's on his last report card and the nightmare he had one night about still being stuck in eighth grade at age thirty, he has cracked down on himself.

Eric writes a capricious series of letters down the answer column— "B S H B how about an H here S's are cool all in a line S S S—until Shawn takes his shredded pencil away. "Stop tapping, man." The rest of the students are working. "C'mon, let's do this."

"I'm done."

Shawn puts his head in his hands. "Why me? Here, Eric, I found number four."

"Whatever. Mrs. Conroy, I'm finished."

"I'll be there in a second." She comes over, checks. "How did you do that?"

"I looked in the book."

"How did you do it so fast? Eric, what's going on?"

Eric chews on his calluses. "I'll get at least one of them right."

"Show me where you found these."

"Why?"

"Because the teacher instructed you to."

"Why?"

"Because that's the assignment."

"Why?"

"I'll be back when you're ready to succeed."

Mrs. Conroy, too, has read all about middle schoolers' being just like toddlers. She knows how a class with them can feel more like managing than teaching. She knows that when teachers get into power struggles with middle schoolers the kids never give up, and nobody wins. When teachers' frustrations get the better of them and they stop trusting the kids and focus above all on keeping them docile, the class is doomed.

Another thing she has noticed: Behavior has deteriorated over the years, especially when there are family problems but even when there are not. So, six months after the postive-and-negative-consequences sessions, six months after the sixth graders were stunned to see classmates talking back to the teacher and getting away with it, the way the misbehavior of the recalcitrant minority changes the tone of a classroom is part of the landscape. The kids have become acutely aware of the teachers whose threats are empty, who when a boy shouts "Piss!" say, "You can't use that type of language in this class," but he does, again and again. Even when the obstruction doesn't involve cussing, it can be equally insidious, like Eric's at the moment, in the amount of teacher attention it sucks up.

In Eric's case, he is just pissed off. But many middle-school boys know what research has proved: that, the more aggressive and defiant they are, the more popular their peers will perceive them to be. More than anything in the world they want to look cool, and doing extra credit and paying attention in class instead of goofing off do not win points with their pals. Class schedules at Wilde Lake are assigned by a secretary with a click of the mouse—"Too many there, I'll move some here"—so tinderbox combinations occur, of kids who might behave fine when apart. By this late in the year, it has gotten to the point where, even if an event demands audience participation, the immediate instinct of the teachers is to shush everyone.

After misbehaving and being sent to the principal to fill out action forms, which ask, "Why do you think you were sent to the office?" students write things like "Because Mrs. Wright blamed me for talking and I wasn't even talking." The most commonly uttered sentence at Wilde Lake Middle School? "But I didn't do anything!" If you believe the kids, teachers have made up 95 percent of the infractions out of thin air. Sometimes parents back the teachers; just as often, they don't. "It's like *Divorce Court*," one guidance counselor says. "It's never anyone's fault."

The teachers love their kids, love their jobs at the core. But for many it has become beyond hard. After thirty-three years at this, Mr. Wolfe, a seventh-grade social studies teacher, sums it up: "I'm tired of the kids' talking back, the parents' talking back, the lack of interest in learning. It used to be fun. I'm not having fun anymore." And he's one of the teachers the kids really like, and behave for.

In math, Ms. Adams starts a lesson on surface area, but Eric and David are talking on their calculators:

Wassup
Nottin
I want to go home
That's always
I broke the kingpin on my back trucks

Ms. Adams is filling out a sheet on the overhead: How many sides does a cylinder have, how many faces, what's the formula for area. David says, "My stomach hurts." "Mine, too." "What did you have for lunch?"

I got peperroni
Pepporoni—delete. Pepperoni
Uuuhh

Ms. Adams holds up the wooden cylinder and a ruler. "What's the diameter of this circle? The radius is two-point-five."

Dude I hate school

While half the class is making its way to SA = 2B + 2H = 19.63, Eric tells David, "I bought this new CD yesterday, it's so cool. Slipknot. I'm going to make chicken patties and chicken-flavored Oodles of Noodles when I get home." Prisms make their way across the room, and kids measure and calculate, while Eric and David's side conversation segues to looks. Except for his toes, Eric thinks he's "ugly as heck," and it's not low self-esteem to say so if it's true. Most of the class is figuring out the formula at hand, but Eric is typing the alphabet, forward and back. David types the lyrics to "Paranoid" by Green Day.

"What are we supposed to do?" Eric asks David.

David shrugs.

"I can't go to Homework Club today, because I can't stay in school another minute. It's only two o'clock!"

Ms. Adams catches them talking. "This is worth twenty points of classwork," she warns.

"Well, I just lost twenty points."

"Eric, look at what I just wrote."

"That's, like, half the song." Eric and David think about doing the problem the other groups did four problems ago, but then they'd have to erase the song. They try calculating on paper, but they think the diameter is the circumference and the radius is the diameter.

"Two and a half is the circumference, so half of that is one and a half."

"No, 'cause one and a half and one and a half is three, so it's one-point-five." They demonstrate skateboarding moves with the rectangular prism. "Man, I was so close to a kickflip yesterday. Then my truck broke while I was ollieing off the curb."

Eighteen minutes of this, then the bell rings.

Beulah has just found out she's pregnant, and Eric, who has no idea how he'll ever get any work done with a baby around, enjoys coming home to a quiet house while it lasts. Well, if not quiet, at least the kind of noises he is used to. Rap booms from upstairs as Eric sits on the sofa with his math book; Thomas's stereo is so good and so loud, it sounds like there's a live show up there. It's distracting, but Eric figures there's no use asking him to turn it down. *Hey Arnold!* is on TV. "Aw, Jesus, man," Thomas shouts upstairs, as something falls to the ground. Eric writes the answers to eight of his math problems quick and tiny across two lines of torn-out loose-leaf, and skips the other two.

He doesn't know his science assignment and doesn't know the number of Homework Hotline, so he lies down for a while. When he gets up, he calls Shawn for the hotline number and hears page 159, numbers one to nine. One fifty-nine doesn't have any questions, though, so he does the ones on 172. Thomas yells down that he's getting in the shower and leaves instructions on what to say if various girls call. Eric drinks Kool-Aid and eats wings. The phone rings; Thomas comes downstairs and says nobody's coming home tonight. Beulah's gone out with their dad to spend the night in his truck.

Eric plays with his skate, which is missing the middle wheel, and decides to go outside. He blades back and forth across the same seven squares of sidewalk. His skates are so strong, he says, that the only way they'd break is if you landed on them after doing five somersaults from the roof. He likes to fall, because falls are "learnable," meaning they tell you what to do better next time. He likes to do a Macchio, in which he skates to the stoop, jumps, and stops himself on the edge of the first step. Hockey practice starts Saturday. It will be the best day of his life.

Behind the building, as the light fades, younger kids play kickball with a squashy old soccer ball, rutted patches of dirt for bases. Eric joins in, but the kids argue after every other play, and he wearies of trying to defuse the anger. Inside, he soaks up the peace of nobody's-home. He rings his mom at work, gets through after three tries, three times lowering his voice: "Yes, may I have extension seventy-seventy, please? May I speak with Tenacious Epps, please?"

He tells her about the Ping-Pong and the gym clothes. "We'll buy a lock," she says. "Mr. Jackson has better things to do than watch your stuff." He tells her how he likes Ms. Drakes but she's boring, and Tenacious says, "I know. You've just got to deal with it. Middle school is over. This is preparation for high school." When he says, "Ma, it's eighth grade," she says, "Yes, a stepping stone to ninth grade." "Trust me," she always says, about algebra, English, whatever. "I know you don't see the connection, but there is one."

This morning, when Tenacious saw the A + Eric had gotten on an English vocab quiz, she said, "Great! That's awesome. Why can't you do work like this all the time?" She's the best encourager of all time. After he gets off the phone, Eric sees a Hot Wheels commercial and imagines the house they're going to live in one day, maybe as soon as his mom has her next paycheck. He's going to collect Hot Wheels in the basement. Catonsville, he imagines, near his friend James, who says it's a good school even though, after there was a food fight once, lunch was like a prison—no snacks, no fries. If he can't move, Eric at least wants a bomb to blow up Wilde Lake, or, rather, every Howard County school, so they can't find another place to transfer everyone.

Before he walked home today, Eric told Mrs. Conroy about the locker-room incident, and she said he could finish his worksheet at home. But instead he watches *As Told by Ginger* and *Rocket Power* and wrestling, and at eight goes to Safeway for a Three Musketeers. When he returns, he sees the kickball boys pushing each other hard and spinning out in an abandoned red plastic toddler-car. The red looks extra good illuminated by the parking-lot lights. Eric takes a turn. Somewhere there is a sad two-year-old without his wheels, but these boys are thrilled.

After Eric got a second-quarter report card with an F in science, Tenacious said hockey would be over if he didn't bring his grades up. So he starts doing his work, simple as that—not the research paper due in May ("due in May": that means "do in May," right?) but at least what's due the next day. Plus, for the last month Eric's brother Tim, who's taking a semester off from college, has been staying on the couch with him. Whether Eric wants to or not, Tim brings him in the kitchen every night to go over homework. He explains why certain answers are wrong and makes Eric explain why other answers are right. Especially in math, Tim is a good explainer. This feels good, both the doing it right and the doing it with someone.

"I know I should do my work anyway," Eric says, "but it's nice to have somebody care." And it makes a difference. It says so right there on the awards bulletin board:

Ms. Adams' March Student of the Month is Eric Ellis because he has found that working hard—and persevering—has rewards both academically and personally.

For third quarter he gets A's in gym and band and a B in math and brings his English and academic-enrichment grades up, too. Eric jumps around, proclaiming this the best report card ever, though it isn't, and science is still an F. There are GT kids who cry over 89.7's, but most of Eric's classmates say they did well even if they didn't. One girl, bummed about one C, takes a look at Eric's report card and can't believe he's all excited about *that*. "My mom is going to be so happy!" Eric says.

But as quickly as it started, Tim gets into an argument with his father and has to move out. Eric starts tagging along with Ms. Adams as she packs up after class, sitting in her office as she marks grades, sitting in the computer lab as she enters them in the computer, sometimes as late as seven. He still does the work—enough so that roller hockey won't be at risk—but he goes back to doing it sloppily, incompletely, not showing his work. "I don't care," he tells Ms. Adams as he eats her snacks, " 'cause no one else does."

"You've got to do the work," she says, and even lets him do makeup work, against her policy. She doesn't want to tell parents they're making unwise decisions or butt in, but as soon as Eric leaves one evening at six, Ms. Adams calls Tenacious.

"Eric seems really sad about not living with you. He seems very unhappy."

Tenacious says she knows; she wants to change it but doesn't know how. She suggests that Ms. Adams set up a meeting with William. The social worker, whom Eric has told recently that people are teasing him about his weight, comes to the meeting. His seventh-grade reading teacher is there, too.

It's no mystery to the staff that Eric's home situation has a huge amount to do with his academic problems and his behavior, and that worse problems could emerge soon if it doesn't improve. Eric feels cared for at school right now, which helps—and it's because he feels that way that he spends so much time at school when he doesn't have to—but that's no replacement. At home Eric does not feel at all "connected," to use the experts' word.

"He used to always talk about you," the teachers tell Eric's father. The social worker says she's impressed by Eric's maturity, his openness, how family means a lot to him. "Eric is grieving," the teachers tell William. He misses his mom and is sad that he doesn't get one-on-one time with his dad anymore. William says he travels a lot and because of company policy can no longer take Eric with him in the truck on weekends, though that might change back. He says his Masons time and motorcycle time are sacred, his only pure indulgences.

William has sensed Eric's mood changing, but at the same time, he has always figured Eric tells him everything and would say if something was wrong. Whenever William calls home from the road, he asks whoever answers, "Is everything okay?" The answer's always yes, so he has no idea the tension is building. Eric feels deserted by his dad and deserted by his mom and deserted by his brothers, but he loves them too much to get mad at them—so he gets mad at Beulah. He complains in the meeting that Beulah doesn't want to cook or clean. He scrubs the floor, doesn't feel important, doesn't feel like his housework is acknowledged. Eric talks about a recent time when he asked Beulah for a hug and she wouldn't give it, and about the assignment he wanted to put on the refrigerator.

"Sometimes I wanna say stuff," Eric says, "but I don't wanna say stuff, 'cause I don't want to hurt anyone's feelings."

William feels caught in the middle. "Son, you can tell me anything."

"But I can't tell *her* anything. Sometimes I don't get her."

It's not like anything is solved, but it feels good to open up. Oh, the teachers tell William, one other thing. Eric really wants to be taken to skating. And so the conversation moves to the logistics of driving Eric on Friday nights, as if a ride to the roller rink will solve his problems.

Chapter eighteen

another survivor of the woods

Even though at his house Jimmy and Will play MechWarrior 4: Reclaim Your Blood right and SSX Tricky, and at Will's house they tell ghost stories with flashlights under their chins and wrestle, even though whoever's the guest always fights his parents when it's time to go home, even though they can discuss for ages whether you can drown in your own spit and whether your balls can pop while you climb the rope in PE, even though the photo of the two of them still smiles over both boys as they sleep, Jimmy doesn't put Will on his cabin-request form for the sixth-grade camping trip.

After all, Will still brags that he knows where Andorra is and makes Jimmy feel bad about his grades and stuffs his gray binder so fat and heavy that he spends all day scooching it up with his right thigh. Jimmy has added Will to his teasing list at school, while he himself has discovered that a well-timed belch in music class makes popular boys laugh.

"I'm not going to be friends with Will," he says, "because he's not going to be cool. Unless he's the first person to go up on one of those rocket things, and he's on TV and famous."

Jimmy does get Rich Stoessel in his cabin. Bad enough the boys have found out Camp Ramblewood is a nudist colony in the summer, but to have to spend two nights in a cabin with someone they're sure is gay? Because they don't want Rich taking pictures of them naked, the group makes a rule: no going in the bathroom while someone is showering.

As they stand around a science-room table the day before the trip, gluing felt letters to their cabin banner, one of the boys announces, "Rich has no dick."

"He probably has a dick," Ben says.

"But a small one," Jimmy says. "I'm so much taller than you it's, like, not even funny."

"You're so much *what*?"

"I'm so much taller than you it's, like, not even funny. Stand up."

"No."

"Why not?"

"I don't like being made to feel short."

"You can't take any pain. You can't even take a spider bite." He pinches Ben's skin with his thumb and middle finger and presses his index finger in.

"Don't!"

In the room next door, a tube of fabric paint squirts all over Mia's pants leg. Her eyes tear up, and Lily comes to the rescue with her gym shorts. Of course she put Mia and Beth on her cabin-request form. Mia told her friends she put them all down, even though the teacher said to list only two, and winds up with Alexandra and not Lily. Lily is unhappy about this, but she's glad at least to be with Beth, and glad to see Mia out on the soccer field wearing her very own shorts.

The next morning there are four buses for kids and two for luggage, which includes many hair dryers and stuffed animals and Jimmy's Batman pillow and even some blankies. Lily and Beth are first in line, and behind them is Mia, who has decided to sit by herself. They take the very last seats, which they never get to do when eighth graders are around. They make HELLO signs on loose-leaf and press them to the back window, so Jimmy and his friends can see. The boys sing "Ninety-Nine Bottles of Beer," but the health teacher stops them, so instead they strum air guitars and make up goofy rhymes and get truckers to honk.

When they arrive at Camp Ramblewood, nobody is nude, fortunately, and the activities begin right away. Two dads lead Jimmy's group down a path to the confidence course and explain: Cross a wobbly log suspended between two trees, hug the tree, and scooch around to a rope, cross that while holding on to a more flaccid rope, swing through a set of five tires suspended just far apart enough to be tricky but not impossible, traverse a series of ropes hung like U's and then another set of loose double ropes, walk a very high log (this one at least secure), then scale a rope web to a platform way up in a tree. If your feet touch the ground, start over.

Two boys and a girl go before Jimmy, and from his perspective they have no trouble. Some people scooch across the first log on their butts, Colin dashes across it, and Jimmy crawls on his tummy, getting it on his first try, along with stains on his long white T-shirt. He makes it through the first rope okay, nicks the ground twice from the tires but nobody sees, and then gets to the ropes crossed like an X.

He freezes. He leans backward, his belly slight but visible under his shirt. "I'm scared," Jimmy tells the dad. "I can't do it. I'm scared."

It looked so easy for everyone else. It always looks easy for everyone else.

Times like this, it's clear to Jimmy that God all of a sudden has anointed a privileged section of the sixth-grade jocks, and he is not one of them. The second he misses a catch in kickball he's yelled at, and the second he misses a kick the pitcher says, "You can't kick!" "You can't pitch!" he shouts back. Flag football gives him cramps, and when he misses a high spiral off the tip of his fingers, a girl—a girl!—says, "Bum!"

"I'm not a bum."

"You should be glad I'm making you something."

Jimmy quit his lacrosse team last month because he didn't like getting hit or hitting back, and went to Play It Again Sports to trade his stick and pads for a skateboard. In floor hockey there's always this one boy who appoints himself center forward, plays the whole court, yells at everyone who does anything minutely wrong, which often enough includes Jimmy. As for his plan to start running, it turns out Jimmy is dog-tired when he gets home from school. And, typical of a boy in puberty, lazy in ways he never used to be. At soccer, he's not bad but isn't aggressive, is only half in the game. Before practice he prays for rain and, though he is afraid of storms, blesses the lightning that eventually arrives.

It's not like he wants to be a jock. There's something appealing about how comfortable they are in their bodies, but you know what's sad about them? They're so cocky that they drive crazy. "A lot of them die in car accidents," Jimmy says. "It pisses me off."

Still and all, it would be nice to be able to cross these goddamn ropes, since everyone's watching.

"Yes, you can," the dad says.

I'm gonna fall, Jimmy thinks, I should start lifting weights and doing curl-ups. Out loud, barely, he says, "I can do it. I can do it."

He inches across the low rope, gripping the high rope tight, wobbling. Wobbling. His arms feel weak. The lighter boys had it easier, the lacrosse boys had it easier, maybe he never should have quit the team.

"I can do it."

Even though Jimmy Schissel may never be a Jock with a capital "J," there is a part of him that can take his blue Mongoose around the cul-de-sac three times in 27.4 seconds. There is a part of him that once in a while magically catches passes in the end zone. There is a part of him that, when the spiky-haired little neighbor boy mouths off, takes chase, sending the eight-year-old tearing away in fear. There is a part of him that last week couldn't keep himself from checking with his lacrosse stick in gym class. When Darnell checked back, Jimmy kept going, and when Darnell said "Fuck you, stupid," even though he knew it might turn every black kid in the school against him, Jimmy took a swing.

On the ropes a part of Jimmy still wobbles. And the other part impels himself across.

Then—the tall log. "I'm scared," he announces, and inches forward on his stomach, his blue surf shorts riding up. Slowly, he makes it across, and leaps to the wobbly web of ropes. If I drop, he thinks, nothing will be holding me but the net, and that will hit the ground, too. Some kids scaled this in four swift scampers, but Jimmy Schissel has not yet been bitten by a magic spider, and it takes him a while.

"Another survivor of the woods," he declares from atop the platform, a thicket of leaves crowning his head.

The buzzword for outdoor education is "team-building." Remove students, teachers, and parents from the normal school atmosphere, let them unify into a cohesive group, and in the meantime have some educational fun in a world some kids never get to explore. In several ways, the planned bonding takes place. But, just like in a Victorian costume drama, being in the country lays everything bare, and inhibitions collapse. Some teams fall apart.

At the arts-and-crafts table Lily is knotting pink, blue, green, and purple embroidery floss into a bracelet for Mia. Mothers sit in the shade nearby, sharing snippets of love that their boys have allotted—he hugged me in front of everyone at the buses this morning! he made pancakes with me! "Last week," one mom says, "I came home and there was a bouquet of roses on the kitchen table from my eighth grader, and he wrote a note. He said, 'Mommy, thank you for helping me on the *Odyssey.*' "

"Awwww," the other moms say, jealous of the note, not the flowers.

One mother says that her boy, Joe, has gotten moodier, that "he is the one on the outside now," but she doesn't want to be one of those mothers who call and complain, and anyway, "they're nice boys." On the other side of camp, on a rolling green lawn, the nice boys play tag with Joe around an old blue metal swing set.

"One two three NOT IT!"

"You're It."

"No fair. I heard Paul last."

"You're It. Just be It. I swear I will beat you up."

During freeze tag with movie titles, they quickly run out of options, after everyone has tried *Star Wars Episode II: Attack of the Clones* at least twice. (Memories don't go far past *The Sandlot*, and *The Lion King* is as old-fashioned as it gets.) Jimmy drops to a squat with a movie title every time It nears, rather than run. The boys trap Joe on the slide and decide he's It. Every time he tags someone, they change the rules to somehow invalidate the tag. A dad watches from a porch nearby, but from the middle distance the torture is invisible.

"Get Joe!" Jimmy says. "You're not It yet." Somebody bangs the slide, and the metal reverberates under Joe's feet. "You're not It yet."

"I didn't know."

"You didn't know? That's brilliant."

"You have to count, stupid. You can't catch him really fast. It's not hide-and-seek, it's freeze tag."

"Oh my gosh, Joe, you're going in the wrong area."

"He can't even get up the slide!"

"I'm not playing," Joe says.

"Yes, you are."

"No, I'm not."

"You're a wuss."

Joe heads off and bumps Jimmy on the way.

"He kicked Jimmy!" Joe goes off to his cabin. "Did you guys see Joe last year in the music room? He was yelling, 'I quit everything!' He was crying and throwing stuff."

Lily's cabin, which they've named "The Bubbles," is stuffy, but the girls don't want to open the wooden shutters because then ghosts will come through the window screens. Not ghosts "like *wooo-hoooo*," one girl explains, wiggling her fingers, but, rather, "like spirits." Not ghosts that will kill you, just ghosts that will possess your body and loot your belongings. There has got to be some reason for the blood on the ceiling.

Bugs—they're creepy, too. The girls ask each other to stand sentry by the shower in case of spiders—"I'll wear my swimsuit, don't worry." By day's end the stories about what's transpired in the cabins have intensified in the telling: the cockroaches that sallied forth from the drain during someone's shower, the frog that jumped from the toilet drain, one girl's nosebleed oozing from her eyes so bad they were going to pop out of their sockets, the tarantula as big as a saucer that Mrs. Lewinsohn killed.

Besides Lily and Beth, the five swimmers are in the cabin, all of whom Lily likes. It might be that, it might be a sugar high from the warehouse-club sacks of Jolly Ranchers and Twizzlers Beth's mom and the other chaperone brought—whatever the reason, she is a cyclone whenever she's inside these wooden walls. When visitors see the loot splayed out on the cots, Lily says, "Hey, our candy, not yours!" When the girls do the cancan and sing, "We're the Bubbles, the slippery sticky Bubbles," as Beth and Lily blow soap bubbles, Lily stops and says, "I stink like shit." She puts scented lotion in her armpits. When she changes, she declares, "Close your eyes, Lily's going down!"

That night at the assembly, the talent-show acts—a rock trio, a Britney Spears dance, two piano solos, a long skit about a birthday party, a house-stopping dance to "Thriller," a soul trio—receive honest and sustained applause, though each group rushes off the stage when done, embarrassed. The teachers don clown suits and wigs and goofy shoes for a completely zany version of *Cinderella*, which brings the kids to the edge of their seats. They say they are glad they didn't have to make "idiot fools" of themselves, but that's exactly what they loved so much about their teachers for one night.

Back in the cabin Lily nurses her sunburn. "This lotion has no freakin' aloe!"

"Lily," Beth's mom says, "I'm gonna spank you."

Beth says, "Lindsey thinks Lily's a lesbian, because she saw her giving me a piggyback ride."

Lily marches around the cabin comparing her legs with everyone's: "Mine are sexier." On Beth's bed, the two sing, "Apples and bananas in my soup, loopdy loopdy loopdy loop." Lily lies on her back with a pillow between her knees, kicking her legs, clapping her hands. She lets out a huge belch. She flips back and forth. She stomps to the other side of the cabin. "Bethie said I peed in the bed!" She leaps from bed to bed.

"Don't bounce on the beds," Beth's mom says.

"I didn't bounce, I leapt. Oh, pillow, how I love you, pillow. I could kiss you, pillow."

"Please, Lily."

She bangs her leg. "Shit."

"She just said the 's' word!"

"Lily, stop cussing."

Lily gives another sturdy belch. "Belches are loud and burps are silent. Farts are loud and poots are silent."

"I'm going to get dressed," Maddy says. "That means if my towel falls don't look at my butt."

"Drawers have two holes in them," Lily continues, "for the boy's thing to go through. Underwear has elastic around the waist."

"What's the difference between Lily and Beth?"

"Lily's much more politer and Beth's more bossier."

"What's the difference between boys and girls?"

"Boys have one thing that sticks out straight and two things that"— Lily cups her hands.

"What's the difference between socks and shoes?"

And on and on, until the chaperones shut it down. Lily announces good nights around the cabin: "Good night, Abby!" "Good night, Lily." "Good night, Beth!" "Good night, Lily." "Good night, Dale!" "Good night, Lily." Six more times, until finally she is silent, though far from asleep.

Four cabins away, Alexandra and a girl named Lynn won't shut up. "Be quiet!" girls yell from the other side of the cabin partition. "We're trying to go to sleep!" Finally, after a half-hour, one of the mothers says, "Cut it out, you guys." In the morning, their side of the cabin tries to sleep in and the other side makes noise. They tell them to shut up, as if they have that right, and Mia goes over to make a truce. She is shooed away.

The second night, things get bizarre. One girl says another girl took her bandana, as if there is no possibility in the universe they could own the same bandana, and tensions are so high the teachers separate them at dinner. Someone started a rumor that Valerie said she was going to dump her boyfriend and go out with Devon, and her friends are desperate to diffuse the situation before she gets beaten up. Devon would have killed for this kind of attention last year. "But now," he says, "you don't know how annoying this is." Valerie keeps her eye out for anyone who looks like she's flirting with Devon ("Oh no, not Alexandra!"). In one cabin a boy is dancing and another boy says, "That's my move." "No, it's mine." Poom, there's a punch, and the kid who did the hitting packs up and heads into the dark, where a teacher sees him during a cabin check and he is sent home. Abigail Werner's cabinmates had left her out of their talent-show act, saying the dance steps were too confusing. She stews over it and when she gets back to the cabin tries to hold it in as long as possible, which isn't that long, and says, "You didn't let me in the cabin song because I'm white."

"Are you calling me racist?" asks Felicia, her best friend since second grade.

"Yes."

Whoops. She's mad at herself for saying that and winds up crying all night, and her mom, who is chaperoning, doesn't feel comfortable stepping in, and on the other side of the cabin the girls listening to the fight complain of stomachaches and headaches, cry because there is no night-light, beg to go home. Ms. Thomas sends three girls from Abigail's cabin to Mia's, where Alexandra has moved out because she felt like being with Tamika ("I guess she doesn't like me that much now," Mia tells her mom), and Carla's crying because she's never been away from her mom, much less in a place like this, and Lynn's leaving, too, because she was pretending she was struck blind, even though a chaperone who happened to be an ophthalmologist said she was fine, and she miraculously regained her sight for the talent show and lost it again afterward, at which point everyone, including Mia's mom, Leigh, had to help her around. The teachers told her if she was blind she should lie down in the infirmary, and she said that would give her a headache, so they said, "Okay, you're going home." At ten-thirty Leigh Reilly is packing Lynn's bags in the dark, and Mia is wondering if her cabin situation could be any worse.

When Lily arrives home the next day, her mother asks how the trip was.

"Fine."

"How was your cabin?"

"Fine."

"How was Mia's cabin?"

"Better."

spring

why is it that when we are mad at someone we tend to wait right by the phone for them to call and tell us that they are ok but they never call and you mad at them and you

she started humping me!
and i was like :-o

It comes in the spring sure as tulips, the time when sixth graders turn into middle schoolers. The dramas that unfolded on the camping trip weren't a simple case of cabin fever; they were a harbinger of things to come.

It takes Mr. Vega, who student-taught last year only in the fall, by surprise: the snobbiness, the cattiness, the spleen. They'll just announce, "I don't like Jordan, Mr. Vega." A girl comes up to him after school and says, "Mr. Vega, the rumors are true." Please, he thinks, don't let someone be pregnant. "Alicia and Julie and them are talking about me behind my back." One girl issues Mr. Vega an ultimatum: Let me switch from clarinet to sax, or I'll quit. He kinda wishes he'd said, "Okay, quit band," for all the trouble it's caused. After making the switch, she gets to practice in the hall with another girl, and they goof off for the first fifteen minutes, at least. When he calls her on it she shoots back, "Not fair," or "Whatever."

At least fifteen kids ask to go to the bathroom during each half-hour practice. They stand up as if sleepwalking and head across the room; they stop in the middle of a song while the other fifty kids play and say, "My folder is broken," or "Can I show you my practice chart?" The trombones are suddenly paranoid that someone is moving their music. "I guess their hormones are changing so fast," Mr. Vega says, "they can't remember anything."

"They're getting crazy," Ms. Thomas says. The last two months of the year, fights break out, physical and emotional. Friendship groups split apart—for the moment, anyway. Your supposed best friend invites you to her lake house and then the weekend comes and she's at the lake with two other girls. Another friend is mad because you both thought to bring cupcakes for the reading teacher's birthday, another friend is mad because you said you do the Cha-Cha Slide better, and another friend is all of a sudden saying you insult her too much, even though you've been insulting each other all your lives, as a joke. This girl has removed you from the "I wanna say hi to all my friends" part of her IM profile, and you get so mad you can't remember why.

"It seems like everyone is ganging up on me these days and taking sides, like I'm a nobody," one seventh grader says. "Like, one day we'll be really cool and hanging out, and the next day one of them is all mad at me for saying the wrong thing." The girls are wondering if it's worth it to be popular, if having thirty "friends" you talk to only in school but who always pull you into some sort of drama is any better than the way it used to be, when they each had three good friends, three true friends. It seems small to an outsider, but these spells are huge to the girls who suffer them. They will make up in weeks, days, hours; the friendships are restored and the cruelty disappears. The anxiety, however, is there to stay. Even if a girl makes new friends, it doesn't compensate for the intense crisis of confidence she's endured, a crisis that her athletic skills or her intelligence or her good relationship with her family can mitigate but not erase. Her mother, who used to know her all daughter's friends, who orchestrated their play dates, may ask why those girls don't call anymore. She shrugs. "They're just jealous of you," her mom says. "You're so wonderful." This means nothing to her in the scheme of things, and she kind of wants to explain the whole thing to her mom, but at the same time she doesn't, because she wants to handle it on her own.

God, this sort of thing drives Ms. Thomas nuts. "Best friends one day and the next day they hate each other. And the girls just don't let it go. Boys, if they have an issue, they get it out and it's over. Girls, it can linger for quite a while. So dramatic. Ugh. They're looking for ways to be more independent, they see slights that aren't there, they're overly sensitive. That can be a bit wearing." Girls and their meanness are all over the literature right now, the subject of the hottest sessions at educational conferences and the hottest books in stores (with diagrams and code names for where people stand in the social web). Consultants visit schools to help with "clique-busting." Ms. Thomas attempts her own clique-busting, but the effort is Sisyphean. For example, she convenes what she thinks is a successful meeting of a group of seventh-grade girls who are getting in each other's business and yelling at each other for getting in their business, but an hour later, at lunch, one of the girls is ragging another about a fight her little sister got in and she storms out of the cafeteria yelling "Shut! The! Fuck! Up!"

Chaos like this isn't Mia's or Lily's style. Their modus operandi, when they are annoyed, is gossip, though only so much as they consider good-natured and harmless. Gossip is the glue that holds together many middle-school friendships, a conflict-avoidant way to let people know what bugs you about them—word almost always gets back, after all—but in such an indirect fashion that the gossiper remains protected, and so does the friendship. Alone, Mia and Lily discuss which of their friends are mean and which are posers, in that they copy everyone else (as if they'd be spared a hard time if they didn't).

Mia spends as many as four hours a day on the Internet, instant-messaging the two hundred kids on her buddy list. Usually kids' profiles include lists of inside jokes, and many are meant for Mia:

> **Mimi~DOGS DOGS . . . lol . . . chic yet humorus, sophisti-cated yet sexy. . . . 123456 . . . u ripped my jacket!! . . . say it like u mean it. . . . im a bluie!!! . . . she grabbed ur butt @ da rink! ooooo we have soo many more insides.**

Mia's insides:

> **lisa and alexandra—Cheerleading! Dancing! Guuurls! haha lylas!***
> *lisa—oh too many insides!!:-/ lylas!*
> **Lunch table—the most beautiful pringle display i have seen in my WHOLE life!!**

alexandra—she started humping me! and i was like :-O

If Lily ever went online—she rarely does; she has maybe thirty girls on her IM list, "but they don't even talk to me"—she might see that her affections for Mia have become an inside joke among the girls: "She started humping me!" "She grabbed ur butt . . . !" This relevation serves as a litmus test: In elementary school we goofed all over each other, but we're in middle school now, we're being watched, is this okay? And in some way it's not about Lily at all. It's about appearing to know a lot of good juice without appearing to be the one who spread it. It's about discovering who stands where in the organizational chart of life. It's about turning something uncomfortable into a joke. It's about the seductive power of having people listen to you, of having this thing you started become an *inside*!

This kind of gossip could wreck a girl for good—it doesn't take much at this age—but it never gets back to Lily, it's not really about her anyway, and nobody shuts her out. Mia and Lily are true friends, after all, and Mia has no desire to ruin that.

Lily knows that her best friend has several worlds she will never be a part of, that Mia doesn't *need* the relationship as much as she does, but that's the price of friendship with the popular girl. With her other friends Mia plays sports, she kicks around the neighborhood, she talks online. She had thirty people—twice as many as Lily even *knows*, she figures—to the roller rink for her birthday party in February. The present Lily carefully picked out, a stuffed bunny with buck teeth and a pink T-shirt that says HUGS in little rhinestones, looked so insignificant on the huge gift-wrapped pile. Tonya was there, a girl from Clemens who goes to a different middle school, skating around loud and bossy. Mia doesn't quite comprehend that she's popular, but Tonya, she knows, *she's* popular. Lily avoided her, because a few weeks earlier they all went to the mall and Tonya wouldn't go to the store Lily wanted to, so she practically cried until Mia went with her, and then they were late for their ride home. Alexandra said she'd be at the party but she didn't show up, which happens with her sometimes. Even though two months ago Mia agreed with Lily that no sixth-grade boys are cute, four boys were at her party, though they stayed away from the girls. Lily and Beth kept to themselves, too, without much to say, and during cake time watched as the other girls noisily plunged sporks in their hair.

When school lets out early, Mia sometimes goes to the Giant with her other friends. They never invite Lily, so she misses out on teasing the boys by the dried-up fountain, gossiping about whose hair is ugly, dancing with stuffed Easter Bunnies in the Seasonal aisle, going back to Mia's rec room to watch a man discuss his diaper obsession and a woman practically rape her sister on *Jerry Springer*.

"We live less than a mile away from the Giant," Lily says. "But if I'm not invited, then I won't ask."

Another other world of Mia's is that all of a sudden Alexandra is back in the picture as if she never disappeared. Lily barely acknowledges her. "I couldn't come to *Peter Pan*," Alexandra nicely tells Lily, who turns the other way. At lunch Alexandra says, "I'm going to Bingo Night with my mom and Mia." Lily says she already invited Mia, who turned her down for a soccer game, and later rolls her eyes and tells Mia, "*Alexandra* said you're going to bingo." The way Lily sees it, she's been paying her dues all year with Mia, and Alexandra hasn't. How fair is that for her to hop right back in? The way Mia sees it, she's friends with both, and she and Alexandra had a lot of fun together playing stupid-dress-up not long ago, purple lipstick all over their mouths and dresses hanging from their legs. At the end of the play date, Alexandra lent Mia her best teddy bear. In math, when they can work with partners, Mia never moves and Alexandra and Lily come to her, one on either side.

Lily realizes maybe she needs to be accepting of Alexandra. Not just because of Mia, but because of one of the life lessons you start to learn when you're twelve: Sometimes, *not* being friends with a person can take up as much of your psychic energy as being friends with her. She may resent Alexandra, but Lily, less emotionally sophisticated than her friends, less aware of what her values are and how to stand by them, is a pleaser. If it pleases Mia for her to get along with Alexandra, she'll suck it up. At lunch Lily offers Alexandra her chocolate chips, and at recess they practice a cheerleading routine. Mia invites both Lily and Alexandra to sleep over one night, and they're all excited, but then her dad makes plans over hers, so she has to cancel.

Avy doesn't get it. "I can't imagine Mia chose to be friends with

Alexandra again," she says. She and Jack are not subtle about letting their daughter know what they find irritating about Alexandra, mostly reflecting what Lily tells them and how she always comes home cranky after spending time with her. But Avy realizes that it wouldn't be productive to invade, that Lily's friendship choices may be annoying but they're not dangerous.

Parents have to accept that their kids will shed some friends, gain others, and their best role is to help their children figure out what's motivating their choices and remind them of that. You don't want to manipulate a child's friendships, turn her into a hothouse flower too precious to grow on her own, become part of the problem. You don't want to get upset over your kid's friendships, because your kid, upset to see you upset, will stop sharing. And you certainly don't want to choose ignorance.

The middle ground is to act as a supportive coach, on her team but never part of the game yourself. Sneak through windows of opportunity to help your child see patterns and connections ("Didn't Andrea blow you off like that last summer?"), discuss what she does and doesn't like about her friends, let her know what are okay ways to be treated and what are not. Rather than discourage the friendships that feel wrong, which backfires, encourage the ones that feel right. "Do you think Dana wants to come to Six Flags with us?"

Remembering all the while that you don't see everything, so you don't have a perfect read on who's worthy and who's not.

As a goal, trying to improve your status in a social group isn't always complementary to nurturing the most rewarding friendships. Lily's affections for Mia don't abate—she will always think Mia's cabin is better, no matter how much fun she has in hers—but she's realizing she'll never win that contest. Nobody will win; Mia is too kind to alienate any of her many best friends. The asymmetry Mia and Lily have in their relationship is commonplace, but it's good for a child, less stressful, to have friendships that are as close as theirs but more reciprocal. Reciprocity, knowing you are both committed to each other, is the hallmark of friendship, after all. Which is why it's nice to see her friendship with Beth blossom. "We didn't know each other at all," Lily says, "and now we're like best friends." She corrects herself: "We're really good friends."

In Lily's eyes Mia is still first, then Beth, then her instant third-best friend, Ashley, though she hasn't spent time with Ashley since her birthday party, and never one-on-one. Lily still asks people, "Do you like my haircut? It reminds you of Mia," and at the spring dance has a Polaroid taken only with Mia, and on the playground hangs out with Beth only as a second resort. But her new, equal friendship is causing some change: When Mia's not around, Lily has been coming out of her shell, acting more like she does in the neighborhood, emboldened, like the way she took over the cabin on the camping trip.

It's hard to say if how a child interacts with her friends at age twelve has much to do with how she will when she's thirty, but certainly experiences have impact. A shy girl can find a niche and hide, but the fact that Lily has learned to cope with people of higher social status, watched them operate at a higher level of social skill, will help her later, and is helping her now. She has more people to hang out with than at the beginning of sixth grade, far more than in Louisiana, and is more comfortable opening up. While doing BigTop Math in the computer lab, she narrates, "What's seven times seven? Okay. Six times nine. I'm stupid right now. What's four times eight? Isn't that thirty-two? What's eight times seven? Isn't that fifty-six? What's eight times eight? How many do you have, Maddy?"

She gets back at Abigail Werner by taking her sweet time at her locker, talking with Beth.

"Hurry up," Abigail says.

"I don't have to hurry up. You always talk at your locker, so why can't I?"

Abigail says, "If I get five late notes I have to go to Saturday school."

"It's your problem that you get late notes."

With Beth, "I can talk to her whenever I need," Lily says, "because her friends, they don't bug her or hang around her when I talk to her." At recess Lily and Beth do dances Lily made up and one-handed cartwheels. She looks forward to swimming in Beth's outdoor pool when it gets warm. "It used to be 'Mia' all the time," Avy says. "Now it's 'Mia and Beth.'" Which is fine, nice even, except for the fashion obsession that seems to have rubbed off. Clothes are one thing Lily loves about Beth, who can fit into extra smalls at Forever 21. The Children's Place doesn't cut it anymore. Lily comes home from school and tells Avy, "We have to go to Limited Too—there's this shirt I saw in the catalogue and it's like this, thick right here on this strap, and it goes to here, and it has a tiny strap right here that's removable, and it has American flags—"

"Who had the catalogue?"

"Beth." Always Beth now, setting the trends, on top of it all. Beth has two sets of parents, and Mia's dad is a professor and her mom a dentist, Avy tells Lily, so that's why Beth can shop from catalogues and Mia can buy new sneakers even though her old ones are still very white and too big, kicked off easily on the playground.

When Avy's underwires snap in her only two bras, Lily accompanies her to the mall, and, walking by the shoe store, she says, "I need sandals," even though she left five pairs of shoes by the stairs the other day, including three pairs of sandals.

"I just bought you sandals."

"You didn't buy them—I paid for some," Lily says, having chipped in for one-quarter of one pair. "How many pairs are you buying me for back to school?"

That's four months away, and anyway, Avy says, it's not a matter of how many they're buying but, rather, how many she needs. As opposed to Gabrielle, who says, "I don't need everything fancy name-brand, but could I have just one pair of Gap shorts?" Lily wants a new tankini from Limited Too, because her one-pieces from Sam's Club "aren't in fashion." Lily has six short-sleeved shirts, but she wishes they didn't fit, because there's a new style this year. "Roxy—their shirts are more like classic modern. They look better—funkier. And not just plain. 'Cause my clothes sorta stick out from everyone else."

Beth doesn't have any problem with Lily's clothes. What she does think is strange is how Lily and Mia say they're best friends even when she's the one who plays with Lily all the time these days. "I don't care," Beth says, "but it's weird, because Mia barely talks to Lily, and then she says I'm her second-best friend." When they get together, though, Lily is just as spastic as she is with Mia, and though she wouldn't admit it later, has just as much fun.

One day at recess, Lily tells Beth, "My brother's friend Matt is coming over and my sister's friend Mara is coming over and she's annoying, so my mom said I could invite someone, and I invited Mia and she's busy, so I'm inviting you." At Lily's house they dress up her neighbor Rick in a skirt and blue eye makeup. Lily decides he has a crush on Mia because of the way his lips tauten when she shouts her name in his face: "Mia Reilly! Mia Reilly! Mia Reilly!" Inside, Lily belches loud and Beth says, "That's all you ever do." They turn the video camera on and dance, take close-ups of butts, giggle, wrestle, tangle themselves up in each other, do their special handshake (wave a hand around your head, grab hands, jump up and down like maniacs), sing the H-A-P-P-Y song, and after they've tumbled to the ground in exhaustion, they face the camera, which is propped up on a chair.

"This is Lily."

"And her old pal Beth."

chapter twenty

now you have the persentage
of your love

When kissing games escalate from peck to French, Jackie begs out. Still, by the end of seventh grade, she has come to love the boy-girl party and its rituals: movies she could never watch at home, junk food the girls will only eat once the boys have left, so they don't look like pigs, post-party dishing about spin-the-bottle. They discuss whose tongues were slow and whose fast, whose moved horizontally and whose vertically. "I felt dirty," one girl usually says, and the rest agree. There's something distasteful about making out with guys you don't even like, or have never even talked to. Watching is better than kissing, sort of. Couples are allowed to opt out with impunity, but there's always one single boy who won't play, which gets him teased (and makes him wonder why it appeals to everyone but him). The guys crack the lesbian joke every time the bottle lands in a girl-girl combo. How can boys like the idea of two girls kissing when *they* don't like the idea of two boys kissing? Maybe, just maybe, they could deal with three-way kisses if it were two boys.

By the time you're thirteen, some very grown-up concepts have probably started to tumble around in your mind. In Jackie they don't take full shape, she is not a sexual being yet, but her sexuality is emerging. She has some of the vocabulary, less of the knowledge, and even less of a desire actually to partake in the activities she and her peers joke about constantly. Still, phrases float in the air, and from listening to other people she knows what some mean ("giving head"), though not others ("blow job"). Before social studies, Anton asks what he could put on his penis when he gets head, and Jackie makes suggestions. While Jackie is playing at her friend Meghan's, they come across a videotape called *Amazing Penises*. For five minutes it plays, and Jackie sees what she's never seen before, things being done that almost nobody has seen before. She's neither intrigued nor exactly grossed out. Her mind just goes blank.

At the same time, Jackie's behavior is changing some, and as spring blossoms, Sara Taylor can see fourteen coming. Five minutes before she needs to leave for a trampoline meet, Jackie knocks on the bathroom door, clutching a crusty old tube of purple mascara. "Mom, because it's the Cherry Blossom Invitational, can I put purple streaks in my hair?" Sara says no. The next week, Jackie comes home from school with purple streaks Leslie gave her, and Sara gives her the "What the hell were you thinking?" look. Whether it's renewing *YM* or her strange pleas to take cheerleading, which she hated ten minutes before, or wearing Leslie's stud collar—Leslie is trouble, they think, but what can they do?—Jackie's parents are suddenly always having to shut her up with, "Jacquelyn, you're on the gray line."

"Sometimes," her mother says, "she just doesn't know when to stop."

Jackie's teachers are getting that idea, too. In reading she gets all goofy during her presentation, and her teacher has to tell her to stop running chalk lines back and forth across the blackboard. By day's end the social-studies teacher wishes Jackie wore a muzzle. In science the kids get in partners to cut out little ghost monsters, flipping coins to determine their recessive and dominant traits and genotypes and phenotypes, then breed them with each other. Jackie tap-dances. She bounces. She has named her ghost thing Joe.

"Nobody likes Joe," she says. "Joe was on *Blind Date*. He was rejected on *Blind Date*."

"He's so sexy," Leslie says.

Trista comes up to breed, and they squish their monsters together. Leslie does, too.

"Hey, Mr. Shifflett," Jackie says, "we started mating but Leslie put hers on top. Joe likes to be on top."

"They're standing up. Hey, they're taking a shower."

"Ladies!"

"They're taking a shower because they're *dirty*."

"No!"

As the spring dance starts, on the one hand Jackie is scared boys are going to freak her, and on the other hand she hopes boys will freak her. She likes that little circle that forms, the way everyone says, "Go, Jackie! Go, Jackie!" and she thinks, "Go, me! Go, me!" Who would want to dance the old way anyway? "Do the Monkey"?

Teachers approach each group from time to time, trying to diffuse the magnetic force pulling the kids together, stopping the mosh pit from taking casualties, but the sentries are imperfect. When Lil' Bow Wow sings, "You run through my mind like all the time," Jackie's got her groove on. Her hair runs down her red T-shirt and her hands run through her hair, top to bottom. She piles it atop her head, lets it fall, twirls her hands in the air. You wouldn't have thought she had hips until you see them swivel, getting closer and closer to the ground, her jeans tight and pocketless, this nonsexual body looking all of a sudden very sexual. A nearby couple get their freak on, fast, and Jackie says, "Oh my God," hand to her braces. After the shock, she smiles.

One boy has six girls freaking on him, including Leslie and Kristina. Then the music switches and the children become children, clapping and stamping to "If You're Happy and You Know It." Adam appears, sweaty from the effort of pushing his way into groups of dancing girls. He's not having much luck or much fun: "I can't get any ass or I'm in trouble."

Truth be told, Adam doesn't actually ever "get ass"; by his own admission, 90 percent of his boasts are empty. And Jackie feels no more inclined to make out with anyone than she did before getting her groove on. But it's still worrisome, what this supposed freeing of sexuality for girls and boys portends as they grow older, as they actually do get involved in relationships. *If* they get involved in relationships. The idea that a boy can practically hump any one of a large group of girls from behind on the dance floor, that he can call her a ho with impunity, that she thinks it's funny to be flashed, unthinkingly indulges his conversations about blow jobs, that they both agree that blow jobs aren't really sex, gives lie to the conventional wisdom that somehow girls have the power now. When they finally do get together, will boys and girls meet face to face? Or will the girls be on their knees?

Plenty of social scientists study teenage sex, but few study romance—too frivolous, too fickle. So little is known of how relationships affect development, whether the crushes you have in middle school say anything about your romantic adulthood. The kids themselves think that it all could be just a phase, that it doesn't predict anything, though they occasionally speculate on who will become a stripper and who will become gay.

Studies have shown that kids who initiate dating earlier are more likely to become sexually active sooner and have more partners; those with lots of sexual partners misbehave more in other ways, too. But researchers haven't discovered anything predictive about crushes per se. Some girls who are totally boy-crazy in middle school remain overly focused on boys, but others become very self-possessed by high school. Usually these are the kids with solid family structures; research has shown that the stability of a child's relationship with his parents predicts the stability and quality of his romantic relationships in adolescence.

And the quality of the relationship makes a difference in how much stress it induces. Of Jackie's friends, the girls with the most unhealthful attachments to boys tend to be the ones who developed early, the ones whose parents don't have real authority in the house—even if they think they're strict on the small things, they don't pay attention to the hours she spends online with strangers. They tend to be the ones whose parents aren't married, who bring boyfriends or girlfriends around, who engage in needy romantic relationships themselves, giving the idea that it's all about courtship, about pleading, about conflict.

The most romantically balanced of Jackie's friends are the ones, including her, whose parents keep track of whom they hang out with and control their time. They have close, realistic marriages; they don't delude themselves into thinking that "he's such a nice boy, he wouldn't do anything," or that coed sleepovers are okay because "nothing could happen when they're all together." At this age, when they're all together is precisely when things happen.

As a parent, you can't control the crushes and the obsessions; you might never know about them, and that's okay. It's productive, at this age, for boys to get to know girls, and girls to know boys; kids who can navigate a healthy romantic relationship feel more competent. Mom and Dad shouldn't freak out over spin the bottle—it takes some of the mystery out of kissing and can be harmless, especially if Mom comes downstairs occasionally to replenish the soda.

Most of all, adults should be careful not to belittle their children's crushes, and should show sympathy when it's needed. Romance can exacerbate depression in adolescents: They're sad or ashamed when things don't work out; they're let down when things do work out but fall short of their expectations; even being the subject of someone else's crush can be difficult. And rejection, simply put, is never fun. Jackie sees this all the time with her friends. Even if you want the freedom to flirt, and you're not allowed to hang out with the guy anyway, when you hear he wants to break up with you, you are miserable. And even if you are one of the few couples at Wilde Lake who are actually comfortable together, who actually talk to each other regularly about your lives, you hide in the bathroom stall, too scared to say anything, as your friends bombard you: "Are you gonna break up with him first? When?"

Despite this, Jackie has found it impossible to go without a crush. That's what makes up at least 60 percent of your friends' conversations, and, well, you just *should* have one. "When you have a crush on someone," Jackie says, "even them saying 'Bye' makes you feel special." Besides, at recess Adam keeps poking Jackie—and Jackie alone, she is certain—in the side.

"Don't touch me."

"What you say?"

"Don't touch me."

"What you say?"

"Don't touch me."

"What you say?"

"That's unwanted touching. Sexual harassment!"

Adam stretches a girl's elastic necklace two feet, to demonstrate how long his penis is, and simulates masturbation with a Lipton Brisk bottle. But Jackie knows he is all talk. Leslie tested it once, by offering him a blow job after school. At first he said okay, but in two minutes he came back and said, "Nah, I don't like you like that."

QED.

So, when Jackie overhears Anton behind her in social studies saying to Adam, "You'd be lucky if she says yes," she swings around.

"What did you say?"

"Adam wants to know if you'd go out with him."

"Did you say that?"

Adam shrugs, smiles.

"Yeah," Jackie says, "sure."

At lunch, she asks Adam, "What you said during social studies, did you mean it?"

"Sure."

She hugs him and spends the afternoon jumping around Leslie's bedroom listening to Staind, yelling, "I have a boyfriend!" The two of them go to the roller rink and wait for Adam, who said he would be there.

Each Friday night, Columbia's middle schoolers line up outside the door to enter the one place that is, for the moment, *theirs*. Girls wear the spaghetti straps they can't wear in school; bellies see the light. Boys wear pants so baggy it's an insult to physics that they stay up while in motion. A Rollerblade under each arm, a girl says to her father, "I need money." "I gave you money." "Whatever." "Do you have it? Take it out." "I *have* it. *Dad*, leave." "Are you sure you have it?" A kid in a Redskins jersey gets his wrist run over—he shakes it and stomps his feet but he will not cry. The lone mother, a woman who has never left her boy without a parent, watches from behind the glass, and she and her son wave to each other as he skates by. A group of eighth-grade girls with O-rings up their arms plot a secret mission to Wendy's.

Adam has a history of being not exactly the most fulfilling roller-skate date. Ann, a subtle, big-eyed princess who tosses her hair and fends off all comers with a straight line of closed lips, would eventually hook Jay Starr, but in the fall Adam, her boyfriend at the time, blew even her off at the roller rink. She spent couples skate sitting on the bench crowded with shoes as Adam begged off with a supposedly hurt ankle and then trolled the parking lot for a ninth grader named Jennifer. Tonight, as Jackie circles the rink with her eye toward the entrance, Adam never shows up. He is "studying" in the bedroom of a girl from church, a girl with boobs.

And so it ends much as it began, much as these things do. During social studies on Monday, Anton tells Jackie that Adam cheated on her. She had an idea something was up, because at recess one of her friends asked Adam why he liked Jackie and he said, "I don't." After Anton opens his big mouth Adam hits him in the head, three times. Jackie is sad, but not so much she has to cry.

Jackie has created a compatibility test on the computer:

Boys And Thier Love for You
THIS IS THE SURVAY TO SEE HOW GOOD OR HOW BAD A GUY IS FOR YOU. JUST FILL OUT A CARD TYPING HOW YOU THINK THAT GUY RATES FROM A SCALE OF 1–10, THEN ADD UP HIS SCORE.
Looks
Personality
Athletic Ability
Things in Common With You
Favorite color (red, orange, yellow = 10, green, blue, purple = 9, all others like black = 5)
The gifts he gives you
Kisses
Hugs

Now subtract these next questions points to your total from the top questions for the total score.

Times he forgets you
Times he doesn't like your friends
Times he has cheated (on anyone)

Now take this score (that you have subtracted from the top) and put it over 90 and divide and now you have the persentage of your love.

Part of the reason that Jackie is so resilient—that she doesn't cry over boys, as some of her friends do—is that she's taken the time to figure things out for herself. She's getting to know who she is, what she wants. Aside from "favorite color," the criteria in her formula make sense. This is the kind of thing a parent can discuss with a child. "What do you like about him?" "What would make a good girlfriend?"

Jackie still sits next to Adam and in front of Anton in social studies, which is in one way a pain, because "I hate all my ex-boyfriends," but in another way not a pain, because she doesn't really. She and Adam whisper all the time, and Mr. Wolfe talks to them sternly about not paying attention. They are filling in maps of the United States. Jackie has colored the Rockies brown and the Great Plains green and the East Coast Megalopolis red and labeled all the rivers and cities. Adam's map is blank, and he wants the answers from Jackie.

"What have you done for me lately?"

"He bought you a toothbrush for your birthday," says the boy next to Anton.

"Yeah, I bought you a toothbrush. Your breath stinks. You need a Tic Tac."

That is not the way to get the answers. Jackie continues her work, hands it in, gets an extra-credit word search of cities around the world, and Adam continues to pester her for help.

"Take back what you said."

"Okay, your breath doesn't stink, you don't need a Tic Tac, you don't smell," he murmurs.

"Say it like you mean it."

He says it again, clearer.

"You're lucky I'm nice." She puts aside the word search. "Okay, look on the map. Missouri. Do you see the state of Missouri? Do you see the Missouri River anywhere near there?" She goes through the map like this, nudging him to search the book for the Mississippi, the Rio Grande, until Adam says, "There's only seventeen minutes left. I don't have time to look in the index."

By the time Jackie gets to the St. Lawrence River, she just shows him where it is.

chapter twenty-one

she's lost to us

When the buses arrive at Wilde Lake in the morning, the kids are supposed to stay aboard until the school doors open. Sometimes the drivers let kids off anyway, and this is what Elizabeth's driver does one day, until the art teacher notices and heads to the bus—just as Elizabeth is getting off.

"Get back on the bus," Mr. Mitchell tells her. "Hey, don't let people off the bus yet," he tells the driver.

The bus driver says Elizabeth was getting off the bus because she has diarrhea. The word amplifies in Elizabeth's head as she stands in limbo on the bus stairs—diarrhea—Diarrhea!—DIARRHEA!!—**SHE HAD DIARRHEA!!!**—to the point where she figures the jerk couldn't have yelled it louder if he had a megaphone in his hand.

If he had said, "Don't get off the bus because I don't want to get in trouble," she wouldn't have, and anyway why is she being singled out, and double anyway he doesn't have to keep calling her "bad girl" after Mr. Mitchell walks away, and triple anyway why would she even come to school if she had diarrhea? By the time she arrives late to first period, after spending ten minutes tearfully explaining herself to Mr. Mitchell, the kids on her bus have spread the word, and now *everyone is asking about it*, which makes her cry.

"Look," Mrs. Rashid scolds, "now you made her cry." If anyone on earth ever felt more pathetic than this, Elizabeth can't imagine.

The kids talk about making a petition to get the bus driver fired, but it goes nowhere, like all the petitions about getting bus drivers fired. Elizabeth doesn't bring the issue home, except to write:

omg, my bus driver is a jerk an idiot and should b fired.
he is such a lier
he imbarresed me so much
he needs 2 go back 2 school and learn responsibility

Days later, on the way to her math tutor, she and Ellen fight, Ellen angry that Elizabeth left her math book at school the night before a quiz. It escalates into screaming and crying, and sullenness sets in for the whole afternoon. Seems to Elizabeth—this is the way it looks when you become a teenager—that her mom is the one changing, becoming more irritable, harder to manage. When Joseph gets home and sees them both upset, he offers to take Liz to Starbucks for a Frappuccino. He watches Elizabeth's eyes tear up as she drinks, Ellen's strategies running through his head: Don't micromanage. Don't ask questions. Be patient. Just listen. So, even though Joseph is dying to know what this is all about, he doesn't say a word. He listens, and what he hears is his daughter sipping through a straw, sniffling occasionally.

He is so proud of himself for keeping his mouth shut.

What can a parent do, besides keeping quiet sometimes? Well, that's a start. So is whisking the kid off to a neutral territory, especially one as cool as Starbucks. He can acknowledge the pain inherent in her problems without trying to fix them, without overreacting. He can accept that she isn't totally grown up yet, which affects not just her sometimes babyish television choices but her ability to stay sane in the face of the small annoyances that seem so huge. All the while, he can't be insulted about what she doesn't share; he needs to realize that his attempts to help just increase her anxiety, and what may seem like absence of action *is* doing something after all.

At the last strings concert of the year, Joseph asks Mr. Shifflett about Elizabeth's science project, testing the effect of vinegar on swimsuit finding. "They've found out how to do the tanks of water, and Elizabeth found a chemist. Is she supposed to be a mentor-type person? Because maybe you could tell Elizabeth that. Could you write something down for her? Because she doesn't listen to me." Supposedly she's in the middle of a three-year experiment, but the science department drags these things out, and a year and a half into it, she hasn't soaked one swimsuit. It's the most difficult thing about parenting a thirteen-year-old, Joseph thinks: deciding when to hold her close and when to let her solve her own problems. If she waits till the last minute, like last year, she'll freeze. She won't take any guidance this year, which is good in the maturing sense, "but at the same time we could talk a little bit about the design or something," Joseph says. "A give-and-take."

The schoolwork thing is particularly hard for fathers, who want to teach their children how to do the work, the facts, of course you can do it, it all goes back to mx + b. But that's not what Liz needs sometimes; it's not really about the facts of the homework but about her insecurity over it, in which case she needs to hear reassurance that her struggles are normal, that he understands how she's feeling, that he had a hard time with this kind of project, too, once.

After the concert, the children emerge from backstage and hook up with their parents, except Liz. Joseph and Ellen sit at the bottom of the staircase, waiting. Backstage, Elizabeth begs for an end-of-year party and no more practice charts for the year. It bewilders Miss Colyer the way a kid who supposedly disliked her so much all of a sudden cleaves to her, is now saying, "I'll bring you flowers next year."

"Have things gotten better with Miss Colyer?" Joseph asks in the car.

"I don't want to talk about it."

With Joseph, it's all about Miss Colyer and the science project and swimming. The more he made it about sushi and *Buffy the Vampire Slayer*, the more he met his daughter on her turf, the better his luck would be.

"She's lost to us," Joseph keeps saying. Months after Elizabeth's Bat Mitzvah, her supposed entry into adulthood, as far as her parents can tell she hasn't changed at all, responsibility-wise. The brush-offs continue, and feel massively significant. She seems to have more secrets.

But really—hard as it is for them to see—Elizabeth isn't lost to them.

Ellen and Joseph are her biggest influence, maybe not on whether she likes blues, but on the things that matter. They never give up. They provide the activities she wants, and insist on the ones that she needs. They always, always put her first. She knows when they're arguing, which is fine to a degree, because it shows parents can have conflicts and work them out, but they never, ever weigh her down with their burdens. They don't toss out rules when it's hard to enforce them. Liz cares, still, about their approval. She likes herself, in large part because they like her, too. In her Mother's Day cards—Elizabeth couldn't decide on which, so she bought both—she gives credit to Ellen. "I don't know about you Mom, but I think I turned out pretty good . . . Especially considering I had fifty percent of Dad's genes to overcome," and "Mom, it's because of you that I turned out the way I did. . . . Cheer up. That was supposed to be a compliment."

Elizabeth keeps a lot from her mom and dad, but at least they know that. Plenty of her peers have parents who think their kids are their best friends, who are deluded into thinking that "she tells me everything" and that easy banter and the erasing of generational lines are somehow good for a child. But a child needs her parents to be her parents, not her best friends, and if that means there will always be somewhat of a disconnect, so be it. The important thing is not that Joseph and Ellen are her best pals—they will never be that, at least not in her adolescence—but that they keep providing the combination of warmth, control, and expectations that raises good people. And that they have faith that, in the mystery world Elizabeth navigates without them, she is truly growing up, and making good decisions for herself.

The Sterns next door are divorcing, and though Elizabeth isn't one of the kids whose parents threaten divorce in front of them or stomp out on each other, the news sends Elizabeth into extreme sensitivity every time her own parents argue. Mitch, the boy in her social-studies class who shows his affection by teasing her, is getting more aggravating, if that was even possible. Worst of all, she receives a note to be signed by her parents warning that she has been tardy too many times; the next time, she'll have to go to the reinforcement room. Elizabeth only remembers being

late twice. Once was excused, and the other time was in the very beginning of the year, "when I didn't know." As she walks out of school, Elizabeth feels the tears in the corners of her eyes, feels Hanna trying to get
a look at the note, which is really none of her nosy little business. Reinforcement room? That's where the bad kids work when they're sent out
of class. Never in her life.

She ponders quickly. Maybe her parents could call the principal, tell
them how she really wasn't late those two times. Maybe she'll get more
Frappuccino out of it. Then Elizabeth thinks back to the way Ellen asks
her, "How was strings?" every single afternoon, the never-ending e-mails
between Miss Colyer and Joseph, how even though the Frappuccino was
very delicious, after she drank it she was still crying inside and no less
pissed at her mom.

She decides that being thirteen means her problems are her own. On
her way to the bus, she crumples the note and tosses it in the trash.

And Elizabeth isn't late to class again.

chapter twenty-two

this is the most i ever typed in one day!

If Eric were the boss of school—well, if Eric were the boss of school, he would abolish it. But if Eric were realistic about being the boss of school, "kids would have some power to say how they would like to have some projects done. 'Cause some kids have very creative talents. And if they gave ideas to their teachers the teachers would be like, 'Yeah, whatever. We can't do that. It's not part of the curriculum.' But if the kids had some say, then the school might actually be interesting to them, and there wouldn't be so many dropouts."

If Eric were the boss of school, American-history students would re-enact battle scenes, and at least half the class would be spent learning the story of African Americans.

In May, like just about every eighth-grade social-studies teacher in the state, Mrs. Conroy races through the Civil War. If she had the luxuries of time and student attentiveness, she would like to explain more social aspects of history, families split apart, espionage, riots in the North. Her classes would do activities she tried long ago, skits and a mock *Meet the Press*. "A lot of things I'd like them to *discover*," she says, "instead of me saying, 'This happened.'" During the Reconstruction video, Eric sleeps, he reads a magazine article called "Tony Hawk's Pro Skater 4: The Spine-Tingling Sequel," he watches the kid next to him draw Mrs. Conroy with a fireball heading toward her skull. In the video, a Northerner is

teaching a black child when a man approaches on a horse. "Do you realize the harm you're doing to that child? That colored child will lose his
desire to work." Eric looks up. "This child's parents see the value in education," the teacher says. The man on the horse shoots the place up,
yelling, "Leave, Yankee scum!"

"That was part of my history," Eric says later. "I don't know, that
might be my great-great-great-grandmoms and -dads. It's always interesting to see people on that TV screen who could be somebody that's in
your family. Somebody that you knew come back to life."

If Eric were the boss of school, teachers would choose more books
like *Beowulf*. He likes it not because he relates to the themes, although he
could. He's got a mother as loyal as Grendel's, he feels as abandoned as
Beowulf. Mainly, it's catchy: Tore him limb from limb and swallowed
him whole, "sucking the blood in streams," crunching the bones. But,
still, disorganization intrudes. One day, after school, Eric asks Mrs.
Brown his grade on the quiz. A seventy-two, she says.

"Yes! I passed!"

"A C isn't enough for you."

"Why?"

"Because you're you." Mrs. Brown looks in her grade book. "You
have only a sixty percent, darling." The *Beowulf* Part I quiz a parent was
supposed to sign and his Gilgamesh essay are missing. "You've gotta do
this stuff!"

"Can I just have my dad sign a piece of paper with the information
on it?"

"Yes, but that'll only be three out of five—a sixty! It's sixty!"

"As long as you don't call my mom."

"That's what I need to do!"

"Please don't give her a call, because then I'll be punished."

"I'm not trying to get you in trouble, I'm trying to get you to do
your work. Eric, did you do the Gilgamesh paragraph?"

"Yeah, you were sitting right there."

"What did you do with it?"

"I probably cleaned my binder," he says. "Can I do makeup? Can I
do extra credit?"

"You're an enigma, Eric."

"I'm an egg man?"

"Enigma. E-N-I-G-M-A. Look it up."

He doesn't.

But he shows up for the after-school study group to prepare for the next test, nine kids sitting in a small circle of desks. The conversation is gentle. It ranges from vocab ("Unswert calls him a what? And what does 'braggart' mean?") to plot ("What's the point of the whole thing with Brecka the sea monster?" "How do they know he made it back to the lair?") to language (" 'Bolts burst apart'—what's that?" " 'Torch flaming in his eye'—is there really a torch in his eye?") to form ("What do we see here that makes him an epic hero?"). Eric listens, he participates—"the more you participate," he says, "the more you remember"—and exudes a joy of mastery.

With Mrs. Brown, Eric is finally learning that onomatopoeia is more than just a stumbling block in spelling bees. He learns about metaphor. And he learns words, some of them big and some of them little, but all of them juicy: Unfettered. Torrent. Keening. Gluttonous. Clamorous.

He likes it when Mrs. Brown explains words. For "turret": "Like in some of the video games you play." For "round": "Remember in the movie *Back to the Future*—I watched it this weekend with our niece— when he turns around and says, 'Nobody calls me chicken!' He's *rounding* to his enemy." All of a sudden this feels important to Eric, and he studies. His vocab quizzes come back with a huge *A+* written on the top, and when he can remember he squeezes the words into conversation later. He defines them—"Tyrant, that's an unjust, harsh ruler"—in case you didn't know.

Sometimes in music it seems all they do is fill out worksheets, but one day, after labeling the parts of a guitar, they finally take down the instruments from the rack, and discover the magic moment when you find the one string that turns your hapless, dissonant chord into something lovely. They are picking out "Ode to Joy" and Eric gets it first. "I did it! That sounds good!" His grin is huge. "Good thing I play sax! I got rhythm!"

Ms. Drumm asks if anyone plays bass. "I do!" Eric says. "I'm learning it now." He has been tooling around on the bass in the band room after school—students who hate school and students who don't, all hang out there every afternoon, jamming and getting Mr. Vega to teach them drums. "Man, I kill at bass! I bought a little book. I'm saving money to

buy a bass—I'm gonna get one that's two hundred or three hundred dollars."

"Come up here. Would you be willing to show everyone how it
works? In two weeks we're doing a special song for the grade."

"Oh yeah, that would be cool!"

This is the middle-school philosophy in play: Yes, Eric is learning the
parts of a guitar, which is part of the curriculum. He's also getting to explore, try something self-directed, and this makes him feel great. It's no
coincidence that learning works best when these elements happen together. Too often the false debate between content and self-concept,
academics and self-esteem, turns middle school into a muddle, where
students bounce back and forth from useless goal-setting, what-kind-of-
learner-am-I exercises to cram sessions for standardized tests. Instead,
present the material in a way that gets kids enthusiastic about learning it,
and enthusiastic about their lives, and you will be amazed at how well
they do.

When music class is over, Eric is reluctant to put the guitar away. He
is so excited about the bass demonstration that when he leaves Ms.
Drumm has to chase him down the hall: He forgot his guitar-part worksheets.

It's no surprise that this surge in enthusiasm coincides with smoother
sailing at home. The pregnancy has cheered up Beulah, he thinks. One
day at home it's just the two of them, and she says, "Wanna go see a
movie?" They do, and laugh. He is starting a band with two friends,
called Beef. The football coach at the high school says he has shoulder
pads awaiting Eric. With the help of his mom, he's gone on a diet. Sick of
the teasing, he eats apples and Lean Cuisine instead of junk all the time,
milk instead of juice, and Tenacious and Eric walk-run around the track,
two miles each time. The weight disappears like that, ten pounds in a
month. For Mother's Day he buys his mom an outfit and takes her to
Pizza Hut and *Spider-Man*. She drives him each week to roller hockey,
where he has started playing goalie, a position that feels like it was made
for him. After getting paintballs at Dick's Sporting Goods with his old
friend James, James pushes him in the shopping cart through the parking
lot. The world zooms by, and it is good.

The study-skills packet Eric highlighted in the fall had it only partly right: Sure, it's important to have a dedicated, well-lit place to study each day. But that's not nearly so important—for kids from affluent, stable families as well as those from poorer ones, as much for Jimmy as for Eric—as having at least one person in your family who consistently takes an interest in you and your schoolwork. That means "schoolwork," not "grades." Bribes and threats work—like Tenacious's roller-hockey/science-grade contingency—but only for the short term, and they don't help a child become a learner, just an achiever. When Eric's brother stayed with him and sat him down at the kitchen table for study sessions every day, his grades improved. When his parents show up not just for concerts and conferences but also at home, his grades improve. Now, at the end of the year, when his mother has more time for him, when he feels part of something, he is getting somewhere.

To a degree.

If Eric were the boss of school, he wouldn't change a thing about his research project for Mrs. Cook. "That's giving the kid his time to go ahead and pick a subject he wants to do a project on. Can't get any better than that. It's your choice; you ain't gotta read what you don't want to. I'd read tons of books on cars if there was a lot of books on them."

That doesn't means Eric does the assignment thoroughly, or promptly. It was assigned in November, but the week in May before it's due, Eric hasn't started. The class is in the computer lab, some students studiously typing the What I Learned and Questions I Asked sections of their reports on karate or teen pregnancy or what you must do to become a lawyer. Some students are checking out e-mail, or mtv.com, or rampage.com, which interests Mrs. Cook, because she wants a new black shirt. Eric aimlessly searches car sites: King of the Street, Fastest Street Cars (1/4 Mile) in the USA, bakersfieldstreetracing.com. "Look at that cobra look on that Civic. That's the way my car is going to be—the brake pedal. Mrs. Cook, wanna see the world's fastest truck? It goes three sixty-five mph. It has thirty-six thousand horsepower."

On Saturday he goes to work with his dad, then to Baltimore for a haircut with his mom, then to hockey (where he scores twice), then to James's for the night, where they play video games. He stays at James's till nine Sunday night, eleven hours before his six-month project is due. At James's he hears a stale rumor that his favorite skateboarder died. He has the same skates as him! Once home, Eric stays up all night watching cartoons and thinking about the news. When Tenacious arrives to pick Eric up Monday and finds out his paper isn't done—isn't started, even— she's exasperated. Instead of searching the Internet for roller skates and paintball guns, why can't he use that time to start his research paper? They rush into Mrs. Cook's room late, Tenacious says something about the computer, and Mrs. Cook gives Eric an extension.

After school, and after playing drums in the band room, he goes to the computer lab. It is quiet in there, nearly dark, and the seats down the rows and rows of blue Macs are empty save for a girl named Mary. Mary has arranged fifty note cards for her research project, a PowerPoint presentation on Civil War photographers. Deep in Eric's reading folder, untouched, are a series of reminders and checklists for the research paper. First is this note: "Your product is up to you. This counts as a major grade for the third quarter. Use your time wisely and do a fantastic job." Then the requirements: an outline, a timeline, note cards gathered with a rubber band, a daily journal about your research, the explanation at the outset of the questions you wanted answered, the explanation at the end of how you did your research. If Eric did that part, it might go like this:

> Most of the stuff about cars I knew off the top of my head. I didn't actually open a book or do any interviews like you told us to. But I found some car Web sites last night using Google. And Mrs. Brown happened to be in the computer lab at the time, so she suggested where you can keep your nitrous oxide so the cops don't find it and how to explain what racing-style tires are for.

A bibliography with five or more sources. Final copy typed and double-spaced, with a clear plastic cover and a creative design. The paper itself is worth fifty points, all the other things together worth one hundred.

In the lab, the many things Eric knows about race cars want to spill out of his head through his fingers. But he doesn't use a computer much—too much of a bother to ask his way into his dad and Beulah's room, where it's kept at home—and when academic-enrichment class meets in the computer lab for Mavis Beacon Teaches Typing, Eric selects

Beginner and taps A-S-D-F exercises, "fad daff dad ada sad," eleven words per minute, while kids nearby zip through the advanced exercises about squawking gorillas and weightlifters quipping jovially, well practiced from all that instant-messaging.

Eric does frequent word counts, stopping occasionally to consider which photo in a sheaf he's printed out would be good for the cover. He doesn't know how to insert text in Microsoft Word, he doesn't know that if you type a paragraph the paragraph below it will push down by itself, but to Eric this feels like cruising. He writes and writes and writes about the specs of the best possible quarter-mile race car in the land.

"Mrs. Brown, can you come read this and tell me how it sounds from a car person's point of view?"

"It looks good. It looks professional. I think it's one of the best pieces you've written all year."

"Four hundred and ten words! This is the most I ever typed in one day! And I still have homework. Oh, man. I'll write a paragraph about turbo exhaust. Then I feel like Rollerblading."

Which he goes home to do, the paper still unfinished.

Does it do Eric any good that, when he hands in the assignment a day later, mediocre and incomplete, he gets a B? Certainly it boosts his mood, but the good grade is clearly charitable. Teachers and administrators like Eric, they know his circumstances aren't ideal, they know his mother tries hard, very hard. They want him to succeed. They give him a million breaks. Absent true success, absent true academic progress, you can't help feeling the teachers are manufacturing the success for him, relaxing their standards and expectations so that this lovable boy can stay afloat. His parents do the same: "D's are out of the question," Tenacious said in September, and William agreed. Since then, D's, and even an F, have arrived without consequence. Perhaps he'll always be so buoyed by those around him. Or perhaps the sinking is merely being delayed.

On his fourth-quarter interim, Eric gets a C in science. This sends him over the moon but clearly does not impress Ms. Thomas, who calls him in for a meeting. With a mother who cares like his does, Ms. Thomas figures he'll be fine in high school, so she tells Eric he's going to pass. But, she says, the extracurricular activities are still in question, pending improvement in science. Eric says he doesn't care: "There ain't nothing new there. I know the whole marching band's songs before they start playing them." Band or no band, Eric knows for the sake of his mother he has to keep his science grade up so he doesn't get an F for the year. Hearing he's passing middle school is a huge relief. Now, he figures, he doesn't have to make up all the work his teachers are bugging him for.

"Next year," he says, "will be totally different. I'll be with my mom, and I'll be doing good in school." The plan is for an aunt to sell Tenacious her house in Baltimore, and she'll drive him a half-hour to school every day, and William will move into the city, too.

Ms. Thomas thinks his indifference to the band is a cover for insecurity. Insecurity about high-school work, about not having his hand held, not getting the nurturing he does here. For someone who hates school so much, he sure spends a lot of time there, even walking back after going home. Often the students who most frustrate the teachers during the school day are the most pleasant company once the bell rings; Wilde Lake Middle School is a refuge, and they don't know if high school can take its place. At a jazz-band concert later that week, Tenacious snaps photos and worries about Eric worrying about high school. At the concerts she always stands at the side, often in her nursing uniform, with a small, proud smile. Eric sees her and winks. She's glad that he feels so nurtured here, that in the sea of feeling alone he chooses school as his island instead of one of many bad choices.

She's spoken with Ms. Drakes on the phone and knows Eric is teetering on the edge. A D, please. Just a D. Ms. Drakes thinks only an A would pull up his F's to a D for science for the year, but she won't let him do makeup work; she only lets seventh graders do that. "You've got to prepare them for high school," she says. Along those lines, she hasn't really gone to Eric; he comes in for help occasionally, and after all, "he knows what he has to do. He didn't care. He cares now."

One morning Eric wakes up sick, and Tenacious tells him to stay home with his Kleenex and orange juice and chicken soup. But he wants to go to school, because he stayed home yesterday. *He wants to go to school.* First period, in science, his eyes run, his nose runs; he makes his way back to the sink for paper towels every seven minutes, sticks wads of it out his nostrils, then trudges up front to the trash can to throw it all away. He emits noises that disgust his classmates and make them laugh, which brings him to hang his head low. Maybe then all this gunk will clear out. He coughs into the neck of his T-shirt. He can't focus. He is under water.

"Five, four, three, two, one. If you're talking, you're not listening." The class is going through the steps of mitosis, sketching cells on paper and using playing cards as chromosomes. They draw spindle fibers and simulate the fibers' shrinking and pulling the chromatids apart. Eric wipes his hand under his nose. His mouth is open. A haze coats his eyes.

Eric manages to fill out the mitosis worksheet and hand it in. "For the quiz," Ms. Drakes says, "you might want to take home your activity sheet and index cards so you can study. It's going to be a ridiculously stupid quiz."

The F flashes before Eric's eyes, but so does Ms. Thomas telling him he's passing. He is dizzy. He asks to go to the nurse, and on the way there to be sprung from school stows his binder on top of the lockers. Eric has a quiz in reading and a quiz in science, but he goes home bookless. His policy is that he doesn't have homework tonight, since he won't be around to get it. He walks home, enters the dark apartment, flops on the couch, and searches for the remote.

chapter twenty-three

why do people always take sex as a play thing?

Dear Mia,
I hope you know you extremely sexy. The way you walk your legs look so sexy. The way you look blow my. Your legs must be tired because you are running through my mind all the time. Bye Bye my love.
Love,
Jimmy S.

Mia has received this note from a messenger named Nicole. Something smells; the text is written in a light, scrawly hand, whereas the signature is heavy. Mia asks Jimmy if this is his work.

"Yes," he says. "So—will you go out with me?"

"No way."

In the principal's office, Ms. Thomas meets with a girl suspected of leaving science class to smoke, one of a small group of eighth graders who are appalled that a year ago they wore Abercrombie shirts, and now etch their pain lightly on their forearms with steak knives and ink it on their binders: "I always knew looking back on tears would make me laugh, but never knew looking back on laughs would make me cry." They cut school to hang out with their nineteen-year-old boyfriends, read up on Wicca at the library, and sneak cigarettes. Just as with sexuality, there is a broad range of experience in a middle school regarding substance abuse, and Dawn, the girl in Ms. Thomas's office, is particularly fond of poems like, "Weed is a seed that grows in the ground. If God didn't like it it wouldn't be found."

She picks at a long skinny scab on the white of her forearm, pulling down the sleeve of her T-shirt to dab at the blood, and explains that she was not out smoking, just getting a tampon from her locker. Ms. Thomas begs—gently, kindly—that, if Dawn wants to finish the last nineteen days of middle school and avoid the Saturday-morning smoking-cessation program with its revolting slide show, she not bring cigarettes to school. Ms. Thomas asks about the small round scar on Dawn's cheekbone, which she says she got wrestling with her boyfriend while smoking. Dawn goes on: Her father put her in a choke hold until all she was aware of was her big sister screaming for him to stop; her sister ignores her, because she has stolen from her too many times; Zoloft makes her so tired that all she wants to do after school is sleep, except for the one day she didn't take the pill and got all her homework done.

"I'm glad you're getting help."

"I'm getting everything there is," Dawn says—everything working for nothing, as far as she can tell.

Like all Wilde Lake students, Dawn takes health class every year, but she can be told a million times that cigarettes are poison and still smoke. Then there are the kids like Jimmy, who wouldn't touch the stuff even without the never-ending series of overheads and quizzes. As Ms. Thomas meets with Dawn, Jimmy sits down the hall in health. The room is filled with boys who wear DARE T-shirts without irony and girls who run inside proclaiming an emergency when they find an empty cigarette pack in the backyard. Health class is where middle-school students who don't eat breakfast and are handed only carbohydrates and fat by the lunch ladies and wash down the brownies and pizza they make in home ec with pink Country Time lemonade learn about a well-balanced diet and heart disease. "It doesn't cost you any more to put that orange on your tray," Ms. Rouiller pleads, "to put that salad on that tray, to take your milk and drink it." What wall space there is—this cramped, odd-angled room was once a storage space—is covered by posters cautioning

against peer pressure, pregnancy, HIV, anorexia, smoking ("tumor causing, teeth staining, smelly, puking habit"). Most of the sixth graders,
Jimmy included, can't imagine why anyone would smoke.

The antismoking poster Jimmy is creating says, in green and orange
bubble letters, "Tobacco makes you a wacko!" The dot of the exclamation point is a frowny face of a dead smoker, "X"s for eyes. Next to him
Jacob draws blood dripping down cigarettes: "Smokers Are Jokers. Don't
add yourself to the pile of bones." "I love Joe Camel," Jimmy says as he
draws. He sings: "Tobacco, tobacco, I love ya, tobacco!"

Under the surface of Jimmy's cheekbones, begging to emerge, are
pimples the same color as his skin. Jacob's nose has broadened since the
year started, and he's got a little fuzz over his lip, which you can see from
certain angles. Jimmy tells him, "Did you hear about the kid who was
walking down the hall, he scratched his balls, they stuck to the wall? His
girlfriend screamed, his thing turned green, and that was the end of his
rubber ding-a-ling."

Jacob smiles, and Jimmy glimpses his mouth. "Your teeth are yellow.
You're smoking."

"Maybe all those people in the World Trade Center died from smoking."

"It should say smoking supplies terrorists with money."

"That's drugs."

"Smoking is a drug."

Will asks Jimmy if he's going to the aquarium-club barbecue and
Jimmy says no, he has homework and piano. "But they have a huge yard,
and this train that goes around the whole yard."

"A baby train? Sounds like fun."

Jimmy turns back to Jacob and says, "Don't smoke! No dope!"

"Just say no, unless you want to be a ho!"

The students have learned that Americans lose five million years of
potential life to cigarettes each year; they've searched in the textbook for
tobacco's ill effects on each body part and copied it all onto a line drawing of a woman (when Jimmy sees "bladder" he thinks about the pee he's
holding in, and says to no one in particular, "My bladder hurts"); they've
learned that to Just Say No effectively you should use "proper body language, tone of voice, and repetition." Discussion then takes off, as it always does in health class, smoking and sex and their bodies far more

interesting and mysterious than the Bill of Rights.

"I saw some high-school students who were late for school," Devon says, "and they were smoking, and one guy wanted a cigarette, but the other guy said no because he didn't want to share."

"That's not the kind of 'no' we're talking about."

"What if they're teenagers, and they ask if you want to smoke and you keep saying no and you can't really run away from them?"

"It doesn't ever really happen like that," Ms. Rouiller says.

"I saw it in a movie."

"My neighbor, her friend stopped being friends with her because she didn't smoke."

"I have some friends who smoke," Ms. Rouiller says, "but they know I'd never smoke."

"How come people in movies smoke?"

"Is it true that secondhand smoke is worse than firsthand smoke?"

"If you just put a cigar in your mouth and don't light it, is it still bad for you?"

"If someone is smoking weed in front of you and they exhale, can you get high?"

"That's not a good question," Alexandra says.

"Why not?" says Ms. Rouiller. "She can ask that. We don't really get into marijuana in this class because it's illegal. You shouldn't put yourself in a situation like that, because it's illegal."

"What if your mom and dad smoke? What do you do?"

"I suggest you talk to them, discuss it with them—how it makes you feel. Show them information and ask them, 'Did you know this? Did you know what smoking does to you?' "

"I have a friend, his dad used to smoke. He hid his cigarettes, and it worked."

"For the record, I'm not telling you to take their cigarettes."

"I ask people why they smoke, they say it relaxes you."

"In reality it doesn't. It's a stimulant. Those people it relaxes because they're addicted. They need the nicotine."

"Are you married, Ms. Rouiller? Rick thought you like Mr. Juliano."

"What does this have to do with nicotine?"

"Well, if one of you smokes, and you kiss, you'll get nicotine in the other person's mouth."

Jimmy raises his hand halfway, elbow bent.

"Could kids have heart attacks?"

Though the topic of health class is an eleven-year-old's favorite—himself!—Jimmy says he hates it. Every year it's Your Changing Body, Drugs Are Bad, Breakfast Is Good, blah blah blah. He says he knows it all. His classmates say they know it all. On the first day of the family-life unit, one boy says, "My mom kept asking me, 'What do you know?' I said, 'I don't know. What *do* I know?' More than she does."

Even if there were something Jimmy was curious about, if he wanted to look at a pamphlet from the rack he'd have to ask Ms. Rouiller's permission. Before embarrassment set in last year, he asked his parents whatever he wanted to know about sex. Now he'll just talk about the clinical things. His mother will creep further, things like, "Do girls sit on boys' laps on the bus?" Jimmy says no, but even if the answer were yes he wouldn't say, "because then they would think the school is really bad," and they might call, and his teachers might take it out on him.

Marie sat in on the sex ed Jimmy had at religious school earlier in the year, saw the explicit pictures of diseases the kids were given, and on the ride home clarified her morals on certain points the minister made, like when he said gays are okay but not gays having sex. Gays having sex, she said, was okay, too. It felt to her like Jimmy was comfortable enough with this conversation, more than if Paul were trying. Jimmy doesn't discuss this kind of stuff with his dad at all.

A lot of what he needs to know he now asks his sister. Brianna is three years older and a better confidante than a parent would be. She tells Jimmy to eat with his mouth closed at the dinner table in a not-very-polite way and says, "That's so pointless," when he's playing GameCube, but at least is over her Valley Girl phase, when she would tell him, "Get a-waaaay!" Now he comforts her when she's sad. When a friend of hers committed suicide in the winter, Jimmy himself didn't cry, because he had only played with the guy three or four times, but he put up with Brianna's crying for an hour and a half, even though he couldn't hear the TV. She hugged him, which he was cool with, though eventually he felt squished and thought, "Okay, enough." In return for his empathy, she tells him about what she does with her boyfriend, which to Jimmy sounds "kind of funky," but, still, there is a limit, he feels, to what he can find out from other people and what he'll just have to come to know himself one day—whenever that day may be.

Jimmy sees girls talk about their puberty. But his friends talk about their physical changes in such coded and macho ways, mainly with mistruths about sex and jokes about penises and homosexuality. Any remotely related topic brings a boy Jimmy's age to giggles. In the library one day, when he and John have to look up Michelangelo, they get to the page in *The History of Art* with the statue of David—naked!—and begin laughing. They slam the book shut. They crack it open just enough to get the info they need without seeing the genitals they don't. He and his friends make up words like "dickonary" for "dictionary" and derive great humor from the fact that Australians say "fag" when they mean cigarette and that Billy Mara's uncle's middle name is Gay.

In middle school, everyone is changing at such different rates that there's little indication of whether the same thing is happening to anyone else. Some of Jimmy's friends have entered the lust phase. Jacob, for example, has testosterone running and pubic hair and the erections they giggle over in class. A boy at Jacob's stage thinks constantly about sex, as much as an adult times ten. *American Pie* wasn't so unreal: Every object and every female is sexualized, in his mind, a potential outlet for his energies. He wonders if he is the only one in the world who thinks these thoughts.

Jimmy wonders if he's the only one who doesn't. Why, he thinks, does Jacob look at porn all the time on the computer? Jimmy tried once. He typed in www.sex.com, and what came up was a tiny bit interesting, but mostly gross. As for the lurid note to Mia: Though he owned up to it, Nicole wrote it. In fact, Jimmy never even read it—he just signed it. His grammar and spelling would have been better, and for sure he would have been less explicit. It's not like he thinks Mia's legs are sexy, it's not like he even knows what it is to think someone's legs are sexy, it's not like he thinks about what it would be like actually to touch her. He just thinks she's cute. It's more like Nicole put *him* up to the note, not the other way around.

What Jimmy knows: The ovaries produce estrogen and progesterone, and puberty is triggered by hormones secreted by the pituitary gland, and the pituitary gland is the size of a pea, and testosterone causes body hair to grow, your voice to deepen, your sex organs to develop (as well as your sexual desire, which Ms. Rouiller explains as the "development of romantic feelings toward others"), and when such desire exists, semen enters the female's body through sexual intercourse and travels through the vagina and fallopian tubes to fertilize the egg. Jimmy raises his hand to give these answers as he folds tiny bright-pink origami in the back of the room, laughing occasionally with his classmates at a hilarious term such as "pelvic region" or "testes" or "uterus."

What Jimmy really wants to find out is buried with the rest of life's great mysteries in the daily Question Box, from which Ms. Rouiller plucks questions one by one, to answer or not.

Why do only women have their period, and why does it hurt?

"My mom, when she gets her period, she gets really agitated."

"My friend says it's called PMS."

"My teacher said it's like a roller coaster: Sometimes you're happy and sometimes you're sad."

"That roller coaster," Ms. Rouiller says, "is something you're all going to be riding the next few years. The boys, too."

Can you die if you have a baby?

"Yes, but it's not common."

If the baby's too big will it pop the uterus?

How does the baby come out of the vagina if it's so small?

What is masturbation?

"When a person handles their own genitals. That's all I'm allowed to say. You'll have to ask your parents."

"I can't ask my parents that! I'd get in trouble."

"I don't think you would. I think you'd be surprised. Tell your parents this question came up in health class and the teacher couldn't answer it."

Yeah, right.

What if sperm is injected into another male what would happen?

"It's kind of hard to inject sperm into a male," Ms. Rouiller says. "You can't do that."

"But on the *Men in Black* cartoon, Will Smith gets pregnant with an alien's baby."

Jimmy has just begun knotting a bracelet he started at outdoor ed when Ms. Rouiller picks his folded-up question from the box. She opens it, looks, and places it on the pile next to her without answering. *Why do people always take sex as a play thing instead of a life thing?* Jimmy's question is the same one he asked in health last year, when the teacher at least gave it a try. "It's different for everybody," she said then.

Beyond the fact that answering would take Ms. Rouiller into the realm of morals, where she's not allowed to go, what would she say, anyway? Could she explain why so many of the kids who are having sex these days (or a facsimile thereof) have no idea there's supposed to be meaning to it, not just about making babies but about making connection and love? Could she explain why they do it not just outside of marriage but outside of any relationship at all? Could she explain why a group of girls from a rival middle school were caught recently in the back row of a movie giving oral sex to a group of boys? These are the kinds of activities and attitudes that get written up in front-page newspaper stories, that shock politicians into pushing for abstinence-only sex ed, and that still produce a refreshingly sweet sentiment once in a while in a child like Jimmy.

Why do some people have sex every single day, he wonders, like it's just something for their pleasure?

As for Jimmy, he knows about the ideas, but it will be a small while before his body instructs him to feel the desire. His mother tells him it could happen any day now, but Jimmy is counting on more like two years.

All of it, come to think of it, seems further off than it really is. It's hard to imagine being a man, shaving, wet dreams. He's not too worried about those, since his neighbor's well into puberty and hasn't had one yet; Jimmy can't scream like a girl anymore, though, so he figures a voice change isn't far away. He hopes his goes smoother than Peter's did in that *Brady Bunch* special.

chapter twenty-four

there's nothing to be scared of in middle school

If the students of Wilde Lake Middle School could select their own awards for the end-of-year assembly, Jimmy Schissel would get Most Creative in Social Studies. Barring that, Best at Origami.

Lily Mason would get Best at Sewing.

Jackie Taylor would get Most Willing to Go on Any Roller Coaster in the World.

Eric Ellis would get the Good Person Award, signifying a kid who was nice to everybody unless someone teased him and five minutes later came begging for a dollar. Better yet, Most Improved in English.

But for Most Improved you have to have started out super-lousy. Other than that, there are a couple of Citizenship Awards for effort and attitude, but it's mostly Academic Achievement Awards, for the boy and girl with the top final averages in each class. It's repetitive, the same kids over and over. For most students this ceremony is very boring. They expect the Award for Kids Who Got Awards to be next.

If that prize existed, Elizabeth Ginsburg would win it. She gets Academic Achievement for reading and English and Spanish, and Perfect Attendance, too. "They should just give all the straight-A students awards and let the rest of us go home," Jackie says from the back of the cafeteria, where she's sitting with her friends making a gel-pen tattoo on her arm that says "I LOVE_ _ _AND_ _ _ _ _" (Jay, of course, and Danny);

across from her, a clot of nonawarded boys draw Japanese anime characters. But Jackie gets Perfect Attendance, too, and bounces to the front of the room, Leslie whooping.

The jazz band in the front corner is supposed to provide entertainment—when Mr. Vega asks the eighth graders in band to stand, Eric smiles and lifts his sax over his head—but as they get ready to play "Louie Louie," the awards assembly ends. "For those of you who know in your heart that you tried hard, that's award enough," Mr. Wolfe says, and the students head back to class, unconvinced.

The band plays to an empty cafeteria, and ends halfway through the song.

Eric leaves his binder on top of the lockers and his book bag under a table and didn't buy a yearbook, so he can't leave that anywhere. Holding only an old birthday card he salvaged from his locker, he meets his mother outside, to shop for a shirt for the graduation ceremony tonight. Waiting for Eric, Tenacious sees Ms. Drakes, and they exchange hugs.

"We made it through another year," Tenacious says, and Ms. Drakes says, "Sure did," but no word from either about Eric's science grade.

That night, the gym is packed for the ceremony, themed "Stars of Tomorrow." Onstage with the jazz band, Eric picks out Tenacious in her usual side spot with her camera, Thomas and Tim tall in their ball caps, William and Beulah in the back. "Wow," Eric thinks. "Everyone's here. Together even, kind of." The jazz band gives its best performance ever; Eric plays like mad. He doesn't appear in the slide show and officially doesn't care, but unofficially he does a little. One by one the teachers come up to the podium to say how much they liked the eight-grade students. "School may suck," Eric thinks, "but some of these teachers are really nice." First and foremost Eric is contemplating how glad he is that this is *it*, this is over, no more Ms. Thomas, a middle-school career without any suspensions, why are these girls crying when they're going to see each other, like, next week? "I would not cry for nobody at this school."

But there's this other feeling, a tiny pea under the mattress: pride.

Eric was going to skip the dance, but he has time to kill, and in spite of himself he has fun. The cafeteria is dotted with the glittered stars the kids made in class with their names on them. The girls' dresses are all clingy shimmers and flowers; the boys dance with sombreros and plastic top hats on their heads. The huge sheet cake and snacks in the fluorescent-lit hallway go largely uneaten. Besides the line dances, the kids mostly clump in the middle of the room, playing with toys the DJ gives out. "Baby Got Back" comes on, and it's all jiggling near-naked butts on the video screen, and Ms. Thomas alternately laughs and cringes. Parents will arrive soon to pick up their kids, and it's the longest five minutes of her life.

Then Mandy Moore's "I Wanna Be With You" comes on. Eric approaches a girl named Anna, pulls her close, a gray ball cap on his head, and for some reason a balloon inside his gray long-sleeved T-shirt. They dance, arms around each other, Eric's second slow dance in his life, not that you can tell. When the song is over, more balloons—a million, it seems—are released from a net in the sky and tumble down, knocking the last bits of middle school out of their heads.

William is waiting in a car outside, with Eric's pillow and bag in the back seat. "Congratulations," father tells son, and they drive without words to where William's semi awaits. The little refrigerator has drained the truck's battery, and they jump it, *er-er-er-er*, Eric in charge of gunning the gas in the car.

Once on the road, Eric stays awake through Maryland and a quarter of the way into Pennsylvania, then he falls asleep.

The light comes up, and Eric is still on the road when the last day of the school year begins. Ms. Thomas is crying, not because of the boy who cursed the nurse or the vandalism in the boys' locker room or the rash of fistfights this week—boys and girls, two in sixth grade, three in seventh, and two in eight, over some fake slapping in class, a brownie, whatever, victory determined when the other person cries, gets a black eye, or falls to the ground—or even the remnants of today's brawl, three high schoolers and police and ice packs crowded right this moment into Mr. West's office. She is crying because of the typed letter she has gotten signed "Mara Zall aka Bubbles."

Mara, a seventh grader, has been quite a source of stress for Ms. Thomas this year, starting with a notebook filled with writings about sucking dick and ending with notes that said much the same thing, so what the girl has written this time stuns her. Although it seems strange coming from her, Mara writes, Ms. Thomas should be proud of what she has accomplished as principal and with her family, and though Mara can't change the mistakes she herself has made, she wishes she could, and "I think you are the best principal ever, even though I didn't show it."

"You just never know who you're getting through to," Ms. Thomas says, through tears. "That's middle schoolers for you."

In the sixth-grade wing, Lily puts her head down as her teachers sign her yearbook. Most of the kids dart from room to room, but Lily and Beth, wearing light-blue T-shirts and matching ponytails, linger in Ms. Knighten's, the quietest room. Lily has written to Beth, "You're like a third sister to me. Hope I see you over the summer. LYLAS, Lily." She has signed her name on Mia's and written "BBFE" (Best Buds Forever), "but I haven't finished writing in hers. I don't want Alexandra to." Mia has written in Lily's book, "Mia Reilly LYLAS BBFE."

In the cafeteria, Ben comes up to Jimmy: "You're right. Yoda is eight hundred seventy-four years old, not eight hundred forty-seven."

"I knew it was near nine hundred."

"How does he live so long?"

"He waddles."

"He uses the Force to keep his heart beating."

"In *Episode II*, Luke is thirty-two," Jimmy says.

"No, he's in his twenties."

"In *Episode III*, he's going to be forty."

Jimmy has finished his lunch. He gets up from the table, burps, and heads outside. On the way out he sees Joe, who earlier in the day was tussling with another boy over some paper torn from a binder. Jimmy looks down at him—way down, farther down than even a month ago—and says, "I can't believe you were fighting over a blank piece of paper."

On the playground, Alexandra poses for photos with the new friends she's made this year. Mia is on the field practicing a new high-five with Marnie, and when she spots a man shirtless in the distance, she runs back and forth and shouts, "There's a guy running in his underwear! There's a guy running in his underwear!" Lily and Beth stand on edge of the blacktop, kicking their Skechers and talking about amusement parks and pools.

At recess, Jackie tries to write "LOSER" on Dan Pryor's forehead, but the ink pen doesn't work well on his sweaty skin, and she only gets through "LOS." Kevin has drawn a penis on Dan's cheek. Dan doesn't know what's on his face, but whatever it is makes everyone laugh, so he rubs hard.

Jackie had decided that on the last day she was going to have everyone sign her jeans. She would save the butt for Adam and Jay. But when the time came, her mom wouldn't let her, so she settled for a white T-shirt instead.

Elizabeth has been going out with a boy named Dan for a week because she didn't want to hurt his feelings by saying no, and she is trying desperately to get back inside the cafeteria to deliver him a note:

> Hey wat's up? I am writing to say I think we should break up because we never talk or do ne thing. Don't be upset because you shouldn't get upset over me. We can still be friends.

She's left his name off so her nosy friends won't figure out who it is, since everyone on the planet thinks Dan is ugly and utterly gross. Except her—ugly, sure, but sweet, and only sort of gross.

"I have to give someone something," she says to Ms. Rouiller.

"Is it life-threatening?"

"Yes."

"This is Elizabeth," Mrs. Rashid says. "Everything is life-threatening with her."

Denied a pass inside, Elizabeth decides she'll break up on IM later, and now she's shoving Mr. Juliano, a gym teacher, toward Ms. Rouiller so she can take a photo of them together. "Go ask her," Mr. Juliano tells Elizabeth, who says, "I'm scared."

"There's nothing to be scared of in middle school," Mr. Juliano says. "Except all the teachers, and half the students."

In the eighth-grade wing, kids are screaming, signing yearbooks, eating leftover cookies from graduation, watching last night's slide show again, and singing along to its soundtrack. Chris pushes a toy cop car down the hall and says, "I'm a little kid." Dawn sits on a counter in the corner of the math room, thinking of how mean people were here, but she's a tiny bit sad to leave.

When the bell rings, the sixth graders yell and run out the door. The seventh graders are a little more huggy, and slow. Then the eighth graders emerge, through an arbor of clapping staffers. Dawn runs out with her hands up: "I'm free!" Some kids slap the teachers' hands. Some girls hold hands and cry. Liam tosses a tennis ball as he passes down the hall, Chris claps back at those who are applauding him. Some kids hug so hard they won't let go.

And somewhere in southern Michigan, in the silent cab of a truck, Eric tosses sunflower seeds at his father, who tosses them back. The Slip-knot CD is coming through his headphones. Eric smiles, and sits back. He thinks for a very small moment about how certain teachers at middle school were really cool, and he'll miss them.

But mostly he thinks about the music.

epilogue

The F comes in the mail, eventually—Eric's report card having been held up a month because he didn't turn in a textbook. At the bottom of the page it says PROMOTED, and Eric thinks, "Yes. They wanted me out of there, so they passed me." The F is supposed to mean no band, so Eric figures that's a good excuse to quit sax and focus on playing bass with Beef. "You get good at something," he says, "and then you move on. It's like skating, how the good bladers become skateboarders."

But when high school starts, Eric's on the list for band. The county F rule goes unenforced. So Eric sticks with the sax and tries out for All-State, waits for his baby brother to be born (there is no new house with a basement for Matchbox cars), hangs with his friends, old and new. He is impressed that kids can fit in all different ways in high school—he doesn't feel like an outsider. He visits his old teachers at Wilde Lake, except for Ms. Adams, who's gone to teach in a school with a supposedly easier "population." He tells Mr. Shifflett about his new science teacher, who has a real piece of lava rock and is giving him a B. Other than that, his first-quarter interim grades are all C's, which doesn't concern him in the least.

"If I were, like, 'Oh my God, I'm a dummy,' " he says, "I might be worried. But I'm smart."

Over the summer, Jackie develops a crush on Vin Diesel, and finally gets a computer. Her instant-message profile says:

I am so lazy i am just sittin here with a box of Frosted Flakes dipping each little Flake in a glass of milk 'cause I'm to lazy to pour a bowl and to lazy to go to Giant 'cause my other gallon of milk is 3 years rotten. And ur sitten there thinkin is she on drugs? . . . I want some . . . were did she get it?
But, oh well, i sooo brd n i need a boyfriend so if u r single give me a im n i will talk to u lata, I'm OUT! (OF MY MIND BE BACK IN 5 MIN.)
toodles
~Jackie~(worth $100,000 in 10 years)

Days later, at another of Dustin Fried's parties, she's sitting on the couch, damp from the hot tub, when Kevin says, "Adam likes you." Jackie asks Adam if he wants to go out, and he says okay. During truth-or-dare, she gives him a peck.

Four days later, she sees Adam at the pool. She says hi; he says nothing back. He is conferring with Kristina, one of those "You tell her" / "No, you tell her" conversations.

"What is it?" Jackie demands.

"I don't like you anymore."

Jackie is confused, yet sanguine. "He likes you a lot one day and you don't talk with him for a few days and all of a sudden he doesn't like you anymore. Hello? Oh well, there's a million guys out there, and by the time I'm twenty-one, a million more will be born."

Then again: "The one for you could be two years old right now, or ninety. My soulmate could have been Benjamin Franklin."

Elizabeth and her parents go to Seattle for the synchronized-swimming nationals, a fact Joseph tells even to the cashier at Subway, driving Elizabeth mad. Then a family vacation to British Columbia. It's the first time Elizabeth doesn't show interest in a family vacation—she'd prefer to be back east with her friends. She worries every time her mother mentions low cash flow.

"Are we going to be poor?"

"No, sweetie, we have a lot of money in the bank, we just don't have any with us."

The trip turns out to be not so bad, especially the restaurants. While taking pictures of the salmon running at the locks, Elizabeth mentions she might want to be a photographer, and Joseph's heart leaps a tiny bit but he keeps his mouth shut, lest he turn her off. He promises to bring her for Take Your Daughter to Work Day, and she is glad.

Later in the summer, they tour Switzerland, where, although her dad is embarrassing, there is a cute fourteen-year-old boy to talk to, and a group of twenty-year-olds who take her out one night and buy her a bottle of wine. She takes only three sips, because she doesn't want to come back drunk. When Joseph takes Elizabeth's film in to be developed, there are some photos of Miss Colyer, which he finds odd, but "she won't talk to me about it. They got along better, or something."

When eighth grade starts, Ellen assigns Liz one night a week to cook dinner. The first few times she grumbles, and they do have to suffer through spaghetti with hot dogs and meatballs, but she starts to enjoy it, and the meals get more palatable, too.

Over the summer, Lily starts to organize a campaign with the neighborhood kids to rescue pound puppies. She creates a newsletter on the computer, makes plans to alert the local newspapers and television stations, then drops it. Her mother has taken a job as the office manager of Mia's mom's dental practice, which at first seemed like a good way for the two girls to hang out, but it doesn't really happen. She sees a lot of Beth and not as much of Mia, who's pretty busy.

When school starts up, however, the three take gymnastics together on Fridays, at Lily's urging, and Beth and Mia become friends in their own right. Alexandra continues to do her own thing, but during French class she and Lily bond over their dislike of Abigail Werner, who sits at their table. Lily becomes a regular on instant-message and, despite her avowal that she had no interest in speaking to boys for at least a decade, gets herself caught in the middle of online dramas with the boys who like Mia.

"Timothy is mad because I said Beth wasn't online but really she was—she was with me at my house—and then he found out. And so I'm trying to apologize but he won't answer me back so will you apologize to him for me?"

No, it doesn't make sense to her either, but she's enjoying herself.

Jimmy showers every day now, sometimes twice. While he's sailing and camping and swimming and practicing with his magician handbook (so he'll be comfortable getting up in front of groups) and playing with his new friends the Wexler twins (no battle of egos, and he gets to be boss), Jimmy is growing. He adds three inches in three months, and ends the summer at five six and a half.

After clearing off his bedroom floor, Jimmy starts doing thirty crunches a night, plus ten or twelve curls with eight-pound weights—stuff he saw in his father's *Men's Health* magazine. Cheese and crackers have replaced much of the junk regime: "After a while, cookies get old." His belly has flattened. His arms have muscled. Peach fuzz has started to emerge—not like Jacob, who has hair dangling under his arms, but still.

When school starts, his temper, as his parents see it, gets worse. They refrain from checking his homework and only help when asked—and Jimmy does well. The brick wall no longer appeals to Jimmy during recess; he plays football instead, and comes home and tells his mom about the touchdown he makes.

It took a while, but Jimmy has started to see many of his bodily changes as a good thing. He feels like he's not just getting bigger but getting stronger, too. He realizes that this is what makes him more like those older boys he watches, who seem so well adjusted and happy.

He misses what he left behind, but he wants to get there, soon.

notes

000   *The most humiliating experience of their lives:* Giannetti and Sagarese (2001).

000   *They've read to expect contradictions:* Some of these examples, and more, are found in Giannetti and Sagarese (1997, xiv) and Freud (1936).

000   *Children start to fix their values:* The British philosopher Alfred North Whitehead called preadolescence "the years during which the lines of character are graven." According to Albert Schweitzer, "The most important years in life are those between nine and fourteen. This is the time to plant the seeds of knowledge in the mind—afterwards it is too late. This is the time to acquaint the young with the great spirits of mankind."

000   *Middle school pulls in children:* An excellent source on children's changes from sixth to seventh to eighth grade is Judith Baenen, author of several pamphlets on middle schoolers and president of St. Mary's Academy in Englewood, Col.

000   *James Rouse's original planned community:* The early years of Columbia were explored beautifully by the novelist Michael Chabon (2001), who grew up there at its inception.

000   *Thirteen-year-olds can't get interested:* Douglas MacIver, principal research scientist at the Center for Social Organization of Schools at Johns Hopkins University, which helps schools implement what he calls "minds-on" learning practices, has found middle schoolers less likely than third- through fifth-graders to display high-interest, active engagement and high effort and to think what they're taught is valuable. As well, they are less convinced teachers care about their learning.

000   *Anything less than a C is unacceptable:* Temple University Professor Laurence Steinberg (1997, 161) found that black students thought a C-minus

was the grade threshold at which they'd get in trouble; for white students, the threshold was a full letter grade higher.

000 *Means that you put friends number one:* Sullivan (1953, 245–46) and Gesell (1956). Sullivan's work on the nature and importance of these formative friendships, what he calls "chumships," remains the prevailing philosophy today.

000 *Never have more capacity for devotion:* Freud (1968).

000 *Jackie is in the norm:* Data on young adolescents' romantic activity is scarce, thanks in part to a Bush-administration decision in 1991 rescinding funding for such research, on the grounds that asking children questions about sexual behavior might encourage it. Thompson and Grace (2001, 191) report data from the Sexuality Information and Education Council of the United States: 73 percent of girls and 66 percent of boys thirteen and younger had been kissed, 20 percent of thirteen-year-old boys had touched breasts; 25 percent of girls that age had had their breasts touched, and 23 percent of boys and 18 percent of girls thirteen or younger had fondled someone's genitals. In 1999, the Federal Centers for Disease Control and Prevention reported that 12 percent of boys and 4 percent of girls had had sexual intercourse by age thirteen.

000 *Because they aren't so comfortable:* Darling et al. (1999, 476).

000 *The subject of much sociological study:* Both schools of thought are summarized in ibid. Among boys and girls in eighth grade, the study reports, comfort with the opposite sex is a consistent predictor of self-esteem.

000 *To make sure Jackie doesn't grow up too fast:* For more on the value and difficulty of holding on to childhood—and the media's role—see Postman (1994) and Elkind (2001). Pipher (1994, 66–67) writes on media influence and parents as "the enemies of the cultural indoctrination." Although movies, video games, and music are rated, the entertainment industries disregard their own ratings and market to young children products for people seventeen and up, according to a Sept. 2000 study by the Federal Trade Commission.

000 *The most endearing traits of two-year-olds:* Erikson (1968) and Caplan (1983). Some sentences from Caplan could be taken just as easily from a middle-school handbook: "They like to talk even if they have nothing to say." "He wants exactly what he wants when he wants it, cannot adapt, give in, or wait even a moment, perhaps because he is not able to think ahead."

000 *Four-fifths the height he'll attain by adulthood:* Gesell (1956, 72).

000 *Ten times as likely to engage in risky behaviors:* Young and Zimmerman (1998).

000 *Teachers would choose more active parents:* Public Agenda, 2000.

000 *Protects against nearly every possible middle-school health risk:* Resnick et al. (1997, 823–32). Pollack (1998) also cites research that correlates boys' behavior to both their relationships with their parents and their parents' relationships with each other.

000 *Organizations across the country:* They include the National Coalition for Parent Involvement in Education in Fairfax, Va., the National Network of

Partnership Schools in Baltimore, and the National PTA in Chicago.

000 *A disregard for consequences:* Restak (2001) and Gesell (1956).

000 *Show few signs of abating:* American Association of University Women (2001). According to a study of eighth- through eleventh-graders, seven in ten students said their schools had harassment policies in 2000, compared with one-quarter in 1993. Eight in ten girls reported experiencing harassment at some time in their school lives, the same as in 1993. Fifty-six percent of boys said they'd been harassed, compared with 49 percent in 1993.

000 *Sometimes it feels like her body is the only reason:* "Being beautiful can be a Pyrrhic victory. The battle for popularity is won, but the war for respect as a whole person is lost" (Pipher [1994, 55]).

000 *They can't infuse disgrace back into activities:* Ibid., 66.

000 *Trying to appear helpless:* Orenstein (1994, 22).

000 *The boys continue bragging:* Pollack (1998, 16) posits that boys brag to hide a lack of confidence, more pronounced in boys than girls.

000 The number of children living in two-parent households decreased from 77 percent in 1980 to 69 percent in 2001, according to the Department of Health and Human Services. In 1999, 78 percent of mothers of children age six through thirteen worked, according to the U.S. Department of Labor Bureau of Labor Statistics.

000 *She wants to talk more about her schoolwork:* Seventy-two percent of children aged ten to thirteen said this was the case, compared with 48 percent of high-school students (National Commission on Children [1991, 13]).

000 *Boys actually report more conflict:* Wyndol Furman, "The Measurement of Friendship Perceptions: Conceptual and Methodological Issues," in Bukowski et al, eds. (1996).

000 *You will prey upon anyone:* On insulting as a developmental achievement, see Thompson and Grace (2001, 106).

000 *Single most painful thing about middle school:* According to one thousand students surveyed by Giannetti and Sagarese (2001).

000 *Tend to emerge as more self-sufficient adults:* Pipher (1994, 266).

000 *Empowered by groupthink, tinged by guilt:* On the power of groupthink, see Thompson and Grace (2001, 103 and 177).

000 *More upsetting than if he spied on you in the shower:* American Association of University Women (2001, 11).

000 *For the first two-thirds of the twentieth century:* For more on the origins and purposes of middle school, see Dickinson, ed. (2001) and David, ed. (1998).

000 *Able to get themselves around the abstract as well as the concrete:* The Swiss psychologist Jean Piaget originated the concept that children in preadolescence move from concrete thinking to formal operations, in which they can think abstractly and hypothetically for the first time. Donald Eichhorn, one of the fathers of the modern middle school, said in a 1972 speech printed in David (1998, 57), "It is vital that emphasis be placed on higher cognitive processes such as hypothesizing, generalizing, synthesizing, and evaluating" as well as recalling, recognizing, and copying. Good sources

on the changes needed in middle schools include Jackson and Davis (2000); Scales (1996); Erb, ed. (2001); Carnegie Council on Adolescent Development (1995); and the 1997 vision statement by Joan Lipsitz of the Lilly Endowment, M. Hayes Mizell of the Edna McConnell Clark Foundation, Anthony W. Jackson of the Carnegie Corporation, and Leah Meyer Austin of the W.K. Kellogg Foundation, which all study middle-school reform.

000 *Curriculum would let students progress at different rates:* John Lounsbury, a founder of the middle-school movement, noted in 1977, "At this level when young people exhibit greatest diversity, we often present them a more standardized and common program than any other time in the educational process" (in George, ed. [1977]).

000 *70 percent of questions:* Alfred Arth, chairman of the middle-school program at the University of Nebraska School of Education.

000 *Learn what their students need only on the job:* In a 1992 study of middle-school teachers, only half said they had received specific middle-school preparation, and half said it was inadequate or poor. Most had not intended to teach middle school. Nearly a third of respondents had professional preparation that did not include coursework on young-adolescent development, 40 percent didn't include coursework directly on appropriate teaching methods for young adolescents, and nearly 60 percent did not include fieldwork in grades five through nine. The situation has improved since then, to some degree. (Scales and McEwin [1994].)

000 *Shown to have significant academic and other advantages:* Lee and Smith (1993).

000 *The pendulum has swung the other way:* "The once-heralded argument for making a more humane and humanistic institution in the 1960s and 1970s was turned aside by the Conservative Restoration of the 1990s," "rolled back by neo-Puritan critique favoring schools that were less joyful, more stressful focused almost solely on academics, and less concerned about young adolescents as people" (Dickinson [2001, xviii]).

000 *Those emotions literally shrink the space:* O'Neil (1996).

000 *Hanging more with the other black girls:* "As children approach adolescence, they seem to become more selective in their choice of same-race friends," write Frances E. Aboud and Morton J. Mendelson, "Determinants of Friendship Selection and Quality: Developmental Perspectives," in Bukowski et al., eds. (1996, 91). Black girls, they found, have the most other-race friends, white girls the fewest.

000 *The biggest influence is friends.* The 2002 Roper Youth Report, conducted by Roper ASW, asked eight-to-seventeen-year-olds what is their biggest influence in making such decisions. For music, 64 percent said friends and 28 percent said parents; for clothing, 47 percent said friends and 42 percent parents. For television, however, only 26 percent said friends and 43 percent parents; for alcohol use, 20 percent friends and 71 percent parents; and for career plans, 18 percent friends and 53 percent parents.

000 *Spends, on average, fifty-nine dollars a week:* Teenage Research Unlimited, Glenbrook, Ill.

000   *And one theory posits that the rapid pace of video games triggers irrational fear responses:* Sylwester (1997).

000   *Having a parent travel for work:* Elkind (2001, 184).

000   *There are far more niches in which to find acceptance:* On how high school's wide range of activities and subcultures benefits children who didn't fit in during middle school, see Eder and Kinney (1995) and Kinney (1993).

000   *The more aggressive and defiant they are:* Rodkin et al. (2000, 14–24).

000   *Her best friend has several worlds:* For more on what each girl gets from an uneven friendship, see Thompson and Grace (2001, 60).

000   *Lily . . . is a pleaser:* The term "pleaser" is from Wiseman (2002). For more on the organizational chart of middle-school cliques, see Giannetti and Sangarese (2001).

000   *It wouldn't be productive to invade:* On what children want from parents regarding friendships, see Thompson and Grace (2001, 8–11).

000   *She has some of the vocabulary:* On the difference between having vocabulary and having knowledge, see Pipher (1994, 245).

000   *You just should have one:* One study found that the norm for middle-school girls is to think "one should always be in love" (Simon et al. [1992]).

000   *"kids would have some power . . .":* On the value of self-directed learning and why some teachers feel threatened by it, see Pitton, in Dickinson, ed. (2001, 23): "As adults, we know we work harder on things we enjoy, we learn more when we choose to do something and are involved in the decision making, and we strive to do our work well when it means something to us." See also Richard R. Powell, "On Headpieces of Straw: How Middle Level Students View Their Schooling," in ibid. (117–52); and William Alexander's 1966 speech at the Mount Kisko Conference, reprinted in David, ed. (1998, 21).

selected bibliography

American Association of University Women Education Foundation. "Hostile Hallways: Bullying, Teasing, and Sexual Harassment in School." Washington, D.C.: American Association of University Women, 2001.

Asher, Steven R., and John D. Coie, eds. *Peer Rejection in Childhood*. Cambridge: Cambridge University Press, 1990.

Blum, Robert William, and Peggy Mann Rinehart. *Reducing the Risk: Connections That Make a Difference in the Lives of Youth*. Report of the National Longitudinal Study of Adolescent Health. Minneapolis: University of Minnesota Press, 1997.

Bukowsi, William M., Andrew F. Newcomb, and Willard W. Hartup, eds. *The Company They Keep: Friendship in Childhood and Adolescence*. Cambridge: Cambridge University Press, 1996. Reprint, 1998.

Caplan, Theresa and Frank. *The Early Childhood Years: The 2 to 6 Year Old*. New York: Bantam Books, 1983.

Carnegie Council on Adolescent Development. *Great Transitions: Preparing Adolescents for a New Century*. New York: Carnegie Corporation, 1995.

Chabon, Michael. "Maps and Legends." *Architectural Digest*, April 2001, p. 46.

Coles, Robert. *The Moral Intelligence of Children*. New York: Random House, 1997.

Darling, Nancy, Bonnie B. Dowdy, M. Lee Van Horn, and Linda Caldwell. "Mixed-Sex Settings and the Perception of Competence." *Journal of Youth and Adolescence*, vol. 28, no. 4 (1999): pp. 461–80.

David, Robert, ed. *Moving Forward from the Past: Early Writings and Current Reflections of Middle School Founders*. Columbus, Ohio: National Middle School Association, 1998.

Dickinson, Thomas S., ed. *Reinventing the Middle School*. New York: Routledge-

Falmer, 2001.

Eder, Donna, and David A. Kinney. "The Effect of Middle School Extracurricular Activities on Adolescents' Popularity and Peer Status." *Youth & Society*, vol. 26, no. 3. (March 1995): pp. 298–324.

Elkind, David. *The Hurried Child: Growing Up Too Fast Too Soon.* Cambridge, Mass.: Perseus Books, 3rd ed., 2001.

Erb, Thomas Owen, ed. *This We Believe: And Now We Must Act.* Columbus, Ohio: National Middle School Association, 2001.

Erikson, Erik H., ed. *Youth: Change and Challenge.* New York: Basic Books, 1963.

———. *Identity: Youth and Crisis.* New York: W. W. Norton, 1968.

Freud, Anna. *The Ego and the Mechanisms of Defense.* New York: International University Press, 1936.

———. "On Certain Difficulties in the Preadolescent's Relation to His Parents." In *The Writings of Anna Freud, Vol. 4.* New York: International University Press, 1968.

Furman, Wyndol, B. Bradford Brown, and Candice Feiring, eds. *The Development of Romantic Relationships in Adolescence.* Cambridge: Cambridge University Press, 1999.

George, Paul, ed. *The Middle School: A Look Ahead.* Columbus, Ohio: National Middle School Association, 1977.

Gesell, Arnold, Frances L. Ilg, and Louise Bates Ames. *Youth: The Years from Ten to Sixteen.* New York: Harper & Row, 1956.

Giannetti, Charlene C., and Margaret Sagarese. *The Roller-Coaster Years: Raising Your Child Through the Maddening Yet Magical Middle School Years.* New York: Broadway Books, 1997.

———. *Cliques: 8 Steps to Help Your Child Survive the Social Jungle.* New York: Broadway Books, 2001.

Hersch, Patricia. *A Tribe Apart: A Journey into the Heart of American Adolescence.* New York: Ballantine Books, 1998.

Jackson, Anthony, and Gayle Davis. *Turning Points 2000: Educating Adolescents in the 21st Century.* New York: Teachers College Press, 2000.

Kinney, David A. "From Nerds to Normals: The Recovery of Identity Among Adolescents from Middle School to High School." *Sociology of Education*, vol. 66 (Jan. 1993): pp. 21–40.

Lee, V., and J. Smith. "Effects of School Restructuring on the Achievement and Engagement of Middle-Grades Students." *Sociology of Education*, vol. 64, no. 3 (1993): pp. 190–208.

Lipsitz, Joan, M. Hayes Mizell, Anthony W. Jackson, and Leah Meyer Austin. "Speaking with One Voice: A Manifesto for Middle-Grades Reform." *Phi Delta Kappan*, vol. 78, no. 7, March 1997: p. 533.

National Commission on Children. *Speaking of Kids: A National Survey of Children and Parents.* Washington, D.C.: National Commission on Children, 1991.

O'Neil, John. "On Emotional Intelligence: A Conversation With Daniel Goleman." *Educational Leadership*, Sept. 1996, pp. 6–11.

Orenstein, Peggy. *Schoolgirls: Young Women, Self-Esteem and the Confidence Gap.*

New York: Doubleday, 1994.

Pipher, Mary. *Reviving Ophelia: Saving the Selves of Adolescent Girls.* New York: Ballantine Books, 1994.

Pollack, William. *Real Boys: Rescuing Our Sons from the Myths of Boyhood.* New York: Random House, 1998.

Postman, Neil. *The Disappearance of Childhood.* New York: Delacorte Press, 1982. Reprint, New York: Vintage Books, 1994.

Public Agenda. *A Sense of Calling: Who Teaches and Why.* New York: Public Agenda, 2000.

Resnick, Michael D., et al. "Protecting Adolescents from Harm: Findings from the National Longitudinal Study on Adolescent Health." *Journal of the American Medical Association*, vol. 278, no. 10 (Sept. 10, 1997): pp. 823–32.

Restak, Richard. *The Secret Life of the Brain.* Washington, D.C.: Dana Press and Joseph Henry Press, 2001.

Rodkin, Philip C., Thomas W. Farmer, Ruth Pearl, and Richard Van Acker. "Heterogeneity of Popular Boys: Antisocial and Prosocial Configurations." *Developmental Psychology*, vol. 36, no. 1 (Jan. 2000): pp. 14–24.

Scales, Peter C. *Boxed In and Bored: How Middle Schools Continue to Fail Young Adolescents—and What Good Middle Schools Do Right.* Minneapolis: Search Institute, 1996.

——— and C. Kenneth McEwin. *Growing Pains: The Making of America's Middle School Teachers.* Columbus, Ohio: National Middle School Association, 1994.

Simmons, Rachel. *Odd Girl Out: The Hidden Culture of Aggression in Girls.* New York: Harcourt, 2002.

Simon, R.W., Donna Eder, and C. Evans. "The Development of Feeling Norms Underlying Romantic Love Among Adolescent Females." *Social Psychology Quarterly*, vol. 55, no. 1 (1992): pp. 29–46.

Steinberg, Laurence, with B. Bradford Brown and Sanford M. Dornbusch. *Beyond the Classroom: Why School Reform Has Failed and What Parents Need to Do.* New York: Touchstone, 1997.

Stepp, Laura Sessions. *Our Last Best Shot: Guiding Our Children Through Early Adolescence.* New York: Riverhead Books, 2000.

Sullivan, Harry Stack. *The Interpersonal Theory of Psychiatry.* New York: W. W. Norton, 1953.

Sylwester, Robert. "Bioelectronic Learning: The Effects of Electronic Media on a Developing Brain." *Technos: Quarterly for Education and Technology*, vol. 6, no. 2 (Summer 1997): pp. 19–22.

———, ed. *Student Brains, School Issues: A Collection of Articles.* Arlington Heights, Ill.: SkyLight Training and Publishing, 1998.

Thompson, Michael, and Catherine O'Neill Grace, with Lawrence J. Cohen. *Best Friends, Worst Enemies: Understanding the Social Lives of Children.* New York: Ballantine Books, 2001.

White, Emily. *Fast Girls: The Myth of the Slut.* New York: Scribner, 2002.

Wiseman, Rosalind. *Queen Bees and Wannabes: Helping Your Daughter Survive Cliques, Gossip, Boyfriends and Other Realities of Adolescence.* New York:

Crown Publishers, 2002.

Young, Thomas L., and Rick Zimmerman, "Clueless: Parental Knowledge of Risk Behaviors of Middle School Students." *Archives of Pediatric and Adolescent Medicine*, vol. 152 (Nov. 1998): pp. 1137–39.

I have also benefited from the expertise of these authorities:

On brain research, Jay Giedd of the National Institute of Mental Health.

On relationships with parents, Robert Billingham of Indiana University.

On relationships with friends, William Bukowski of Concordia University, Montreal, and Jeffrey Parker of the Pennsylvania State University.

On romance, W. Andrew Collins of the University of Minnesota.

On materialism, Michael Wood of Teenage Research Unlimited, and Marvin Goldberg of the Pennsylvania State University.

On motivation, Douglas MacIver of Johns Hopkins University, and Judith Baenen of St. Mary's Academy, Englewood, Colo.

On teacher preparation, Kenneth McEwin of Appalachian State University.

acknowledgments

This book would be nothing without the honesty and guts of the Wilde Lake children, especially those I wrote about in depth. Thanks for sharing, being fun, tolerating me. Thanks, too, to their warm families, who opened their homes and didn't put on an act. Brenda Thomas not only let me into her school but encouraged me to explore freely, and the staff was one hundred percent helpful. In the Howard County school system, thanks to John O'Rourke, Mike Hickey, Alice Haskins, Ken Gill, and Patti Caplan.

Gail Ross, my agent, took this project beyond where I imagined, and talked me off the ledge. Becky Saletan, my editor, let me tell the story I wanted to, then made it better. I couldn't have asked for any better than the FSG team. At *The Washington Post*, more people than I can name have supported this effort, and my career. The Ucross Foundation provided a beyond-marvelous place to write.

My friends helped in many ways, especially Hanna Rosin, Susan Gates, Marilyn Thompson, Amy Joyce, David Plotz, Lucy Spelman, Hank Stuever, Amy Argetsinger, Cabot Orton, Marina Walsh, Beverly Solochek, Gail and Bill McNulty, Paula McLain, Jennifer Starkweather, Angela Schaeffer, Rene Sanchez, David Finkel, Scott Shapiro, and John Miller. Thanks also to Team Meldrom, Karen Sigel, the Fenland Field kids, and the Black-Perlsteins.

The devotion and humor of my parents, Sandi and Jerry Perlstein, enriched my own middle-school years, and much more. My brothers Rick and Ben are my models of creativity and ambition. My grandparents, Celia and Harry Perlstein and Bernie and Sarah Friedman, have given me more than they know.

Thanks to my cousins, Rachel and Noah Friedman, for being empathic, hilarious, and still huggy after all these years. Most of all, I am indebted beyond words to Lisa Schneider-Friedman and David Friedman, my aunt and uncle, who epitomize goodness—and keep me in tuna.